CSET English

105
106
107
108

Teacher Certification Exam

By Sharon A. Wynne, M.S.

XAMonline, Inc.
Boston

Copyright © 2018 XAMonline, Inc.
All rights reserved. No part of the material protected by this copyright notice may be reproduced or utilized in any form or by any means, electronic or mechanical, including photocopying, recording or by any information storage and retrievable system, without written permission from the copyright holder.

To obtain permission(s) to use the material from this work for any purpose including workshops or seminars, please submit a written request to:

XAMonline, Inc.
21 Orient Avenue
Melrose, MA 02176
Toll Free 1-800-301-4647
Email: info@xamonline.com
Web www.xamonline.com

Library of Congress Cataloging-in-Publication Data

Wynne, Sharon A.
CSET English 105, 106, 107, 108: Teacher Certification / Sharon A. Wynne.
ISBN 978-1-64239-065-0

1. English 105, 106, 107, 108   2. Study Guides.   3. CSET
4. Teachers' Certification & Licensure   5. Careers

Disclaimer:
The opinions expressed in this publication are the sole works of XAMonline and were created independently from the National Education Association, Educational Testing Service, and any state's Department of Education, National Evaluation Systems or other testing affiliates.

Between the time of publication and printing, state specific standards as well as testing formats and website information may change that is not included in part or in whole within this product. Sample test questions are developed by XAMonline and reflect similar content as on real tests; however, they are not former tests. XAMonline assembles content that aligns with state standards but makes no claims nor guarantees teacher candidates a passing score. Numerical scores are determined by testing companies such as NES or ETS and then are compared with individual state standards. A passing score varies from state to state.

Printed in the United States of America   œ-1
CSET: English 105, 106, 107, 108
ISBN: 978-1-64239-065-0

TEACHER CERTIFICATION STUDY GUIDE

Introduction

More than ever before, teachers of English in California's middle and high schools must deliver a complex and dynamic curriculum to students of every socioeconomic, linguistic, and cultural background. Furthermore, society is increasingly technologically and media-oriented. The Reading/Language Arts Framework for California Public Schools: Kindergarten through Grade Twelve (1999) forms the basis for the preparation of English teachers, who must equip their students to meet the challenges of this changing world. In this context, new paradigms and models are required for teaching English/Language Arts. Multiple forms of literacy demand a broad theoretical knowledge of language and literacy acquisition while new information technologies require an emphasis on critical analysis of both print and non-print texts.

Candidates for Single Subject Teaching Credentials in English have a broad knowledge of literature, language and linguistics, rhetoric and composition, and communication studies. Candidates must be able to read and write well for a variety of purposes and communicate effectively within a variety of rhetorical contexts. In addition, candidates must have experience in theater arts, public speaking, journalism, textual analysis of nonfiction and electronic media, and production of technologically-enhanced documents. This broad scope of background and skills ensures a greater degree of success in English/Language Arts classrooms for California's public school children.

California State Credential in English (Single Subject Credential)

A Single Subject Credential authorizes instruction in English in a departmentalized class, primarily in grades 7-12, but available for grades K-12 or adult classes as well.

Requirements:

1. Baccalaureate or higher degree, except in professional education, from a regionally accredited college or university.

2. Passing CBEST (California Basic Educational Skills Test) score.

3. Verification of subject matter competence by one of the following two methods:
   *Pass all four subtests of the English CSET (California Subject Examinations for Teachers).
   OR
   *Complete a commission-approved English preparation program and obtain verification of completion from the authorized person in the department of that program.

TEACHER CERTIFICATION STUDY GUIDE

4. Complete a single-subject teacher preparation program, including successful student teaching and obtaining a formal recommendation for the credential by the California college or university where the program was completed.

About the CSET Examination in English
The English CSET is five hours long, from 1:30 p.m. to 7:00 p.m., and is offered at any of the test sites and on any of the test dates.

The CSET is criterion-referenced, meaning that it measures a candidate's knowledge and skills as compared to an established standard, rather than in comparison to other test takers' performances.

To pass, the candidate must pass each subtest—scored separately—and evaluated against established standards. Passing status is determined by the total subtest performance. The total subtest score is based on the number of raw score points earned on each section and the weighing of each section. Raw scores are converted to a scale of 100-300, with the scaled score of 220 representing a minimum passing score.

A passing score must be achieved at a single CSET exam. If you do not pass one or more of the subtests, you may register for and retake the subtests an unlimited number of times.

	CSET: English		
Subtest	Domains	# of Multiple Choice Questions	# of Constructed-Response Questions
I (105)*	Literature and Textual Analysis, Composition and Rhetoric	40 10	None None
II (106)	Language, Linguistics and Literacy	50	None
III (107)*	Composition and Rhetoric And Literature and Textual Analysis	None	2 extended responses (One based on literary test, one on nonliterary text)
IV (108)	Communications, Speech, Media, and Creative Performance	None	4 short responses

ENGLISH

TEACHER CERTIFICATION STUDY GUIDE

* Subtests I and III (105 and 107) cover the same domains, with differing question formats.

English Subtest I (English 105): Literature and Textual Analysis, Composition, and Rhetoric

Fifty multiple-choice questions (40 for Literature and Textual Analysis, ten for Composition and Rhetoric). This subtest is scored electronically, based on the number of questions answered correctly. There is no penalty for guessing.

English Subtest II (English 106): Language, Linguistics, and Literacy

Fifty multiple-choice questions scored electronically, based on the number of questions answered correctly. There is no penalty for guessing.

English Subtest III (English 107): Composition and Rhetoric, Literature and Textual Analysis

Covers the same domain as Subtest I. Two extended constructed-response questions, taking approximately 45-60 minutes to complete. One is based on literary text, one on non-literary text. This subtest is scored by qualified California educators, using focused holistic scoring (which centers on the product as a whole instead of separate aspects of the test-taker's work and is scored based on an established rubric).

The rubric is based on four characteristics:
1. Purpose - How well the response addresses the question in relation to relevant CSET subject matter.
2. Subject Matter Knowledge - Application of accurate subject matter.
3. Support - Appropriateness and quality of supporting evidence.
4. Depth and Breadth of Understanding - Degree of demonstrated comprehension.

English Subtest IV (English 108): Communications, Speech, Media, and Creative Performance

Four short responses, taking approximately 10-15 minutes to complete. This subtest is scored by the same California educators, using a rubric that excludes the Depth and Breadth of Understanding component.

Additional Information: The CSET is developed by *National Evaluation Systems, Inc.* (NES) of Amherst, MA, and its website (www.cset.nesinc.com), provides additional information, including registration, preparation and testing procedures, and study materials. The California Commission of Teacher Credentialing (CCTC) is charged with the evaluation and issuance of teaching credentials for public school teachers in California. Their website (www.ctc.ca.gov) provides up-to-date teacher credential information for the state.

TEACHER CERTIFICATION STUDY GUIDE

Table of Contents

DOMAIN I.   LITERATURE AND TEXTUAL ANALYSIS

COMPETENCY 1.0   LITERARY ANALYSIS 1

Skill 1.1   Recognize, compare, and evaluate different literary traditions to include 1
- American (inclusive of cultural pluralism)
- British (inclusive of cultural pluralism)
- World literature and literature in translation (inclusive of cross-cultural literature)
- Mythology and oral tradition

SKILL 1.2   Trace development of major literary movements in historical periods 20

SKILL 1.3   Describe the salient features of adolescent/young adult literature 21

SKILL 1.4   Analyze and interpret major works by representative writers in historical, aesthetic, political, and philosophical contexts 33

COMPETENCY 2.0   LITERARY ELEMENTS 36

SKILL 2.1   Distinguish salient features of genres 36

SKILL 2.2   Define and analyze basic elements of literature 37

SKILL 2.3   Articulate the relationship between the expressed purposes and the characteristics of different forms of dramatic literature 42

SKILL 2.4   Develop critical thinking and analytic skill through close reading of texts 43

COMPETENCY 3.0   LITERARY CRITICISM 47

SKILL 3.1   Research and apply criticism of major texts and authors using print and/or electronic resource 47

SKILL 3.2   Research and apply various approaches to interpreting literature 47

COMPETENCY 4.0   ANALYSIS OF NON-LITERARY TEXTS 49

SKILL 4.1   Compare various features of print and visual 49

ENGLISH

TEACHER CERTIFICATION STUDY GUIDE

SKILL 4.2	Evaluate structure and content of a variety of consumer, workplace, and public documents	49
SKILL 4.3	Interpret individual works in their cultural, social, and political contexts	51

DOMAIN II. LANGUAGE, LINGUISTICS, AND LITERACY

COMPETENCY 5.0 HUMAN LANGUAGE STRUCTURES ... 53

SKILL 5.1	Recognize the nature of human language, differences among languages, the universality of linguistic structures, and change across time, locale, and communities	53
SKILL 5.2	Demonstrate knowledge of word analysis, including sound patterns (phonology) and inflection, derivation, compounding, roots, and affixes (morphology)	57
SKILL 5.3	Demonstrate knowledge of sentence structures (syntax), word and sentence meanings (semantics), and language function in communicative context (pragmatics)	59
SKILL 5.4	Use appropriate print and electronic sources to research etymologies; recognize conventions of English orthography and changes in word meaning and pronunciation	62

COMPETENCY 6.0 ACQUISITION AND DEVELOPMENT OF LANGUAGE AND LITERACY ... 65

SKILL 6.1	Explain the influences of cognitive, affective, and socio-cultural factors on language acquisition and development	65
SKILL 6.2	Explain the influence of a first language on second-language development	68
SKILL 6.3	Describe methods and techniques for developing academic literacy	69

COMPETENCY 7.0 LITERACY STUDIES ... 71

SKILL 7.1	Recognize the written and oral conventions of Standard English, and analyze the social implications of mastering them	71
SKILL 7.2	Describe and explain cognitive elements of reading and writing processes	72

SKILL 7.3 Explain meta-cognitive strategies for making sense of text 74

COMPETENCY 8.0 GRAMMATICAL STRUCTURES OF ENGLISH 76

SKILL 8.1 Identify methods of sentence construction 76

SKILL 8.2 Analyze parts of speech and their distinctive structures and functions 77

SKILL 8.3 Describe the forms and functions of the English verb system 79

DOMAIN III.   COMPOSITION AND RHETORIC

COMPETENCY 9.0 WRITTEN COMPOSING PROCESSES (INDIVIDUAL AND COLLABORATIVE) 83

SKILL 9.1 Reflect on and describe their own writing processes 83

SKILL 9.2 Investigate and apply alternative methods of prewriting, drafting, responding, revising, editing, and evaluating 84

SKILL 9.3 Employ such strategies as graphic organizers, outlines, notes, charts, summaries, or précis to clarify and record meaning 89

SKILL 9.4 Integrate a variety of software applications to produce print documents and multi-media presentations 93

COMPETENCY 10.0 RHETORICAL FEATURES OF LITERARY AND NON-LITERARY, ORAL AND WRITTEN TEXTS 94

SKILL 10.1 Recognize and use a variety of writing applications 94

SKILL 10.2 Demonstrate awareness of audience, purpose, and context 94

SKILL 10.3 Recognize and use various text structures 95

SKILL 10.4 Apply a variety of methods to develop ideas within an essay 96

SKILL 10.5 Apply critical thinking strategies to evaluate methods of persuasion, including but not limited to 99
- Types of appeal
- Types of persuasive speech
- Logical fallacies
- Advertising techniques
- Logical argument
- Classical argument

TEACHER CERTIFICATION STUDY GUIDE

COMPETENCY 11.0 RHETORICAL EFFECTS OF GRAMMATICAL ELEMENTS **103**

SKILL 11.1 Employ precise and extensive vocabulary and effective diction to control voice, style, and tone 103

SKILL 11.2 Use clause joining techniques to express logical connections between idea 104

SKILL 11.3 Identify and use clausal and phrasal modifiers to control flow, pace, and emphasis 108

SKILL 11.4 Identify and use devices to control focus in sentence and paragraph 110

SKILL 11.5 Maintain coherence through use of cohesive devices 111

COMPETENCY 12.0 CONVENTIONS OF ORAL AND WRITTEN LANGUAGE **114**

SKILL 12.1 Apply knowledge of linguistic structure to identify and use the conventions of standard edited English 114

SKILL 12.2 Recognize, understand, and use a range of conventions in both spoken and written English, including 115
- Conventions of effective sentence structure
- Preferred usage
- Conventions of pronunciation and intonation
- Conventional forms of spelling
- Capitalization and punctuation

COMPETENCY 13.0 RESEARCH STRATEGIES **118**

SKILL 13.1 Develop and apply research questions 118

SKILL 13.2 Demonstrate methods of inquiry and investigation 119

SKILL 13.3 Identify and use multiple resources, and critically evaluate the quality of the sources 120

SKILL 13.4 Interpret and apply findings 121

SKILL 13.5 Use professional conventions and ethical standards of citation and attribution 122

SKILL 13.6 Demonstrate effective presentation methods, including multi-media formats 124

DOMAIN IV. COMMUNICATIONS: SPEECH, MEDIA, AND CREATIVE PERFORMANCE

COMPETENCY 14.0 ORAL COMMUNICATION PROCESSES 127

SKILL 14.1 Identify features of, and deliver oral performance in, a variety of forms 127

SKILL 14.2 Demonstrate and evaluate individual performance skills 128

SKILL 14.3 Articulate principles of speaker/audience interrelationship 129

SKILL 14.4 Identify and demonstrate collaborative communication skills in a variety of roles 130

COMPETENCY 15.0 MEDIA ANALYSIS AND JOURNALISTIC APPLICATIONS 132

SKILL 15.1 Analyze the impact on society of a variety of media forms 132

SKILL 15.2 Recognize and evaluate strategies used by the media to inform, persuade, entertain, and transmit culture 132

SKILL 15.3 Identify aesthetic effects of a media presentation 133

SKILL 15.4 Demonstrate effective and creative application of these strategies and techniques to prepare presentations using a variety of media forms and visual aids 134

COMPETENCY 16.0 DRAMATIC PERFORMANCE 136

SKILL 16.1 Describe and use a range of rehearsal strategies to effectively mount a production 136

SKILL 16.2 Employ basic elements of character analysis and approaches to acting, including physical and vocal techniques, that reveal character and relationships 137

SKILL 16.3 Demonstrate basic knowledge of the language of visual composition and principles of theatrical design 139

SKILL 16.4 Apply fundamentals of stage directing, including conceptualization, blocking (movement patterns), tempo, and dramatic arc (rising and falling action) 141

SKILL 16.5 Demonstrate facility in a variety of oral performance traditions ... 144

COMPETENCY 17.0 CREATIVE WRITING 146

SKILL 17.1 Demonstrate facility in creative composition in a variety of genres 146

SKILL 17.2 Understand and apply processes and techniques that enhance the impact of the creative writing product 146

SKILL 17.3 Demonstrate skill in composing creative and aesthetically compelling responses to literature 147

Resources 149

Sample Test 154

Answer Key 193

Rigor Table 194

Rationales for Sample Questions 195

TEACHER CERTIFICATION STUDY GUIDE

Great Study and Testing Tips!

What to study in order to prepare for the subject assessments is the focus of this study guide but equally important is *how* you study.

You can increase your chances of truly mastering the information by taking some simple but effective steps.

Study Tips:

1. Some foods aid the learning process. Foods such as milk, nuts, seeds, rice, and oats help your study efforts by releasing natural memory enhancers called CCKs (*cholecystokinin*) composed of *tryptophan*, *choline*, and *phenylalanine*. All of these chemicals enhance the neurotransmitters associated with memory. Before studying, try a light, protein-rich meal of eggs, turkey, and fish. All of these foods release the memory-enhancing chemicals. The better the connections, the more you comprehend.

Likewise, before you take a test, stick to a light snack of energy boosting and relaxing foods. A glass of milk, a piece of fruit, or some peanuts all release various memory-boosting chemicals and help you to relax and focus on the subject at hand.

2. Learn to take great notes. A by-product of our modern culture is that we have grown accustomed to getting our information in short doses (i.e., TV news sound-bytes or *USA Today*-style newspaper articles.)

Consequently, we've subconsciously trained ourselves to assimilate information better in neat little packages. If you scrawl notes all over the paper, you fragment the flow of the information. Strive for clarity. Newspapers use a standard format to achieve clarity. Your notes can be much clearer through use of proper formatting. A very effective format is called the Cornell Method.

> Take a sheet of loose-leaf, lined notebook paper, and draw a line all the way down the paper about 1"-2" from the left-hand edge.
>
> Draw another line across the width of the paper about 1"-2" up from the bottom. Repeat this process on the reverse side of the page.

Look at the highly effective result. You have ample room for notes, a left-hand margin for special-emphasis items or for inserting supplementary data from the textbook, a large area at the bottom for a brief summary, and a little rectangular space for just about anything you want.

3. Get the concept, then the details. Too often we focus on the details and don't gather an understanding of the concept. However, if you simply memorize only dates, places, or names, you may well miss the whole point of the subject.

A key way to understand things is to put them in your own words. If you are working from a textbook, automatically summarize each paragraph in your mind. If you are outlining text, don't simply copy the author's words.

Rephrase them in your own words. You remember your own thoughts and words much better than someone else's thoughts and words, and you subconsciously tend to associate the important details to the core concepts.

4. Ask "Why." Pull apart written material paragraph by paragraph and don't forget the captions under the illustrations.

Pull apart written material paragraph by paragraph, and don't forget the captions under the illustrations.

> Example: If the heading is "Stream Erosion," flip it around to read "Why do streams erode?" Then answer the question.

If you train your mind to think in a series of questions and answers, not only will you learn more, but the training will also help to lessen the test anxiety because you are used to answering questions.

5. Read for reinforcement and future needs. Even if you only have ten minutes, put your notes or a book in your hand. Your mind is similar to a computer: you have to input data in order to have it processed. *By reading, you are creating the neural connections for future retrieval.* The more times you read something, the more you reinforce the learning of ideas.

Even if you don't fully understand something on the first pass, *your mind stores much of the material for later recall.*

6. Relax to learn, so go into exile. Our bodies respond to an inner clock called biorhythms. Burning the midnight oil works well for some people, but not for everyone.

If possible, set aside a particular place to study that is free of distractions. Shut off the television, cell phone, and pager, and exile your friends and family during your study period.

If you really are bothered by silence, try background music. Light classical music at a low volume has been shown to aid in concentration over other music. Music that evokes pleasant emotions without lyrics is highly suggested. Try just about anything by Mozart. It relaxes you.

. **7. Use arrows, not highlighters.** At best, it's difficult to read a page full of yellow, pink, blue, and green streaks.

Try staring at a neon sign for a while, and you'll soon see my point; the horde of colors obscures the message. A quick note: a brief dash of color, an underline, and an arrow pointing to a particular passage are much clearer than a horde of highlighted words.

8. Budget your study time. Although you shouldn't ignore any of the material, *allocate your available study time in the same ratio that topics may appear on the test.*

TEACHER CERTIFICATION STUDY GUIDE

Testing Tips:

1. <u>Get smart; play dumb.</u> Don't read anything into the question. Don't make an assumption that the test writer is looking for something else than what is asked. Stick to the question as written, and don't read extra things into it.

2. <u>Read the question and all the choices *twice* before answering the question</u>. You may miss something by failing to carefully read--and then re-read--both the question and the answers.

If you really don't have a clue as to the right answer, leave it blank on the first time through. Go on to the other questions because they may provide a clue as to how to answer the skipped questions.

If later on, you still can't answer the skipped ones . . . *Guess*. The only penalty for guessing is that you *might* get it wrong. Only one thing is certain: if you don't answer a question, it will be counted as wrong.

3. <u>Turn the question into a statement</u>. Look at the way the questions are worded. The syntax of the question usually provides a clue. Does it seem more familiar as a statement rather than as a question? Does it sound strange?

By turning a question into a statement, you may be able to spot if an answer sounds right, and it may also trigger memories of material you have read.

4. <u>Look for hidden clues</u>. It's actually very difficult to compose multiple-choice questions without giving away part of the answer in the options presented.

In most multiple-choice questions, you can often readily eliminate one or two of the potential answers. This leaves you with only two real possibilities, and automatically your odds go to 50-50 for very little work.

5. <u>Trust your instincts</u>. For every fact that you have read, you subconsciously retain something of that knowledge. On questions that you aren't really certain about, go with your basic instincts. *Your first impression on how to answer a question is usually correct.*

6. <u>Mark your answers directly on the test booklet</u>. Don't bother trying to fill in the optical scan sheet on the first pass through the test.

Be careful not to mismark your answers when you transcribe them to the scan sheet.

7. <u>Watch the clock</u>! You have a set amount of time to answer the questions. Don't get bogged down trying to answer a single question at the expense of 10 questions you can more readily answer.

ENGLISH

TEACHER CERTIFICATION STUDY GUIDE

TEACHER CERTIFICATION STUDY GUIDE

DOMAIN I.   **LITERATURE AND TEXTUAL ANALYSIS**

Candidates demonstrate knowledge of the foundations and contexts of the literature and textual analysis contained in the English-Language Arts Content Standards for California Public Schools (1997) as outlined in the *Reading/Language Arts Framework for California Public Schools: Kindergarten Through Grade Twelve* (1999) at a post secondary level of rigor. Candidates have both broad and deep conceptual knowledge of the subject matter. The candidate's preparation should include breadth of knowledge in literature, literary analysis and criticism, as well as non-literary text analysis.

Literary analysis presumes in-depth exploration of the relationship between form and content. The curriculum should embrace representative selections from different literary traditions and major works from diverse cultures. Advanced study of multicultural writers is also fundamental preparation for teaching these works. Shakespeare remains integral to the secondary school curriculum; advanced study of his work is, therefore, essential to future secondary teachers. Candidates must be enthusiastic readers and writers, who know and apply effective reading strategies and compose thoughtful, well-crafted responses to literary and non-literary texts.

COMPETENCY 1.0   LITERARY ANALYSIS

SKILL 1.1   Recognize, compare, and evaluate different literary traditions to include
- American (inclusive of cultural pluralism)
- British (inclusive of cultural pluralism)
- World literature and literature in translation (inclusive of cross-cultural literature)
- Mythology and oral tradition

American Literature

American literature is marked by a number of clearly identifiable periods. While these stand alone, they can also be useful as histories across the curriculum.

> Check out the
> **Brief Timeline of American Literature**
> http://www.wsu.edu/~campbelld/amlit/timefram.html

Native American Works from Various Tribes
These were originally part of a vast oral tradition that spanned most of continental America from as far back as prior to the fifteenth century.

Characteristics of native Indian literature include
- Reverence for and awe of nature.
- The interconnectedness of the elements in the life cycle.

Themes of Indian literature often reflect
- The hardiness of the native body and soul.
- Remorse for the destruction of their way of life.
- The genocide of many tribes by the encroaching settlement and Manifest Destiny policies of the U. S. government.

The Colonial Period in both New England and the South
Stylistically, early colonists' writings were neo-classical, emphasizing order, balance, clarity, and reason. Schooled in England, their writing and speaking was still decidedly British even as their thinking became entirely American.

Early American literature reveals the lives and experiences of the New England expatriates who left England to find religious freedom.

William Bradford's excerpts from *The Mayflower Compact* relate vividly the hardships of crossing the Atlantic in such a tiny vessel, the misery and suffering of the first winter, the approaches of the American Indians, the decimation of their ranks, and the establishment of the Bay Colony of Massachusetts.

Anne Bradstreet's poetry relates colonial New England life. From her journals, modern readers learn of the everyday life of the early settlers, the hardships of travel, and the responsibilities of different groups and individuals in the community. Early American literature also reveals the

> *"If ever two were one, then surely we.*
> *If ever man were loved by wife, then thee."*
> Read more about
> **Anne Bradstreet**
> http://www.annebradstreet.com/Default.htm

commercial and political adventures of the Cavaliers who came to the New World with King George's blessing.

William Byrd's journal, *A History of the Dividing Line* concerns his trek into the Dismal Swamp separating the Carolinian territories from Virginia and Maryland and makes quite lively reading. A privileged insider to the English Royal Court, Byrd, like other Southern Cavaliers, was given grants to pursue business ventures.

The Revolutionary Period contains non-fiction genres: essays, pamphlets, speeches, famous documents, and epistles.

Major Writers and Works of the Revolutionary Period:
Thomas Paine's pamphlet, *Common Sense*, though written by a recently transplanted Englishman, spoke to the American patriots' common sense in dealing with the issues in the cause of freedom.

Other contributions are Benjamin Franklin's essays from *Poor Richard's Almanac* and satires such as "How to Reduce a Great Empire to a Small One" and "A Letter to Madame Gout."

There were great orations such as Patrick Henry's *Speech to the Virginia House of Burgesses* (the "Give me liberty or give me death" speech) and George Washington's *Farewell to the Army of the Potomac*. Less memorable are Washington's inaugural addresses, which strike modern readers as lacking sufficient focus.

The *Declaration of Independence*, the brainchild predominantly of Thomas Jefferson (along with some prudent editing by Ben Franklin), is a prime example of neoclassical writing—balanced, well crafted, and focused.

Epistles include the exquisitely written, moving correspondence between John Adams and Abigail Adams. The poignancy of their separation—she in Boston, he in Philadelphia—is palpable and real.

The Romantic Period
Early American folktales and the emergence of a distinctly American writing, not just a stepchild to English forms, constitute the next period.

Washington Irving's characters, Icabod Crane and Rip Van Winkle, represent a uniquely American folklore devoid of English influences. The characters are indelibly marked by their environment and

> Find more sites about
> **American Romanticism**
> http://guweb2.gonzaga.edu/faculty/campbell/enl311/romanticism.htm

the superstitions of the New Englander. The early American writings of James Fenimore Cooper and his *Leatherstocking Tales* provide readers a window into their uniquely American world through the stirring accounts of drums along the Mohawk, the French and Indian Wars, the futile British defense of Fort William Henry, and the brutalities of this period. Natty Bumppo, Chingachgook, Uncas, and Magua are unforgettable characters who reflect the American spirit in thought and action.

The poetry of Fireside Poets—James Russell Lowell, Oliver Wendell Holmes, Henry Wadsworth Longfellow, and John Greenleaf Whittier— was recited by American families and read in the long New England winters. In "The Courtin'," Lowell used Yankee dialect to tell the story. Spellbinding epics by Longfellow (such as *Hiawatha*, *The Courtship of Miles Standish*, and *Evangeline)* told of adversity, sorrow, and ultimate happiness in a uniquely American fashion. "Snowbound" by Whittier relates the story of a captive family isolated by a blizzard, stressing family closeness.

Nathaniel Hawthorne and Herman Melville are the preeminent early American novelists, writing on subjects definitely regional, specific, and American, yet sharing insights about human foibles, fears, loves, doubts, and triumphs.

Hawthorne's writings range from children's stories, such as the *Cricket on the Hearth* series, to adult fare of dark, brooding short stories such as "Dr. Heidegger's Experiment," "The Devil and Tom Walker," and "Rapuccini's Daughter." His masterpiece, *The Scarlet Letter*, takes on the society of hypocritical Puritan New Englanders, who ostensibly left England to establish religious freedom but who have become entrenched in judgmental finger-wagging. They ostracize Hester and condemn her child, Pearl, as a child of Satan. Great love, sacrifice, loyalty, suffering, and related epiphanies add universality to this tale. *The House of the Seven Gables* deals with-kept secrets, loneliness, societal pariahs, and love ultimately triumphing over horrible wrong.

Herman Melville's great opus, *Moby Dick*, follows a crazed Captain Ahab on his Homeric odyssey to conquer the great white whale that has outwitted him and his whaling crews time and again. The whale has even taken Ahab's leg and, according to Ahab, wants all of him. Melville recreates in painstaking detail and with insider knowledge the harsh life of a whaler out of New Bedford by way of Nantucket.

For those who don't want to learn about every guy rope or all parts of the whaler's rigging, Melville offers up the succinct tale of *Billy Budd* and his Christ-like sacrifice to the black-and-white maritime laws on the high seas. An accident results in the death of one of the ship's officers, a slug of a fellow, who had taken a dislike to the young, affable, shy Billy. Captain Vere must hang Billy for the death of Claggert but knows that this is not right. However, an example must be given to the rest of the crew so that discipline can be maintained.

The Life and Works of Herman Melville
http://www.melville.org/

Edgar Allan Poe creates a distinctly American version of romanticism with his 16-syllable lines in "The Raven," the classical "To Helen," and his Gothic "Annabelle Lee." The horror short story can be said to originate from Poe's pen. "The Tell-Tale Heart," "The Cask of Amontillado," "The Fall of the House of Usher," and "The Masque of the Red Death" are exemplary short stories. In addition, the genre of detective story emerges with Poe's "Murders in the Rue Morgue."

American Romanticism has its own offshoot in the transcendentalism of Ralph Waldo Emerson and Henry David Thoreau. Emerson wrote about transcending the complexities of life; Thoreau, who wanted to get to the marrow of life, immersed himself in nature at Walden Pond and wrote an inspiring autobiographical account of his sojourn, aptly titled *On Walden Pond*. Thoreau also wrote passionately regarding his objections to the interference of government imposed on the individual in his "On the Duty of Civil Disobedience."

Emerson's elegantly-crafted essays and war poetry still validate several important universal truths. Probably most remembered for his address to Thoreau's Harvard graduating class, "The American Scholar," he defined the qualities of hard work and intellectual spirit required of Americans in their growing nation.

The Transition between Romanticism and Realism
The Civil War period ushers in the poignant poetry of Walt Whitman and his homages to all who suffer from the ripple effects of war and presidential assassination. His "Come up from the Fields, Father" about a Civil War soldier's death and his family's reaction and "When Lilacs Last in the Courtyard Bloom'd" about the effects of Abraham Lincoln's death on the poet and the nation should be required readings in any American literature course. Further, his *Leaves of Grass* gave America its first poetry truly unique in form, structure, and subject matter.

Emily Dickinson, like Walt Whitman, leaves her literary fingerprints on a vast array of poems, all but three of which were never published in her lifetime. Her themes of introspection and attention to nature's details and wonders are, by any measurement, world-class works. Her posthumous recognition reveals the timeliness of her work. American writing had most certainly arrived!

During this period, such legendary figures as Paul Bunyan and Pecos Bill rose from the oral tradition. Anonymous storytellers around campfires told tales of a huge lumberman and his giant blue ox, Babe, whose adventures were explanations of natural phenomena like those of footprints filled with rainwater becoming the Great Lakes. Or the whirling-dervish speed of Pecos Bill explained the tornadoes of the Southwest. Like ancient peoples finding reasons for the happenings in their lives, these American pioneer storytellers created a mythology appropriate to the vast reaches of the unsettled frontier.

> Find more sites about
> **American Literature**
> http://www.wsu.edu/~campbelld/amlit/sites.htm

Mark Twain also left giant footprints with his unique blend of tall tale and fable. "The Celebrated Jumping Frog of Calaveras County" and "The Man who Stole Hadleyburg" are epitomes of short story writing. With the novel, Twain again stands out with his bold, still disputed, oft-banned *The Adventures of Huckleberry Finn*, which examines such taboo subjects as a white person's love of a slave, the issue of leaving children with abusive parents, and the outcomes of family feuds. Written partly in dialect and southern vernacular, *The Adventures of Huckleberry Finn* is touted by some as the greatest American novel.

The Realistic Period

The late nineteenth century saw a reaction against the tendency of romantic writers to look at the world through rose-colored glasses. Writers including Frank Norris (*The Pit*) and Upton Sinclair (*The Jungle*) used their novels to decry conditions for workers in slaughterhouses and wheat mills.

Upton Sinclair
http://www.online-literature.com/upton_sinclair/

In *The Red Badge of Courage*, Stephen Crane wrote of the daily sufferings of the common soldier in the Civil War. Realistic writers wrote of common, ordinary people and events using realistic detail to reveal the harsh realities of life. They breached taboos by creating protagonists whose environments often destroyed them. Romantic writers' created protagonists with indomitable wills that helped them rise above adversity.

Crane's *Maggie: A Girl of the Streets* deals with a young woman forced into prostitution to survive. In "The Occurrence at Owl Creek Bridge," Ambrose Bierce relates the unfortunate hanging of a Confederate soldier.

Short stories, like Bret Harte's "The Outcasts of Poker Flat" and Jack London's "To Build a Fire," deal with unfortunate people whose luck in life has run out. Many writers, sub-classified as naturalists, believed that man was subject to a fate over which he had no control.

The Modern Era

Twentieth-century American writing can be divided into the following three genres: drama, fiction, and poetry.

American Drama: The greatest and most prolific of American playwrights include these playwrights:

- Eugene O'Neill- *Long Day's Journey into Night, Mourning Becomes Electra,* and *Desire Under the Elms*
- Arthur Miller- *The Crucible, All My Sons,* and *Death of a Salesman*
- Tennessee Williams- *Cat on a Hot Tin Roof, The Glass Menagerie,* and *A Street Car Named Desire*
- Edward Albee- *Who's Afraid of Virginia Woolf? Three Tall Women,* and *A Delicate Balance*

American Fiction: The renowned American novelists of this century include these authors:

- Eudora Welty- *The Optimist's Daughter*

- John Updike- *Rabbit Run* and *Rabbit Redux*
- Sinclair Lewis- *Babbit* and *Elmer Gantry*
- F. Scott Fitzgerald- *The Great Gatsby* and *Tender Is the Night*
- Ernest Hemingway- *A Farewell to Arms* and *For Whom the Bell Tolls*
- William Faulkner- *The Sound and the Fury* and *Absalom, Absalom*
- Bernard Malamud- *The Fixer* and *The Natural*

American Poetry: The poetry of the twentieth century is multifaceted, as represented by Edna St. Vincent Millay, Marianne Moore, Richard Wilbur, Langston Hughes, Maya Angelou, and Rita Dove. Usually known more than other poets' work are the layered poems of Robert Frost. His New England motifs of snowy evenings, birches, apple-picking, stone-wall mending, hired hands, and detailed nature studies relate universal truths in exquisite diction, polysyllabic words, and rare allusions to either mythology or the Bible.

American Indian Literature: The foundation of American Indian writing is found in story-telling, oratory, autobiographical and historical accounts of tribal village life, reverence for the environment, and the postulation that the earth with all of its beauty was given in trust, to be cared for and passed on to future generations.

Early American Indian Writers

- Hal Barland- *When the Legends Die*
- Geronimo (Apache; edited by Barrett and Turner)- *Geronimo: His Own Story: The Autobiography of a Great Patriot Warrior*
- C. Eastman & E. Eastman- *Wigwam Evenings: Sioux Folktales Retold*
- L. Riggs and Jace Weaver- *Cherokee Night* - drama

Twentieth Century American Indian Writers

- V. Deloria- *Custer Died for your Sins* (Sioux)
- M. Dorris- *The Broken Cord: A Family's On-going Struggle with Fetal Alcohol Syndrome* (Modoc)
- Linda Hogan- *Mean Spirit* (Chickasaw) - poetry
- C.F. Taylor- *Native American Myths and Legends*

Feminist/Gender-Concern Literature Written by American Women

American women authors have contributed notably to literature in all genres, providing a unique perspective throughout American history.

For example, Edith Wharton's *Ethan Frome* is a heartbreaking tale of lack of communication, lack of funds, the unrelenting cold of the Massachusetts winter, and a toboggan ride which gnarls Ethan and Mattie just like the old tree which they smash into. The *Age of Innocence*, in contrast to *Ethan Frome*, is set in the upper echelons of fin-de-siècle New York and explores the marriage of stifling social protocols.

Willa Cather's work moves the reader to the prairies of Nebraska and the harsh eking out of existence by the immigrant families who choose to stay there and farm. Her most acclaimed works include *My Antonia* and *Death Comes for the Archbishop*, which takes place in New Mexico Territory.

Kate Chopin's regionalism and local color takes her readers to the upper-crust Creole society of New Orleans and the resort isles off the Louisiana coast. Her "The Story of an Hour" is lauded as one of the greatest of all short stories. Her feminist liberation novel *The Awakening* is still hotly debated.

> Find more literary resources about **Feminism and Women's Literature** at http://andromeda.rutgers.edu/~jlynch/Lit/women.html

Eudora Welty's regionalism and dialect shine in her short stories of rural Mississippi, especially in "The Worn Path."

Modern Black Female Writers explore the world of feminist/gender issues as well as class prohibitions.

- Alice Walker- *The Color Purple*
- Zora Neale Hurston- *Their Eyes Were Watching God*
- Toni Morrison- *Beloved*, *Jazz*, and *Song of Solomon*

Feminists

- Louisa May Alcott- *Little Women*
- Betty Friedan- *The Feminine Mystique* and *The Second Stage*
- Elizabeth Janeway- *Man's World, Woman's Place: A Study in Social Mythology*
- Adrienne Rich- *Of Woman Born: Motherhood As Experience and Institution* and *Driving into the Wreck*

British Literature

To appreciate fully American literature, students need to study the deep canon of British literature.

Anglo-Saxon

The Anglo-Saxon period spans six centuries but produced only a smattering of literature. The first British epic is *Beowulf,* anonymously written by Christian monks many years after the events in the narrative supposedly occurred. This Teutonic saga relates the triumph over monsters three times over by the hero, Beowulf. "The Seafarer," a shorter poem, some history, and some riddles represent what we know of the Anglo-Saxon canon.

> Check out this lesson plan
> **An Introduction to Beowulf: Language and Poetics**
> http://www.readwritethink.org/lessons/lesson_view.asp?id=813

Medieval

The Medieval period introduces Geoffrey Chaucer, the father of English literature, whose *Canterbury Tales* are written in the vernacular or street language of England, not in Latin. Thus, the tales are said to be the first work of British literature.

Next, Thomas Malory's *Le Morte d'Arthur* calls together the extant tales from Europe as well as England concerning the legendary King Arthur, Merlin, Guenevere, and the Knights of the Round Table. This work is the generative work that gave rise to the many Arthurian legends that stir the chivalric imagination.

Renaissance and Elizabethan Periods

The Renaissance, the most important period since it is synonymous with William Shakespeare, begins with importing the idea of the Petrarchan or Italian sonnet into England. Sir Thomas Wyatt and Sir Philip Sydney wrote English versions. Next, Sir Edmund Spenser invented a variation on this Italian sonnet form, aptly called the Spenserian sonnet. His masterpiece is the epic, *The Faerie Queene*, honoring Queen Elizabeth I's reign. He also wrote books on the Red Cross Knight, St. George and the Dragon, and a series of Arthurian adventures. Spencer was dubbed the Poet's Poet. He created a nine-line stanza, with eight lines in iambic pentameter followed by an extra-footed ninth line or iambic hexameter (alexandrine). Thus, he invented the Spenserian stanza as well.

> Examine links to
> **Renaissance: The Elizabethan World - Related Sites**
> http://elizabethan.org/sites.html

William Shakespeare, the Bard of Avon, wrote 154 sonnets, 39 plays, and two long narrative poems. The sonnets are justifiably called the greatest sonnet sequence in all literature. Shakespeare dispensed with the octave/sestet format of the Italian sonnet and invented his three-quatrain sonnet concluding with one heroic couplet. His plays are divided into comedies, history plays, and tragedies.

ENGLISH

Great lines from these plays are more often quoted than from any other author. The "Big Four" tragedies, *Hamlet*, *Macbeth*, *Othello*, and *King Lear* are acknowledged to be the most brilliant examples of the genre of tragedy.

Seventeenth Century

John Milton's devout Puritanism was the wellspring of his creative genius that closes the remarkable productivity of the English Renaissance. His social commentary in such works as *Aereopagitica*, *Samson Agonistes*, and his elegant sonnets would be enough to solidify his stature as a great writer. It is his masterpiece based in part on the Book of Genesis that places Milton very near the top of the rung of a handful of the most renowned of all writers. *Paradise Lost*, written in balanced, elegant neoclassic form, justifies the ways of God to man.

The well-known allegory about man's journey to the Celestial City (Heaven) was written at the end of the English Renaissance by John Bunyan in the book *Pilgrims Progress*. The allegory describes virtues and vices personified, and this work was for a long time second only to the Bible in numbers of copies printed and sold.

The Jacobean Age gave us the marvelously witty and cleverly constructed conceits of John Donne's metaphysical sonnets as well as his insightful meditations and his version of sermons or homilies. "Ask not for whom the bell tolls" and "No man is an island unto himself" are famous epigrams from Donne's *Meditations*. His most famous conceit is that which compares lovers to a footed compass traveling seemingly separate, but always leaning towards one another and conjoined in "A Valediction: Forbidding Mourning."

Eighteenth Century

Ben Jonson, author of the wickedly droll play, *Volpone,* and the Cavalier *carpe diem* poets Robert Herrick, Sir John Suckling, and Richard Lovelace also wrote during King James I's reign.

The Restoration and Enlightenment reflect the political turmoil of the regicide of Charles I, the Interregnum Puritan government of Oliver Cromwell, and the restoring of the monarchy to England by the coronation of Charles II, who had been given refuge by the French King Louis. Neoclassicism became the preferred writing style, especially for Alexander Pope. New genres, such as *The Diary of Samuel Pepys*, the novels of Daniel Defoe, the periodical essays and editorials of Joseph Addison and Richard Steele, and Alexander Pope's mock epic *The Rape of the Lock* demonstrate the diversity of expression during this time.

Writers who followed were contemporaries of Dr. Samuel Johnson, the lexicographer of *The Dictionary of the English Language*. Fittingly, this Age of Johnson, which encompasses James Boswell's biography of Dr. Johnson, Robert Burns' Scottish dialect and regionalism in his evocative poetry, and the mystical pre-Romantic poetry of William Blake ushers in the Romantic Age and its revolution against Neoclassicism.

Romantic Period

The Romantic Age encompasses what is known as the First Generation Romantics, William Wordsworth and Samuel Taylor Coleridge, who collaborated on *Lyrical Ballads,* which defines and exemplifies the tenets of this style of writing. The Second Generation includes George Gordon, Lord Byron, Percy Bysshe Shelley, and John Keats. These poets wrote sonnets, odes, epics, and narrative poems, most dealing with homage to nature.

Read about
The Romantic Period
http://www.wwnorton.com/college/english/nael/romantic/welcome.htm

Wordsworth's most famous works are "Intimations on Immortality" and "The Prelude." Byron's satirical epic *Don Juan* and his autobiographical *Childe Harold's Pilgrimage* are irreverent, witty, self-deprecating and, in part, cuttingly critical of other writers and critics. Shelley's odes and sonnets are remarkable for sensory imagery. Keats' sonnets, odes, and longer narrative poem *The Eve of St. Agnes* are remarkable for their introspection at this tender age of the poet who died when he was only twenty-five.

In fact, all of the Second Generation died young. Wordsworth, who lived to be eighty, outlived them all, including Coleridge, his friend and collaborator.

Others who wrote during the Romantic Age are the essayist Charles Lamb and the novelist Jane Austin. The Brontë sisters, Charlotte and Emily, wrote one novel each, which are noted as exceptional: *Jane Eyre* (Charlotte) and *Wuthering Heights* (Emily). Mary Anne Evans, also known as George Eliot, wrote several important novels: *Middlemarch*, *Silas Marner*, *Adam Bede*, and *Mill on the Floss*.

Nineteenth Century

The Victorian Period is remarkable for the diversity and proliferation of work in three major areas. Poets typified as Victorians include Alfred, Lord Tennyson, who wrote *Idylls of the King*, twelve narrative poems about the Arthurian legend; and Robert Browning, who wrote chilling, dramatic monologues, such as "My Last Duchess," as well as long poetic narratives such as *The Pied Piper of Hamlin*. His wife Elizabeth wrote two major works, the epic feminist poem, *Aurora Leigh*, and her deeply moving and provocative *Sonnets from the Portuguese,* in which she details her deep love for Robert and, to her, his startling reciprocation.

http://www.victorianweb.org/

Gerard Manley Hopkins, a Catholic priest, wrote poetry with sprung rhythm. A. E. Housmann, Matthew Arnold, and the Pre-Raphaelites--especially the brother and sister duo, Dante Gabriel Rosetti and Christina Rosetti--contributed much to round out the Victorian Era's "poetic scene." The Pre-Raphaelites, a group of 19th-century English painters, poets, and critics, reacted against Victorian materialism and the neoclassical conventions of academic art by producing earnest, quasi-religious works, inspired by medieval and early Renaissance painters up to the time of the Italian painter Raphael.

Robert Louis Stevenson, the great Scottish novelist, wrote his adventure/history lessons for young adults. Victorian prose ranges from the incomparable, keenly woven plot structures of Charles Dickens to the deeply moving Dorset/Wessex novels of Thomas Hardy, in which women are repressed and life is more struggle than euphoria. Rudyard Kipling wrote about Colonialism in India in his works *Kim* and *The Jungle Book* that create exotic locales and a distinct main point concerning the Raj, the British colonial government during Queen Victoria's reign. Victorian drama is a product mainly of Oscar Wilde, whose satirical masterpiece *The Importance of Being Earnest* farcically details and lampoons Victorian social mores.

Twentieth Century

The early twentieth century is represented mainly by the towering achievement of George Bernard Shaw's dramas: *St. Joan*, *Man and Superman*, *Major Barbara*, and *Arms and the Man,* to name a few. Novelists are too numerous to list, but Joseph Conrad, E. M. Forster, Virginia Woolf, James Joyce, Nadine Gordimer, Graham Greene, George Orwell, and D. H. Lawrence are among some of the century's very best.

Twentieth century poets of renown and merit include W. H. Auden, Robert Graves, T. S. Eliot, Edith Sitwell, Stephen Spender, Dylan Thomas, Philip Larkin, Ted Hughes, Sylvia Plath, and Hugh MacDarmid. This list is by no means complete.

World Literature

North American Literature

North American literature was created by writers from the United States, Canada, and Mexico. Canadian writers of note include feminist Margaret Atwood (*The Handmaid's Tale*); Alice Munro, a remarkable short story writer; and W. P. Kinsella, another short story writer whose two major subjects are North American Indians and baseball. Mexican writers include 1990 Nobel Prize winning poet Octavio Paz (*The Labyrinth of Solitude*) and feminist Rosario Castillanos (*The Nine Guardians*).

Central American/Caribbean Literature

The Caribbean and Central America encompass a vast area and cultures that reflect oppression and colonialism by England, Spain, Portugal, France, and The Netherlands. The Caribbean writers include Samuel Selvon from Trinidad and Armando Valladares of Cuba. Central American authors include dramatist Carlos Solorzano, from Guatemala, whose plays include *Dona Beatriz, The Hapless, The Magician,* and *The Hands of God.*

> **The Norton Anthology of World Literature**
> http://www.wwnorton.com/college/english/nawol/

South American Literature

Chilean Gabriela Mistral was the first Latin American writer to win the Nobel Prize for literature in 1945. She is best known for her collections of poetry, *Desolation and Feeling.*

Chile was also home to Pablo Neruda, who, in 1971, also won the Nobel Prize for literature for his poetry. His 29 volumes of poetry have been translated into more than 60 languages, attesting to his universal appeal. *Twenty Love Poems* and *Song of Despair* are justly famous. Isabel Allende carries on the Chilean literary standards with her acclaimed novel *House of Spirits*. Argentine Jorge Luis Borges is considered by many literary critics to be the most important writer of his century from South America. His collections of short stories, *Ficciones*, brought him universal recognition. Also from Argentina, Silvina Ocampo, a collaborator with Borges on a collection of poetry, is famed for her poetry and short story collections, which include *The Fury* and *The Days of the Night*.

Noncontinental European Literature

Horacio Quiroga represents Uruguay, and from Brazil is Joao Guimaraes Rosa, whose novel, *The Devil to Pay*, is highly regarded.

Continental European Literature

With its long history of great writers, continental European literature expands the world of students and broadens their exposure to different cultures and values. This category excludes British literature as it was covered previously.

Germany

German poet and playwright Friedrich von Schiller is best known for his history plays *William Tell* and *The Maid of Orleans*. He is a leading literary figure in Germany's Golden Age of Literature. Also from Germany, Rainer Maria Rilke, the great lyric poet, is one of the poets of the unconscious or stream of consciousness. Germany also has given the world Herman Hesse, (*Siddartha*), Gunter Grass (*The Tin Drum*), and often considered the greatest of all German writers, Goethe.

Scandinavia

Scandinavian literature includes the work of Hans Christian Andersen of Denmark, who advanced the fairy tale genre with such wistful tales as "The Little Mermaid" and "Thumbelina." The social commentary of Henrik Ibsen in Norway startled the world through drama exploring such issues as feminism (*The Doll's House* and *Hedda Gabler*) and the effects of sexually-transmitted diseases (*The Wild Duck* and *Ghosts*). Sweden's Selma Lagerlof is the first woman to win the Nobel Prize for literature (1909). Her novels include *Gosta Berling's Saga* and the world-renowned *The Wonderful Adventures of Nils*, a children's work.

Read more about **Henrik Ibsen**
http://www.hf.uio.no/ibsensenteret/index_eng.html

Russia

Russian literature is vast and monumental. Who has not heard of Fyodor Dostoyevski's *Crime and Punishment* and *The Brothers Karamazov* or Count Leo Tolstoy's *War and Peace*? These are examples of psychological realism.

Dostoyevski's influence on modern writers cannot be over-stressed. Tolstoy's *War and Peace* is the sweeping account of the invasion of Russia and Napoleon's taking of Moscow. Further advancing Tolstoy's greatness was his ability to create realistic and unforgettable female characters, especially Natasha in *War and Peace* and Anna in *Anna Karenina*. Pushkin is famous for great short stories; Anton Chekhov for drama (*Uncle Vanya*, *The Three Sisters*, *The Cherry Orchard*); and Yevgeny Yevtushenko for poetry (*Babi Yar*). Boris Pasternak won the Nobel Prize (*Dr. Zhivago*) in 1958, and he felt he had to reject it. Aleksandr Solzhenitsyn (*The Gulag Archipelago*) returned to Russia after years of expatriation in Vermont. Ilya Varshavsky, who creates fictional societies that are dystopias, or the opposite of utopias, represents the genre of science fiction.

France

France has a multifaceted canon of great literature that is universal in scope and that almost always champions some social cause. Examples include the poignant short stories of Guy de Maupassant; the fantastic poetry of Charles Baudelaire (*Fleurs du Mal*); the groundbreaking lyrical poetry of Rimbaud and Verlaine; and the existentialism (a philosophical and literary movement, variously religious and atheistic, stemming from Kierkegaard) of Jean-Paul Sartre (*No Exit*, *The Flies*, *Nausea*); Andre Malraux (*The Fall*); and Albert Camus (*The Stranger* and *The Plague*), recipient of the 1957 Nobel Prize for literature.

Drama in France is best represented by Rostand's *Cyrano de Bergerac* and the neo-classical dramas of Racine and Corneille (*El Cid*). Feminist writers include Simone de Beauvoir and Sidonie-Gabrielle Colette, known for her short stories and novels. The great French novelists include Andre Gide, Honore de Balzac (*Cousin Bette*), Stendel (*The Red and the Black*), and Alexandre Dumas (*The Three Musketeers* and *The Man in the Iron Mask*). Victor Hugo is the Charles Dickens of French literature, having penned the masterpieces *The Hunchback of Notre Dame* and *Les Miserables*. The stream of consciousness of Proust's *Remembrance of Things Past* and the Absurdist theatre of Samuel Beckett and Eugene Ionesco (*The Rhinoceros*) attest to the groundbreaking genius of the French writers.

Learn more about **Jean Paul Sartre**
http://www.users.muohio.edu/shermalw/honors_2001_fall/honors_papers_2001/detwilerj_Sartre.htm

Slavic Nations

Austrian writer Franz Kafka (*The Metamorphosis*, *The Trial*, and *The Castle*) is considered by many to be the literary voice of the first-half of the twentieth century. Poet Vaclav Havel represents the Czech Republic. Slovakia has dramatist Karel Capek (*R.U.R.*). We can be reminded of Romania when we read Elie Weisel (*Night*), winner of the Nobel Prize in 1986.

Spain

Spain's great writers include Miguel de Cervantes (*Don Quixote*) and Juan Ramon Jimenez. The anonymous national epic, *El Cid*, has been translated into many languages.

Italy

Italy's greatest writers include Virgil (*The Aeneid*), Giovanni Boccaccio (*The Decameron*), Dante Alighieri (*The Divine Comedy*) and the more contemporary Alberto Moravia.

Ancient Greece

Greece will always be foremost in literary stature because of Homer's epics, *The Iliad* and *The Odyssey*. No one except Shakespeare is more often cited. The works of Plato and Aristotle in philosophy; of Aeschylus, Euripides, and Sophocles in tragedy, and of Aristophanes in comedy further solidify Greece's pre-eminence. Greece is the cradle not only of democracy, but of literature as well.

Africa

African literary greats include South Africans Nadine Gordimer (Nobel Prize 1991) and Peter Abrahams (*Tell Freedom: Memories of Africa*), an autobiography of life in Johannesburg. Chinua Achebe (*Things Fall Apart*) and the poet, Wole Soyinka, hail from Nigeria. Mark Mathabane wrote an autobiography *Kaffir Boy* about growing up in South Africa. Egyptian writer, Naguib Mahfouz, and Doris Lessing from Rhodesia, now Zimbabwe, write about race relations in their respective countries. Lessing won the 2007 Nobel Prize for Literature. Because of her radical politics, Lessing was once banned from her homeland and the Union of South Africa, as was Alan Paton whose seemingly simple story, *Cry, the Beloved Country*, brought the plight of blacks and the whites' fear of blacks under apartheid to the rest of the world.

> Learn more about
> **Postcolonial Literature in English**
> http://www.thecore.nus.edu.sg/post/misc/africov.html

Far East Literature

Asia has many modern writers who are being translated for the western reading public. India's Krishan Chandar has authored more than 300 stories. Rabindranath Tagore won the Nobel Prize for literature in 1913 (*Song Offerings*). R. K. Narayan, India's most famous writer (*The Guide*), is interested in mythology and legends of India. Santha Rama Rau's work *Gifts of Passage* is her true story of life in a British school where she tries to preserve her Indian culture and traditional home.

Revered as Japan's most famous female author, Fumiko Hayashi (*Drifting Clouds*) by the time of her death had written more than 270 literary works.

In 1968 the Nobel Prize for literature was awarded to Yasunari Kawabata (*The Sound of the Mountain*, *The Snow Country*). His *Palm-of-the-Hand Stories* take the essentials of haiku poetry and transform them into the short story genre.

Katai Tayama (*The Quilt*) is touted as the father of the Japanese confessional novel. His works, characterized as naturalism, are definitely not for the squeamish. The "slice of life" psychological writings of Ryunosuke Akutagawa gained him acclaim in the western world. His short stories, especially "Rashamon" and "In a Grove," are greatly praised for style as well as content.

China, too, has given to the literary world. Li Po, the T'ang dynasty poet from the Chinese Golden Age, revealed his interest in folklore by preserving the folk songs and mythology of China. Po further allows his readers to enter into the Chinese philosophy of Taoism and to understand feelings against expansionism during the T'ang dynastic rule. The T'ang dynasty, which was one of great diversity in the arts, saw Jiang Fang help create the Chinese version of a short story. His themes often express love between a man and a woman.

Modern feminist and political concerns are written eloquently by Ting Ling, who used the pseudonym Chiang Ping-Chih. Her stories reflect her concerns about social injustice and her commitment to the women's movement.

Mythology and Oral Tradition

Literary allusions are drawn from classic mythology, national folklore, and religious writings that are supposed to have such familiarity to the reader that he can recognize the comparison between the subject of the allusion and the person, place, or event in the current reading. Children and adolescents who have knowledge of proverbs, fables, myths, epics, and the Bible can understand these allusions and thereby appreciate their reading to a greater degree than those who cannot recognize them.

Classical Mythology

Much of the mythology that produces allusions in world literature is a product of ancient Greece and Rome because Greek and Roman myths have been liberally translated. Some Norse myths are also well known.

Children are fond of myths because those ancient people sought explanations for what happened in their lives in a manner accessible and familiar to children. These stories provide insight into the order and ethics of life. In them, ancient heroes overcome the terrors of the unknown, and explanations are given for thunder and lightning, the changing seasons, the origin and function of magical creatures of the forests and seas, and frightening natural phenomena. There is often a childlike directness in the emotions of supernatural beings. Many good translations of myths exist, but Edith Hamilton's *Mythology* is the definitive choice for adolescents.

Fairy Tales

Fairy tales are lively fictional stories involving children or animals that come in contact with super beings via magic. They provide happy solutions to human dilemmas. The fairy tales of many nations are peopled by trolls, elves, dwarfs, and pixies, child-sized beings capable of fantastic accomplishments.

Among the most famous are "Beauty and the Beast," "Cinderella," "Hansel and Gretel," "Snow White and the Seven Dwarfs," "Rumplestiltskin," and "Tom Thumb." In each tale, the

> Check out
> **Sur La Lune Fairy Tales and Folklore**
> http://www.surlalunefairytales.com/introduction/index.html

protagonist survives prejudice, imprisonment, ridicule, and even death to receive justice in a cruel world.

Older readers encounter a kind of fairy tale world in Shakespeare's *The Tempest* and *A Midsummer Night's Dream*, which use pixies and fairies as characters. Adolescent readers today are as fascinated by the creations of fantasy realms in the works of Piers Anthony, Ursula LeGuin, and Anne McCaffrey. An extension of interest in the supernatural is the popularity of science fiction that allows us to use current knowledge to predict the possible course of the future.

Angels (or sometimes fairy godmothers) play a role in some fairy tales, and in *Paradise Lost* and *Paradise Regained* Milton also used symbolic angels and devils.

Biblical stories provide many allusions. Parables, moralistic-like fables but with human characters, include the stories of the Good Samaritan and the Prodigal Son. References to the treachery of Cain and the betrayal of Christ by Judas Iscariot are oft-cited examples.

Fables and Folktales

This literary group of stories and legends was originally orally transmitted to the common populace to provide models of exemplary behavior or deeds worthy of recognition and homage.

In fables, animals talk, feel, and behave like human beings. Fables always have a moral, and the animals depict specific people or groups indirectly. For example, in Aesop's *Fables,* the lion represents the King and the wolf represents the cruel, often unfeeling, nobility. In *The Lion and the Mouse, the* moral is that "little friends may prove to be great friends." In *The Lion's Share,* it is "might makes right." British folktales (*How Robin Became an Outlaw* and *St. George Slaying of the Dragon)* investigate the interplay between power and justice.

American Folk Tales

American folktales are divided into two categories: tall tales and legends.

Imaginary tales, also called **tall tales,** are humorous tales based on non-existent, fictional characters developed through blatant exaggeration.

- John Henry is a two-fisted steel driver who beats out a steam drill in competition.

- Rip Van Winkle sleeps for twenty years in the Catskill Mountains and upon awakening cannot understand why no one recognizes him.

- Paul Bunyan, a giant lumberjack, owns a great blue ox named Babe and has extraordinary physical strength. He is said to have plowed the Mississippi River while the impression of Babe's hoof prints created the Great Lakes.

Real tales, also called **legends,** are based on real persons who accomplished the feats that are attributed to them even if they are slightly exaggerated.

- For more than forty years, Johnny Appleseed (John Chapman) roamed Ohio and Indiana planting apple seeds.

- Daniel Boone, scout, adventurer, and pioneer, blazed the Wilderness Trail and made Kentucky safe for settlers.

- Paul Revere, a colonial patriot, rode through the New England countryside warning of the approach of British troops.

- George Washington cut down a cherry tree, which he could not deny. Or did he?

SKILL 1.2 Trace development of major literary movements in historical periods

There are four major time periods of writings: Neoclassicism, Romanticism, Realism, and Naturalism. Certain authors, among these Chaucer, Shakespeare, and Donne, though writing during a particular literary period, are considered to have a style all their own.

Neoclassicism

Patterned after the greatest writings of classical Greece and Rome, this type of writing is characterized by balanced, graceful, well-crafted, refined, elevated style. Major proponents of this style are poet laureates, John Dryden and Alexander Pope. The eras in which they wrote are called the Ages of Dryden and Pope. The self is not exalted, and focus is on the group, not the individual, in neoclassic writing.

Romanticism

These writings emphasize the individual. Emotions and feelings are validated. Nature acts as an inspiration for creativity; it is a balm of the spirit. Romantics hearken back to medieval, chivalric themes and ambiance. They also emphasize supernatural, Gothic themes and settings, which are characterized by gloom and darkness. Imagination is stressed. New types of writings include detective and horror stories and autobiographical introspection such as those by William Wordsworth.

There are two generations in British Literature: First Generation includes William Wordsworth and Samuel Taylor Coleridge whose collaboration, *Lyrical Ballads*, defines romanticism and its exponents. Wordsworth maintained that the scenes and events of everyday life and the speech of ordinary people were the raw material of which poetry could and should be made. Romanticism spread to the United States, where Ralph Waldo Emerson and Henry David Thoreau adopted it in their transcendental romanticism, emphasizing reasoning. Further extensions of this style are found in Edgar Allan Poe's gothic writings.

Second Generation romantics include the ill-fated Englishmen Lord Byron, John Keats, and Percy Bysshe Shelley. For some, Byron and Shelley epitomize the romantic poet (in their personal lives as well as in their work). They wrote resoundingly in protest against social and political wrongs and in defense of the struggles for liberty in Italy and Greece. The Second Generation romantics stressed personal introspection and the love of beauty and nature as requisites of inspiration.

The Percy Bysshe Shelley Resource Page
http://www.wam.umd.edu/~djb/shelley/gallery/header.jpg

Realism

Unlike classical and neoclassical writing which often deal with aristocracies and nobility or the gods, realistic writers deal with the common man and his socio/economic problems in a non-sentimental way. Muckraking, social injustice, domestic abuse, and inner city conflicts are examples of writings by writers of realism. Realistic writers include Thomas Hardy, George Bernard Shaw, and Henrik Ibsen. Realism denotes a particular kind of subject matter, especially the representation of middle-class life. The extreme of the realistic technique is Naturalism.

Naturalism

This is realism pushed to the maximum, writing which exposes the underbelly of society, usually the lower class struggles. This is the world of penury, injustice, abuse, ghetto survival, hungry children, single parenting, and substance abuse. Émile Zola was inspired by his readings in history and medicine and attempted to apply methods of scientific observation to the depiction of pathological human character, notably in his series of novels devoted to several generations of one French family.

SKILL 1.3　Describe the salient features of adolescent/young adult literature

Prior to twentieth century research on child development and child/adolescent literature's relationship to that development, books for adolescents were primarily didactic. They were designed to address history, manners, and morals.

Middle Ages

As early as the eleventh century, Anselm, the Archbishop of Canterbury, wrote an encyclopedia designed to instill in children the beliefs and principles of conduct acceptable to adults in medieval society. Early monastic translations of the Bible and other religious writings were written in Latin for the edification of the upper class.

Fifteenth-century hornbooks were designed to teach reading and religious lessons. William Claxton printed English versions of *Aesop's Fables*, Mallory's *Le Morte d'Arthur*, and stories from Greek and Roman mythology. Though printed for adults, tales of adventures of Odysseus and the Arthurian knights were also popular with literate adolescents.

Renaissance

The Renaissance saw the introduction of the inexpensive chapbooks, small in size and 16-64 pages in length. Chapbooks were condensed versions of mythology and fairy tales. Designed for the common people, chapbooks were imperfect grammatically but were immensely popular because of their adventurous contents. Though most of the serious, educated adults frowned on the sometimes vulgar little books, they received praise from Richard Steele of *Tattler* fame for inspiring his grandson's interest in reading and in pursuing his other studies.

Meanwhile, the Puritans' three most popular reads were the Bible, John Foe's *Book of Martyrs*, and John Bunyan's *Pilgrim's Progress*. Though venerating religious martyrs and preaching the moral propriety which was to lead to eternal happiness, the stories of the *Book of Martyrs* were often lurid in their descriptions of the fate of the damned. In contrast, *Pilgrim's Progress*, not written for children and difficult reading even for adults, was as attractive to adolescents for its adventurous plot as for its moral outcome. In Puritan America, the *New England Primer* set forth the prayers, catechisms, Bible verses, and illustrations meant to instruct children in the Puritan ethic. The seventeenth-century French used fables and fairy tales to entertain adults, but children found them enjoyable as well.

"I never use it, but I've found it to be a great deterrent."

Seventeenth Century

The late seventeenth century brought the first concern with providing literature that specifically targeted the young. Pierre Peril's *Fairy Tales*, Jean de la Fontaine's retellings of famous fables, Mme. d'Aulnoy's novels based on old folktales, and Mme. de Beaumont's "Beauty and the Beast" were written to delight as well as instruct young people. In England, publisher John Newbury was the first to publish a children's line. These included a translation of Perrault's *Tales of Mother Goose; A Little Pretty Pocket-Book*, "intended for instruction and amusement" but decidedly moralistic and bland in comparison to the previous century's chapbooks; and *The Renowned History of Little Goody Two Shoes*, allegedly written by Oliver Goldsmith for a juvenile audience.

Eighteenth Century

Largely, eighteenth-century adolescents were finding their reading pleasure in adult books: Daniel Defoe's *Robinson Crusoe*, Jonathan Swift's *Gulliver's Travels*, and Johann Wyss's *Swiss Family Robinson*. More books were being written for children, and moral didacticism, though less religious, was nevertheless ever present. The short stories of Maria Edgeworth, the four-volume *The History of Sandford and Merton* by Thomas Day, and Martha Farquharson's twenty-six volume *Elsie Dinsmore* series dealt with pious protagonists who learned restraint, repentance, and rehabilitation from sin.

Two bright spots in this period of didacticism were Jean Jacques Rousseau's *Emile* and *The Tales of Shakespeare*, and Charles and Mary Lamb's simplified versions of Shakespeare's plays. Rousseau believed that a child's abilities were enhanced by a free, happy life, and the Lambs subscribed to the notion that children were entitled to entertaining literature written in language comprehensible to them.

Nineteenth Century

Child/adolescent literature truly began its modern rise in nineteenth-century Europe. Hans Christian Andersen's *Fairy Tales* were fanciful adaptations of the somber revisions of the Grimm brothers in the previous century. Andrew Lang's series of colorful fairy books contain the folklores of many nations and are still part of the collections of many modern libraries. Clement Moore's "A Visit from St. Nicholas" is a cheery, non-threatening child's view of the night before Christmas. The humor of Lewis Carroll's books about Alice's adventures, Edward Lear's poems with caricatures, and Lucretia Nole's stories of the Philadelphia Peterkin family are full of fancy and not a smidgen of morality.

Other popular Victorian novels introduced the modern fantasy and science fiction genres: William Makepeace Thackeray's *The Rose and the Ring*, Charles Dickens' *The Magic Fishbone*, and Jules Verne's *Twenty Thousand Leagues*

Under the Sea. Adventure to exotic places became a popular topic: Rudyard Kipling's *Jungle Books*, Verne's *Around the World in Eighty Days*, and Robert Louis Stevenson's *Treasure Island* and *Kidnapped*. In 1884, the first English translation of Johanna Spyri's *Heidi* appeared.

North America was also finding its voices for adolescent readers. American Louisa May Alcott's *Little Women* and Canadian L.M. Montgomery's *Anne of Green Gables* ushered in the modern age of realistic fiction. American youth were enjoying the adventures of Tom Sawyer and Huckleberry Finn. For the first time, children were able to read books about real people just like themselves.

Twentieth Century

The literature of the twentieth century is extensive and diverse and, as in previous centuries, much influenced by the adults who write, edit, and select books for youth consumption. In the first third of the century, suitable adolescent literature dealt with children from good homes with large families. These books projected an image of a peaceful, rural existence.

> For more information, read
> **Introductory Lecture on Children's & Adolescent Literature**
> http://homepages.wmich.edu/~tarboxg/Introductory_Lecture_on_Children's_&_Adol_Lit.html

Though the characters and plots were more realistic, the stories maintained focus on topics that were considered emotionally and intellectually proper. Popular at this time were Laura Ingalls Wilder's *Little House on the Prairie* series and Carl Sandburg's biography Abe Lincoln Grows Up. English author J.R.R. Tolkein's fantasy, The Hobbit, prefaced modern adolescent readers' fascination with the works of Piers Antony, Madelaine L'Engle, and Anne McCaffery.

Adolescent Development

The social changes of post-World War II significantly affected adolescent literature. The Civil Rights movement, feminism, the protest of the Vietnam Conflict, and issues surrounding homelessness, neglect, teen pregnancy, drugs, and violence have bred a new vein of contemporary fiction that helps adolescents understand and cope with the world they live in.

Popular books for preadolescents deal with establishing relationships with members of the opposite sex (Sweet Valley High series) and learning to cope with their changing bodies, personalities, or life situations, as in Judy Blume's *Are You There, God? It's Me, Margaret*. Adolescents are still interested in the fantasy and science fiction genres as well as popular juvenile fiction. Middle school students still read the *Little House on the Prairie* series and the mysteries of the *Hardy Boys* and *Nancy Drew*.

Teens value the works of Emily and Charlotte Bronte, Willa Cather, Jack London, William Shakespeare, and Mark Twain as much as those of Piers Anthony, S.E. Hinton, Madeleine L'Engle, Stephen King, and J.R.R. Tolkein.

Older adolescents enjoy the writers in these genres.

Fantasy: Piers Anthony, Ursula LeGuin, Ann McCaffrey

Horror: V.C. Andrews, Stephen King

Juvenile Fiction: Judy Blume, Robert Cormier, Rosa Guy, Virginia Hamilton, S.E. Hinton, M.E. Kerr, Harry Mazer, Norma Fox Mazer, Richard Newton Peck, Cynthia Voight, and Paul Zindel.

Science Fiction: Isaac Asimov, Ray Bradbury, Arthur C. Clarke, Frank Herbert, Larry Niven, H.G. Wells.

The Influence of Child Development Theories on Literature

The studies by behaviorists and developmental psychologists in the late nineteenth and early twentieth centuries affected the manner in which the educational community and parents approached the selection of literature for children.

The cognitive development studies of Piaget, the epigenetic view of personality development by Erik Erikson, the formulation of Abraham Maslow's hierarchy of basic needs, and the social learning theory of behaviorists like Alfred Bandura contributed to a greater understanding of child/adolescent development even as these theorists contradicted each others' findings.

Though few educators today totally subscribe to Piaget's inflexible stages of mental development, his principles of both qualitative and quantitative mental capacity, his generalizations about the parallels between physical growth and thinking capacity, and his support of the adolescent's heightened moral perspective are still used as measures to evaluate child/adolescent literature.

Piaget's Four Stages of Mental Development:

Sensimotor intelligence (birth to age two) deals with the pre-language period of development. The child is most concerned with coordinating movement and action. Words begin to represent people and things.

Preoperational thought is the period spanning ages two to twelve. It is broken into several substages.

- Preconceptual (2-4) phase - most behavior is based on subjective judgment.

- Intuitive (4-7) phase - children use language to verbalize their experiences and mental processes.

Concrete operations (7-11) occur when children begin to apply logic to concrete things and experiences. They can combine performance and reasoning to solve problems.

Formal operations (12-15) occur when adolescents begin to think beyond the immediate and begin to theorize. They apply formal logic to interpreting abstract constructions and to recognizing experiences that are contrary to fact.

Though Piaget presented these stages as progressing sequentially, a child might enter any period earlier or later than most children. Furthermore, a child might perform at different levels in different situations. Thus, a fourteen-year-old female might be able to function at the formal operations stage in a literature class but function at a concrete operations level in mathematical concepts.

> Learn more about
> **Piaget's Cognitive Development**
> http://courses.dsu.edu/epsy330/
> theorists/cognitive.htm

Piaget's Theories Influence Literature
Most middle school students have reached the concrete operations level. By this time they have left behind their egocentrism for a need to understand the physical and social world around them. They become more interested in ways to relate to other people. Their favorite stories become those about real people rather than animals or fairytale characters. The conflicts in their literature are internal as well as external.

Paula Fox's *The Stone-Faced Boy*, Betsy Byards' *The Midnight Fox*, and Lois Lenski's *Strawberry Girl* are books that deal with a child's loneliness, confusion about identity or loyalty, and poverty. Pre-adolescents are becoming more aware of and interested in the past, thus their love of adventure stories about national heroes such as Davy Crockett, Daniel Boone, and Abe Lincoln and biographies and autobiographies of real life heroes such as Jackie Robinson and César Chávez. At this level, children also become interested in the future--thus, their love of both fantasy (most medieval in spirit) and science fiction.

The seven- to eleven-year-olds also internalize moral values. They are concerned with their sense of self and are willing to question rules and respond to adult authority. In books such as Beverly Cleary's *Henry Huggins* and *Mitch and Amy*, the protagonists are children pursuing their own desires with the same frustrations as other children. When these books were written in the 1960s, returning a found pet or overcoming a reading disability were common problems.

From twelve to fifteen, adolescents advance beyond the concrete operations level and begin developing communication skills that enable them to articulate attitudes and opinions and exchange knowledge. They can recognize and contrast historical fiction from pure history and biography. They can identify the elements of literature and their relationships within a specific story. As their thinking becomes more complex, early adolescents become more sensitive to others' emotions and reactions. They become better able to suspend their disbelief and enter the world of literature, thus expanding their perceptions of the real world.

In discussing the adolescent's moral judgment, Piaget noted that after age eleven, children stopped viewing actions as either "right" or "wrong." The older child considers both the intent and the behavior in its context. A younger child would view an accidental destruction of property in terms of the amount of damage. The older child would find the accident less wrong than minor damage done with intended malice.

Kohlberg's Theories of Moral Development

Expanding on Piaget's thinking, Lawrence Kohlberg developed a hierarchy of values. Though progressive, the stages of Kohlberg's hierarchy are not clearly aligned to chronological age. The six stages of development correlate to three levels of moral judgment.

Level I. Moral values reside in external acts rather than in persons or standards.

> Stage 0. Premoral. No association of actions or needs with sense of right or wrong.
>
> Stage 1. Obedience and punishment orientation. Child defers to adult authority. Child's actions are motivated by a desire to stay out of trouble.
>
> Stage 2. Right action/self-interest orientation. Performance of right deeds results in needing satisfaction.

Level II. Moral values reside in maintaining conventions of right behavior.

> Stage 3. Good person orientation. The child performs right actions to receive approval from others, conforming to the same standards.

Stage 4. Law and order orientation. Doing one's duty and showing respect for authority contributes to maintaining social order.

Level III. Moral values reside in principles separate in association from the persons or agencies that enforce these principles.

Stage 5. Legalistic orientation. The rules of society are accepted as correct but alterable. Privileges and duties are derived from social contact. Obedience to society's rules protects the rights of self and others.

Stage 6. Conscience orientation. Ethical standards, such as justice, equality, and respect for others, guide moral conduct more than legal rules.

Though these stages represent a natural progression of values to actions relationships, persons may regress to an earlier stage in certain situations. An adolescent already operating at Stage 5 may regress to Stage 3 in a classroom where consequences of non-conformity are met with disapproval or punishment. An adult operating at Stage 6 may regress to Stage 4 when obligated by military training or confronted with a conflict between self-preservation and the protection of others.

Values clarification education based on Piaget's and Kohlberg's theories imply that development is inherent in human socialization. Becoming a decent person is a natural result of human development.

Social Learning Theory

Much of traditional learning theory resulted from the work of early behaviorists, like B. F. Skinner, and has been refined by modern theorists such as Albert Bandura. Behaviorists believe that intellectual, and therefore behavioral, development cannot be divided into specific stages. They believe that behavior is the result of conditioning experiences, a continuum of rewards and punishments. Environmental conditions are viewed as greater stimuli than inherent qualities. Thus in social learning theory the consequences of behavior - that is, the rewards or punishments - are more significant in social development than are the motivations for the behavior.

Bandura also proposed that a child learns vicariously through observing the behavior of others whereas the developmental psychologists presumed that children developed through the actual self-experience.

The Humanistic Theory of Development

No discussion of child development would be complete without a review of Abraham Maslow's hierarchy of needs, from basic physiological needs to the need for self-actualization. The following list represents those needs from the hierarchy that most affect children.

- **Need for Physical Wellbeing.** In young children the provisions for shelter, food, clothing, and protection by significant adults satisfy this need. In older children, this satisfaction of physical comforts translates to a need for material security and may manifest itself in struggles to overcome poverty and maintain the integrity of home and family.

- **Need for Love.** The presumption is that every human being needs to love and be loved. With young children, this reciprocal need is directed at and received from parents and other family members, pets, and friends. In older children and adolescents, this need for love forms the basis for romance and peer acceptance.

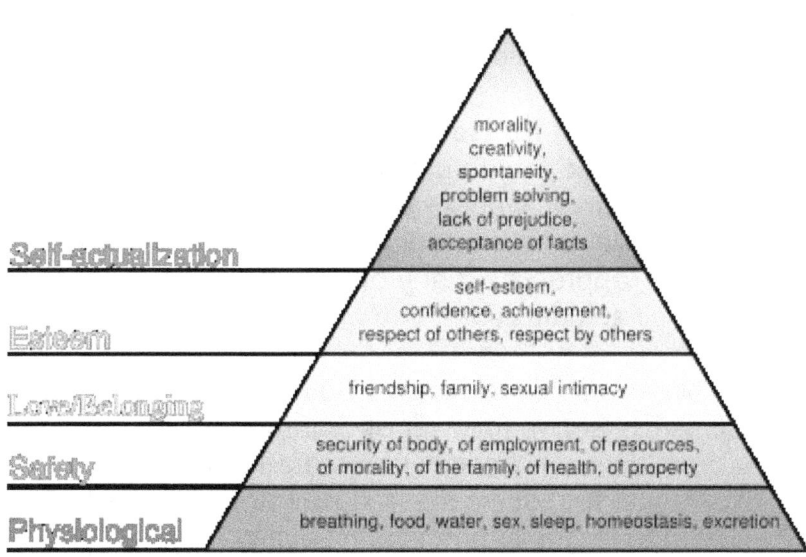

- **Need to Belong.** Beyond the need for one-on-one relationships, a child needs the security of being an accepted member of a group. Young children identify with family, friends, and schoolmates. They are concerned with having happy experiences and being accepted by people they love and respect. Later, they associate with community, country, and perhaps world groups. Adolescents become more aware of a larger world order and thus develop concerns about issues facing society, such as political or social unrest, wars, discrimination, and environmental issues. They seek to establish themselves with groups who accept and share their values. They become more team-oriented.

- **Need to Achieve Competence**. A human's need to interact satisfactorily with his environment begins with the infant's exploration of the immediate surroundings. Visual and tactile identification of objects and persons provides confidence to perform further explorations. To become well adjusted, the child must achieve competence to feel satisfaction. Physical and intellectual achievements become measures of acceptance. Frustrations resulting from physical or mental handicaps are viewed as hurtles to be overcome if satisfaction is to be achieved. Older children view the courage-overcome obstacles as part of the maturing process.

- **Need to Know**. Curiosity is the basis of intelligence. The need to learn is persistent. To maintain intellectual security, children must be able to find answers to their questions in order to stimulate further exploration of information to satisfy that persistent curiosity.

- **Need for Beauty and Order**. Aesthetic satisfaction is as important as the need for factual information. Intellectual stimulation comes from satisfying curiosity about the fine, as well as the practical, arts. Acceptance for one's accomplishments in dance, music, drawing, writing, performing, or appreciating any of the arts leads to a sense of accomplishment and self-actualization.

Theory of Psychosocial Development
Erik Erikson, a follower of Sigmund Freud, presented the theory that human development consists of maturation through a series of psychosocial crisis. The struggle to resolve these crises helps a person achieve individuality as the person learns to function in society.

Maturation occurs as the individual moves through a progression of increasingly complex stages. The movement from one stage to the next hinges on the successful resolution of the conflicts encountered in each stage, and each of the stages represents a step in identity formation. Stage 1 (trust versus distrust), stage 2 (achieving autonomy), and stage 3 (developing initiative) relate to infants and young/middle children. Stages 4 and 5 relate to late childhood through adolescents.

Stage 4—**Becoming Industrious.** Late childhood, according to Erikson, occurs between seven to eleven. The children then have already mastered conflicts that helped them overcome mistrust of unfamiliar persons, places, and things; that made them more independent in caring for themselves and their possessions; and that overcame their sense of guilt at behavior that creates opposition with others. Now children are ready to assert themselves in suppressing feelings of inferiority. Children at this stage learn to master independent tasks as well as to work cooperatively with other children. They increasingly measure their own competence by comparing themselves to their peers.

Stage 5—**Establishing Identity**. From age eleven through the teen years, a person's conflicts arise from the search for identity, as an individual and as a member of society. Because internal demands for independence and peer acceptance sometimes oppose external demands for conformity to rules and standards, friction with family, school, and society in general occur during these years. The adolescent must resolve issues such as the amount of control to concede to family and other rule-enforcing adults as the teen searches for other acceptance models. In the quest for self-identity, the teen experiments with adult behavior and attitudes. At the end of the teen years, this person should have a well-established sense of identity.

Theory of Multiple Intelligences

Howard Gardner's research in the 1980s has been recently influential in helping teachers understand that human beings process information differently and, therefore, communicate their knowledge through different modes of operation. It is important to present language and literature in visual, auditory, tactile, and kinesthetic ways to allow every child to develop good skills through that child's own mode of learning. Then, the child alone must be allowed to perform through the strength of intelligence. The movement toward learning academies in the practical and fine arts and in the sciences is a result of our growing understanding of all aspects of child development.

Modern Society's Role in Child Development

Despite their differences, there are many similarities in the theories of child development. However, most of these theories were developed prior to the social unrest of the 1970s. In industrialized Western society, children are increasingly excluded from the activities of work and play with adults, and education has become their main occupation. This exclusion tends to prolong childhood and adolescence and thus inhibit development as visualized by theorists. For adolescents in America, this prolonging results in slower social and intellectual maturation contrasted to increasing physical maturity. Adolescents today deal with drugs, violence, communicable diseases, and a host of social problems that were of minimal concerns thirty years ago. Even pre-adolescent children are dealing with poverty, disease, broken homes, abuse, and drugs.

Influence of Theories on Literature

All of these development theories and existing social conditions influence the literature created and selected for and by child/adolescent readers.

Child/adolescent literature has always been to some degree didactic, whether non-fiction or fiction. Until the twentieth century, "kiddie" lit was also morally prescriptive. Written by adults who determined either what they believed children needed or liked or what they should need or like, most books, stories, poems, and essays dealt with experiences or issues that would make children into better adults. The fables, fairy tales, and epics of old set the moral and social standards of their times while entertaining the child in every reader/listener. These tales are still popular because they have a universal appeal. Except for the rare exceptions discussed earlier in this section, most books were written for literate adults. Educated children found their pleasure in the literature that was available.

Benefits of Research

One benefit of the child development and learning theory research is that they provide guidelines for writers, publishers, and educators to follow in the creation, marketing, and selection of good reading materials. MacMillan introduced children's literature as a separate publishing market in 1918. By the 1930s, most major publishers had a children's department. Though arguments have existed throughout this century about quality versus quantity, there is no doubt that children's literature is a significant piece of the publishing market.

Another influence is that children's books are a reflection of both developmental theories and social changes. Reading provides children with the opportunity to become more aware of societal differences, to measure their behavior against the behavior of realistic fictional characters or the subjects of biographies, to become informed about events of the past and present that will affect their futures, and to acquire a genuine appreciation of literature.

Furthermore, adults are obligated to provide instruction and entertainment that all children in our democratic society can use. Parents and educators have a further obligation to guide children in the selection of books that are appropriate to their reading ability and interest levels. Of course, there is a fine line between guidance and censorship. As with discipline, parents learn that to make forbidden is to make more desirable. To publish a list of banned books is to make them suddenly attractive. Most children and adolescents, left to their own selections, will choose books on topics that interest them and are written in language they can understand.

Impact of Research on Teachers

Adolescent literature, because of the age range of readers, is extremely diverse. Fiction for the middle group, usually ages ten/eleven to fourteen/fifteen, deals with issues of coping with internal and external changes in their lives. Because children's writers in the twentieth century have produced increasingly realistic fiction, adolescents can now find problems dealt with honestly in novels.

Teachers of middle/junior high school students see the greatest change in interests and reading abilities. Fifth- and sixth-graders in elementary grades are viewed as older children while seventh and eighth graders are preadolescent.

Ninth-graders are either the upper tier in junior high school or the underlings in high school. They definitely view themselves as teenagers. Their literature choices will often be governed more by interest than by ability--thus, the wealth of high-interest, low-readability books that have flooded the market in recent years. Tenth- through twelfth-graders will still select high-interest books for pleasure but are also easily encouraged to stretch their literature muscles by reading more classics.

Because of the rapid social changes, topics that once did not interest young people until they reached their teens—suicide, gangs, and homosexuality—are now subjects of books for even younger readers. Many high-interest books on such subjects are readable for younger children whose reading levels are at or above normal. No matter how tastefully written, some contents are inappropriate for younger readers. It is important to encourage children toward books whose content is appropriate to their levels of cognitive and social development. For example, a fifth-grader may be able to read V.C. Andrews' book *Flowers in the Attic* but not possess the social or moral development to handle the deviant behavior of the characters.

At the same time, because of the complex changes affecting adolescents, the teacher must be well versed in learning theory and child development as well as competent to teach the subject matter of language and literature.

SKILL 1.4 Analyze and interpret major works by representative writers in historical, aesthetic, political, and philosophical contexts

For Fifth and Sixth Grades

These classic and contemporary works combine the characteristics of multiple theories. Functioning at the concrete operations stage (Piaget), being of the "good person," orientation (Kohlberg), still highly dependent on external rewards

> Check out these
> **Online Resources for K-12 Teachers: Children's and Adolescent Literature**
> http://www.indiana.edu/~reading/ieo/digests/d149.html

(Bandura), and exhibiting all five needs previously discussed from Maslow's hierarchy, these eleven- to twelve-year-olds should appreciate the following titles, grouped by reading level. These titles are also cited for interest at that grade level and do not reflect high-interest titles for older readers who do not read at grade level. Some high interest titles will be cited later.

Reading Level 6.0 to 6.9
Barrett, William. *Lilies of the Field*
Cormier, Robert. *Other Bells for Us to Ring*

Dahl, Roald. *Danny, Champion of the World; Charlie and the Chocolate Factory*
Lindgren, Astrid. *Pippi Longstocking*
Lindbergh, Anne. *Three Lives to Live*
Lowry, Lois. *Rabble Starkey*
Naylor, Phyllis. *The Year of the Gopher, Reluctantly Alice*
Peck, Robert Newton. *Arly*
Speare, Elizabeth. *The Witch of Blackbird Pond*
Sleator, William. *The Boy Who Reversed Himself*

For Seventh and Eighth Grades

Most seventh- and eighth-grade students, according to learning theory, are still functioning cognitively, psychologically, and morally as sixth-graders. As these are not inflexible standards, some twelve- and thirteen-year-olds are much more mature socially, intellectually, and physically than the younger children who share the same school. They are becoming concerned with establishing individual and peer group identities that presents conflicts with breaking from authority and the rigidity of rules. Some at this age are still tied firmly to the family and its expectations while others identify more with those their own age or older.

Enrichment reading for this group must help them cope with life's rapid changes or provide escape and thus must be either realistic or fantastic depending on the child's needs. Adventures and mysteries (the Hardy Boys and Nancy Drew series) are still popular today. These preteens also become more interested in biographies of contemporary figures rather than legendary figures of the past.

Reading Level 7.0 to 7.9
Armstrong, William. *Sounder*
Bagnold, Enid. *National Velvet*
Barrie, James. *Peter Pan*
London, Jack. *White Fang, Call of the Wild*
Lowry, Lois. *Taking Care of Terrific*
McCaffrey, Anne. *The Dragonsinger* series
Montgomery, L. M. *Anne of Green Gables* and sequels
Steinbeck, John. *The Pearl*
Tolkien, J. R. R. *The Hobbit*
Zindel, Paul. *The Pigman*

Reading Level 8.0 to 8.9
Cormier, Robert. *I Am the Cheese*
McCullers, Carson. *The Member of the Wedding*
North, Sterling. *Rascal*
Twain, Mark. *The Adventures of Tom Sawyer*
Zindel, Paul. *My Darling, My Hamburger*

For Ninth Grade

Depending upon the school environment, ninth-graders may rank the highest in a junior high school or the lowest in a high school. Much of their social development and thus their reading interests become motivated by peer associations. They are technically adolescents operating at the early stages of formal operations in cognitive development. Their perceptions of their own identities are becoming well-defined, and they are fully aware of the ethics required by society. Ninth-graders are more receptive to the challenges of classic literature but still enjoy popular teen novels.

Reading level 9.0 to 9.9
Brown, Dee. *Bury My Heart at Wounded Knee*
Defoe, Daniel. *Robinson Crusoe*
Dickens, Charles. *David Copperfield*
Greenberg, Joanne. *I Never Promised You a Rose Garden*
Kipling, Rudyard. *Captains Courageous*
Mathabane, Mark. *Kaffir Boy*
Nordhoff, Charles. *Mutiny on the Bounty*
Shelley, Mary. *Frankenstein*
Washington, Booker T. *Up From Slavery*

For Tenth to Twelfth Grades

All high school sophomores, juniors, and seniors can handle almost all other literature except for a few of the very most difficult titles such as *Moby Dick* or *Vanity Fair*. However, since many high school students do not progress to the eleventh or twelfth grade reading level, they will still have their favorites among authors whose writings they can understand. Many will struggle with assigned novels but still read high interest books for pleasure. A few high interest titles are listed below without reading level designations, though most are 6.0 to 7.9.

Bauer, Joan. *Squashed*
Borland, Hal. *When the Legends Die*
Danzinger, Paula. *Remember Me to Harold Square*
Duncan, Lois. *Stranger with My Face*
Hamilton, Virginia. *The Planet of Junior Brown*
Hinton, S. E. *The Outsiders*
Paterson, Katherine. *The Great Gilly Hopkins*

Teachers of students at all levels must be familiar with the materials offered by the libraries in their own schools. Only then can they guide their students into appropriate selections for their social age and reading level development.

COMPETENCY 2.0   LITERARY ELEMENTS

SKILL 2.1   Distinguish salient features of genres

The major literary genres include allegory, ballad, drama, epic, epistle, essay, fable, novel, poem, romance, and the short story.

Allegory: A story in verse or prose with characters representing virtues and vices. There are two meanings, symbolic and literal. John Bunyan's *The Pilgrim's Progress* is the most renowned of this genre.

> Check out more than 180 items
> **Allegories, Fables, Parables & Teaching Tales**
> http://www.insight-books.com/ALLF

Ballad: An *in medias res,* story told or sung, usually in verse and accompanied by music. Literary devices found in ballads include the refrain, or repeated section, and incremental repetition, or anaphora, for effect. Earliest forms were anonymous folk ballads. Later forms include Samuel Taylor Coleridge's Romantic masterpiece "The Rime of the Ancient Mariner."

Drama: Plays – comedy, modern, or tragedy - typically in five acts. Traditionalists and neoclassicists adhere to Aristotle's unities of time, place and action. Plot development is advanced through dialogue. Literary devices include asides, soliloquies and the chorus, which represents public opinion. Greatest of all dramatists/playwrights is William Shakespeare. Other dramaturges include Henrik Ibsen, Tennessee Williams, Arthur Miller, George Bernard Shaw, Tom Stoppard, Jean Racine, Moliére (Jean Baptiste de Poquelin), Sophocles, Aeschylus, Euripides, and Aristophanes.

Epic: Long poem usually of book length reflecting values inherent in the generative society. Epic devices include an invocation to a muse for inspiration, purpose for writing, universal setting, a protagonist and antagonist who possess supernatural strength and acumen, and interventions of God or the gods. Understandably, there are very few epics: Homer's *Iliad* and *Odyssey*, Virgil's *Aeneid*, John Milton's *Paradise Lost*, Edmund Spenser's *The Faerie Queene*, Elizabeth Barrett Browning's *Aurora Leigh*, and Alexander Pope's mock-epic, *The Rape of the Lock*.

Epistle: A letter that is not always originally intended for public distribution but, because of the fame of the sender and/or recipient, becomes public domain. Paul wrote epistles that were later placed in the Bible.

Essay: Typically a limited length prose work focusing on a topic and propounding a definite point of view and authoritative tone. Great essayists include Thomas Carlyle, Charles Lamb, Thomas DeQuincy, Ralph Waldo Emerson and Michel de Montaigne, who is credited with defining this genre.

Fable: Terse tale offering up a moral or exemplum. Geoffrey Chaucer's "The Nun's Priest's Tale" is a fine example of a *bete fabliau* or beast fable in which animals speak and act characteristically human, illustrating human foibles.

Legend: A traditional narrative or collection of related narratives, popularly regarded as historically factual but actually a mixture of fact and fiction.

Myth: Stories that are more or less universally shared within a culture to explain its history and traditions.

Novel: The longest form of fictional prose containing a variety of characterizations, settings, local color, and regionalism. Most have complex plots, expanded description, and attention to detail. Some great novelists include Jane Austin, Charlotte Bronte Emily Bronte, Mark Twain, Leo Tolstoy, Victor Hugo, Thomas Hardy, Charles Dickens, Nathaniel Hawthorne, E.M. Forster, and Gustave Flaubert.

Poem: Verse often rhymed with rhythm. Sub-genres include fixed types of literature such as the sonnet, elegy, ode, pastoral, and villanelle. Blank verse is poetry written in unrhymed iambic pentameter. Dramatic monologue creatively reveals the speaker's character.

Romance: A highly imaginative tale set in a fantastical realm dealing with the conflicts between heroes, villains and/or monsters. "The Knight's Tale" from Chaucer's *Canterbury Tales*, *Sir Gawain and the Green Knight* and John Keats' "The Eve of St. Agnes" are prime representatives.

Short Story: Narrative prose fiction with few characters and aimed toward unity. Edgar Allen Poe emphasized that a successful short story should create one focused impact. Considered to be great short story writers are Ernest Hemingway, William Faulkner, Mark Twain, James Joyce, Shirley Jackson, Flannery O'Connor, Guy de Maupasssant, Saki (H.H. Munro), Edgar Allen Poe, and Alexander Pushkin.

SKILL 2.2   Define and analyze basic elements of literature

Essential terminology and literary devices germane to literary analysis include alliteration, allusion, antithesis, aphorism, apostrophe, assonance, blank verse, caesura, conceit, connotation, consonance, couplet, denotation, diction, epiphany, exposition, figurative language, free verse, hyperbole, iambic pentameter, inversion, irony, kenning, metaphor, metaphysical poetry, metonymy, motif, onomatopoeia, octava rima, oxymoron, paradox, parallelism personification, quatrain, scansion, simile, soliloquy, Spenserian stanza, synecdoche, terza rima, tone, and wit.

Antithesis: Balanced writing about conflicting ideas, usually expressed in sentence form. Some examples are "expanding from the center," "shedding old habits," and "searching never finding."

Aphorism: A focused, succinct expression about life from a sagacious viewpoint. Writings by Ben Franklin, Sir Francis Bacon, and Alexander Pope contain many aphorisms. "Whatever is begun in anger ends in shame" is an aphorism by Benjamin Franklin.

Apostrophe: Literary device of addressing an absent or dead person, an abstract idea, or an inanimate object. Sonneteers, such as Sir Thomas Wyatt, John Keats, and William Wordsworth, address the moon, stars, and the dead Milton. For example, in William Shakespeare's *Julius Caesar*, Mark Antony addresses the corpse of Caesar in the speech that begins: "O, pardon me, thou bleeding piece of earth / That I am meek and gentle with these butchers! / Thou art the ruins of the noblest man / That ever lived in the tide of times. / Woe to the hand that shed this costly blood!"

> For more information, consult **Glossary of Poetry Terms**
> http://www.infoplease.com/spot/pmglossary1.html

Blank Verse: Poetry written in iambic pentameter but unrhymed. Works by Shakespeare and Milton are epitomes of blank verse. Milton's *Paradise Lost* states, "Illumine, what is low raise and support, / That to the highth of this great argument I may assert Eternal Providence / And justify the ways of God to men."

Caesura: A pause, usually signaled by punctuation, in a line of poetry. The earliest usage occurs in *Beowulf*, the first English epic dating from the Anglo-Saxon era. "To err is human, // to forgive, divine" (Pope).

Conceit: A comparison, usually in verse, between seemingly disparate objects or concepts. John Donne's metaphysical poetry contains many clever conceits. For instance, Donne's "The Flea" (1633) compares a flea bite to the act of love; and in "A Valediction: Forbidding Mourning" (1633) separated lovers are likened to the legs of a compass, the leg drawing the circle eventually returning home to "the fixed foot."

Connotation: The ripple effect surrounding the implications and associations of a given word, distinct from the denotative or literal meaning. For example, the word "rest" in *Hamlet's* "Good night, sweet prince, and flights of angels sing thee to thy rest," refers to a burial.

Consonance: The repeated usage of similar consonant sounds, most often used in poetry. "Sally sat sifting seashells by the seashore" is a familiar example.

Couplet: Two rhyming lines of poetry. Shakespeare's sonnets end in heroic couplets written in iambic pentameter. Pope is also a master of the couplet. His *Rape of the Lock* is written entirely in heroic couplets.

Denotation: What a word literally means, as opposed to its connotative meaning.

Diction: The right word in the right place for the right purpose. The hallmark of a great writer is precise, unusual, and memorable diction.

Epiphany: The moment when the something is realized and comprehension sets in. James Joyce used this device in his short story collection *The Dubliners*.

Exposition: Fill-in or background information about characters meant to clarify and add to the narrative; the initial plot element that precedes the buildup of conflict.

Figurative Language: Not meant in a literal sense but to be interpreted through symbolism. Figurative language is made up of such literary devices as hyperbole, metonymy, synecdoche, and oxymoron. A synecdoche is a figure of speech in which the word for part of something is used to mean the whole; for example, "sail" for "boat," or vice versa.

Free Verse: Poetry that does not have any predictable meter or patterning. Margaret Atwood, E. E. Cummings, and Ted Hughes write in this form.

Hyperbole: Exaggeration for a specific effect. For example, "I'm so hungry that I could eat a million of these."

Iambic Pentameter: The two elements in a set five-foot line of poetry. An iamb is an accented syllable followed by an unaccented syllable, per foot or measure. Pentameter means five accented syllables per line.

Inversion: An atypical sentence order to create a given effect or interest. Francis Bacon and Milton's work use inversion successfully. Emily Dickinson was fond of arranging words outside of their familiar order. For example in "Chartless" she writes "Yet know I how the heather looks" and "Yet certain am I of the spot." Instead of saying "Yet I know" and "Yet I am certain," she reverses the usual order and shifts the emphasis to the more important words.

Irony: An unexpected disparity between what is written or stated and what is really meant or implied by the author. Verbal, dramatic and situational are the three literary ironies. Verbal irony is when an author says one thing and means something else. Dramatic irony is when an audience perceives something that a character in the literature does not know. Irony of situation is a discrepancy between the expected result and actual results. Shakespeare's plays contain numerous and highly effective use of irony. O. Henry's short stories have ironic endings.

Kenning: Another way to describe a person, place, or thing so as to avoid prosaic repetition. The earliest examples can be found in Anglo-Saxon literature such as *Beowulf* and "The Seafarer." Instead of writing King Hrothgar, the anonymous monk wrote great Ring-Giver, or Father of his people. A lake becomes the swans' way, and the ocean or sea becomes the great whale's way. In ancient Greek literature, this device was called an "epithet."

Metaphysical Poetry: Verse characterization by ingenious wit, unparalleled imagery, and clever conceits. The greatest metaphysical poet is John Donne. Henry Vaughn and other seventeenth-century British poets contributed to this movement as in *Words*, "I saw eternity the other night, like a great being of pure and endless light."

Metonymy: Use of an object or idea closely identified with another object or idea to represent the second. "Hit the books" means "go study." Washington, D.C. means the U.S. government and the White House means the U.S. president.

Motif: A key, oft-repeated phrase, name, or idea in a literary work. Dorset/Wessex in Hardy's novels and the moors and the harsh weather in the Bronte sisters' novels are effective use of motifs. Shakespeare's *Romeo and Juliet* represents the ill-fated young lovers' motif.

> Share this website with your students
> **NewsHour Extra: Poetry**
> http://www.pbs.org/newshour/extra/poetry/#

Onomatopoeia: Word used to evoke the sound in its meaning. The early Batman series used "pow," "zap," "whop," "zonk," and "eek" in an onomatopoetic way.

Octava Rima: A specific eight-line stanza of poetry whose rhyme scheme is abababcc. Lord Byron's mock epic, *Don Juan*, is written in this poetic way.

Oxymoron: A contradictory form of speech, such as jumbo shrimp, unkindly kind, or singer John Mellencamp's "It hurts so good."

Paradox: Seemingly untrue statement, which when examined more closely proves to be true. John Donne's sonnet "Death Be Not Proud" postulates that death shall die and humans will triumph over death, at first thought not true, but ultimately explained and proven in this sonnet.

Parallelism: A type of close repetition of clauses or phrases that emphasize key topics or ideas in writing. The psalms in the Bible contain many examples.

Personification: Giving human characteristics to inanimate objects or concepts. Great writers, with few exceptions, are masters of this literary device.

Quatrain: A poetic stanza composed of four lines. A Shakespearean or Elizabethan sonnet is made up of three quatrains and ends with a heroic couplet.

Scansion: The two-part analysis of a poetic line. Count the number of syllables per line and determine where the accents fall. Divide the line into metric feet. Name the meter by the type and number of feet. Much is written about scanning poetry. Try not to inundate your students with this jargon; rather allow them to feel the power of the poets' words, ideas, and images instead.

Soliloquy: A highlighted speech, in drama, usually delivered by a major character expounding on the author's philosophy or expressing, at times, universal truths. This is done with the character alone on the stage, as in Hamlet's famous "To be or not to be" soliloquy.

Spenserian Stanza: Invented by Sir Edmund Spenser for use in *The Faerie Queene*, his epic poem honoring Queen Elizabeth I. Each stanza consists of nine lines, eight in iambic parameter. The ninth line, called an alexandrine, has two extra syllables or one additional foot.

Sprung Rhythm: Invented and used extensively by the poet, Gerard Manley Hopkins. It consists of variable meter, which combines stressed and unstressed syllables fashioned by the author. See "Pied Beauty" or "God's Grandeur."

Stream of Consciousness: A style of writing which reflects the mental processes of the characters expressing, at times, jumbled memories, feelings, and dreams. James Joyce, Virginia Woolf, and William Faulkner use stream of consciousness in their writings.

Terza Rima: A series of poetic stanzas use the recurrent rhyme scheme of aba, bcb, cdc, ded, and so forth. The second-generation Romantic poets—Keats, Byron, Shelley, and, to a lesser degree, Yeats—used this Italian verse form, especially in their odes. Dante used this stanza in *The Divine Comedy*.

Tone: The discernible attitude inherent in an author's work regarding the subject, readership, or characters. Jonathan Swift or Pope's tone is satirical. James Boswell's tone toward Samuel Johnson is admiring.

> Read about **Tone and Style**
> http://www.delmar.edu/engl/wrtctr/handouts/ToneStyle.pdf

Wit: Writing of genius, keenness, and sagacity expressed through clever use of language. Alexander Pope and the Augustans wrote about and were said to possess wit.

SKILL 2.3 Articulate the relationship between the expressed purposes and the characteristics of different forms of dramatic literature

In its most general sense, a drama is any work that is designed to be performed by actors onstage. It can also refer to a literary genre broadly divided into comedy and tragedy.

Contemporary usage, however, denotes drama as a work that treats serious subjects and themes but does not aim for the same grandeur as tragedy. Drama usually deals with characters of a less stately nature than tragedy. A classical example is Sophocles' tragedy *Oedipus Rex,* while a modern example is Eugene O'Neill's *The Iceman Cometh*.

Comedy: The comedic form of dramatic literature is meant to amuse and often ends happily. It uses techniques such as satire or parody, and can take many forms, from farce to burlesque. Examples include Dante Alighieri's *The Divine Comedy,* Noel Coward's play *Private Lives,* some of Geoffrey Chaucer's *Canterbury Tales,* and some of William Shakespeare's plays, such as *A Midsummer's Night Dream*.

Tragedy: Tragedy is comedy's other half. It is defined as a work of drama written in either prose or poetry, telling the story of a brave, noble hero who, because of some tragic character flaw, brings ruin upon himself. It is characterized by serious, poetic language that evokes pity and fear.

Read more about
Greek Tragedy
http://depthome.brooklyn.cuny.edu/classics/dunkle/studyguide/tragedy.htm

In modern times, dramatists have tried to update drama's image by drawing its main characters from the middle class and showing their nobility through their nature instead of their standing. Sophocles' *Oedipus Rex* is the classic example of tragedy, while works of Henrik Ibsen and Arthur Miller epitomize modern tragedy.

Dramatic Monologue: A dramatic monologue is a speech given by an actor as if talking to himself or herself, but actually intended for the audience. It reveals key aspects of the character's psyche and sheds insight on the situation at hand. The audience takes the part of the silent listener, passing judgment and giving sympathy at the same time. This form was invented and used predominantly by Victorian poet Robert Browning.

SKILL 2.4 Develop critical thinking and analytic skill through close reading of texts

Reading literature involves a reciprocal interaction between the reader and the text.

Types of Responses

Emotional: In an emotional response, readers can identify with the characters and situations so as to project themselves into the story. They feel a sense of satisfaction by associating aspects of their own lives with the people, places, and events in the literature. Emotional responses are observed in readers' verbal and non-verbal reactions—laughter, comments on its effects, and retelling or dramatizing the action.

> Learn more about
> **Reading Response Journals**
> http://www.education-world.com/a_curr/profdev/profdev085.shtmlreading%20strategies%20index.htm

Interpretive: Interpretive responses result in inferences about character development, setting, or plot; analysis of style elements - metaphor, simile, allusion, rhythm, tone; outcomes derivable from information provided in the narrative; and assessment of the author's intent. Interpretive responses are made verbally or in writing.

Critical: Critical responses involve making value judgments about the quality of a piece of literature. Reactions to the effectiveness of the writer's style and language use are observed through discussion and written reactions.

Evaluative: Some reading response theorists add a response that considers the readers' considerations of such factors as how well the piece of literature represents its genre, how well it reflects the social/ethical mores of society, and how well the author has approached the subject for freshness and slant.

Middle school readers will exhibit both emotional and interpretive responses. Naturally, making interpretive responses depends on the degree of knowledge the student has of literary elements. Children show critical reactions on a fundamental level when they are able to say why a particular book was boring or why a particular poem was sad. Adolescents in ninth and tenth grades should begin to make critical responses by addressing the specific language and genre characteristics of literature.

Evaluative responses are harder to detect and are rarely made by any but a few advanced high school students. However, a teacher who knows what to listen for can recognize evaluative responses and incorporate them into discussions.

For example, if a student says, "I don't understand why that character is doing that," she is making an interpretive response to character motivation. However, if she goes on to say, "What good is that action?" she is giving an evaluative response that should be explored in terms of "What good should it do and why isn't that positive action happening?"

At the emotional level, another student might say, "I almost broke into a sweat when the author was describing the heat in the burning house." An interpretive response says, "The author used descriptive adjectives to bring his setting to life." Critically, the student adds, "The author's use of descriptive language contributes to the success of the narrative and maintains reader interest through the whole story." If he goes on to wonder why the author allowed the grandmother in the story to die in the fire, he is making an evaluative response.

Levels of Response

The levels of reader response will depend largely on the reader's level of social, psychological, and intellectual development. Most middle school students have progressed beyond merely involving themselves in the story enough to be able to retell the events in some logical sequence or describe the feeling that the story evoked. They are aware to some degree that the feeling evoked was the result of a careful manipulation of good elements of fiction writing. They may not explain that awareness as successfully as a high school student, but they are beginning to grasp the concepts and not just the personal reactions. They are beginning to differentiate between responding to the story itself and responding to a literary creation.

Fostering Self-esteem and Empathy for Others and the World in Which One Lives

All-important is the use of literature as bibliotherapy that allows the reader to identify with others and become aware of alternatives while not feeling directly betrayed or threatened. For the high school student the ability to empathize is an evaluative response, a much desired outcome of literature studies. Use of these books either individually or as a thematic unit of study allows for discussion or writing. The titles are grouped by theme, not by reading level.

Abuse
Blair, Maury and Doug Brendel. *Maury, Wednesday's Child*
Dizenzo, Patricia. *Why Me?*
Parrot, Andrea. *Coping with Date Rape and Acquaintance Rape*

Natural World Concerns
Caduto, M. and J. Bruchac. *Keepers of Earth*
Gay, Kathlyn. *Greenhouse Effect*
Johnson, Denis. *Fiskadaro*
Madison, Arnold. *It Can't Happen to Me*

Eating Disorders
Arnold, Caroline. *Too Fat, Too Thin, Do You Have a Choice?*
DeClements, Barthe. *Nothing's Fair in Fifth Grade*
Snyder, Anne. *Goodbye, Paper Doll*

Family
Cormier, Robert. *Tunes for Bears to Dance to*
Danzinger, Paula. *The Divorce Express*
Neufield, John. *Sunday Father*
Okimoto, Jean Davies. *Molly by any Other Name*
Peck, Richard. *Don't Look and It Won't Hurt*
Zindel, Paul. *I Never Loved Your Mind*

Stereotyping
Baklanov, Grigory. (Trans. by Antonina W. Bouis) *Forever Nineteen*
Greene, Betty. *Summer of My German Soldier*
Kerr, M.E. *Gentle Hands*
Reiss, Johanna. *The Upstairs Room*
Taylor, Mildred D. *Roll of Thunder, Hear Me Cry*
Wakatsuki-Houston, Jeanne and James D. Houston. *Farewell to Manzanarr*

Suicide and Death
    Blume, Judy. *Tiger Eyes*
    Bunting, Eve. *If I Asked You, Would You Stay?*
    Gunther, John. *Death Be Not Proud*
    Mazer, Harry. *When the Phone Rings*
    Peck, Richard. *Remembering the Good Times*
    Richter, Elizabeth. *Losing Someone You Love*
    Strasser, Todd. *Friends Till the End*

Caution

Teachers should always use caution with reading materials that have a sensitive or controversial nature. A child who has known a recent death in his family or circle of friends may need to distance him/herself from classroom discussion. Whenever open discussion of a topic brings pain or embarrassment, the child should not be further subjected. Older children and young adults may be able to better discuss issues--with greater objectivity and without blurting insensitive comments.

Teachers must be able to gauge the level of emotional development of the students when selecting subject matter and the strategies for studying it. Students or parents may consider some material objectionable. Should a student choose not to read an assigned material, it is the teacher's responsibility to allow the student to select an alternate title. It is always advisable to notify parents if a particularly sensitive piece is to be studied.

COMPETENCY 3.0   LITERARY CRITICISM

SKILL 3.1   Research and apply criticism of major texts and authors using print and/or electronic resources

Teachers should be familiar with professional resources that aid them in recognizing reader responses and teaching students the process of assessing their responses. One exceptional tool is Laurence Perrine's *Sound and Sense*, cited in the bibliography. Both the text itself and the teacher manual that accompanies it provide excellent activities that contribute to the student's ability to make interpretive and evaluative responses.

In addition, a variety of good student resources are available in most school and public libraries that provide models of critical analyses. The Twayne publications are book-length critiques of individual titles or of the body of work of a given author. *The Modern Critical Interpretations* series, edited by Harold Bloom, offers a collection of critical essays on individual titles in each book. Gale Research Company also provides several series: *Nineteenth Century Literature Criticism, Twentieth Century Literature Criticism*, and *Contemporary Literary Criticism*, to name a few. These encyclopedic sets contain reprints of literary magazine articles that date from the author's own lifetime to the present. Students doing independent research will find these are invaluable tools.

SKILL 3.2   Research and apply various approaches to interpreting literature

Studying literature requires more involvement of the student than traditional discussion or lecture processes have allowed. Literature, whether fiction, non-fiction, poetry, or drama, should not be studied for comprehension alone nor should detailed analyses of the elements of literature be an end in themselves. Literature is to be experienced if it is to be appreciated.

Teaching Strategies

Reading/Discussion: Reading, whether aloud or silently, evokes responses that can be verbalized. For young or below grade-level readers, some sight-reading may be necessary. This should be done in small groups of two or three without teacher intervention. Students should feel free to discuss the text as they read.

Most high school students should be able to participate in small group discussions of literature that has been read outside of class. During silent or at-home reading, the students should take notes of key elements as they read to enable them to contribute to subsequent discussions. Teacher-guided discussion should transpire only after students have had a chance to think through the elements of the literature which are under study. Teacher-led discussions should evolve from student responses to the reading, not from preconceived interpretations by the teacher or recognized critics. Perceptive assessment of student comments will lead to questioning that probes the student's personal reactions and can ultimately be as analytical as any discussion the teacher might have planned.

Rather than involving the whole class, which favors the loquacious and inhibits the shy, let the students form into four or five discussion groups. After the initial discussion, have two groups join to share their reactions.

Dramatization: Young students need little encouragement to retell stories to their classmates and to pantomime action. Older students should be given an opportunity to act out scenes not only from plays but also from other literature as well but only after planning and rehearsal. Treat the performance as a reflection of their appreciation for the work and not as a graded assignment.

Middle school students often become inhibited by solo performances, so allow them to structure group performances. It is also important for students to view and listen to others performing and to show their appreciation for the performers as well as the literature.

COMPETENCY 4.0 ANALYSIS OF NON-LITERARY TEXTS

SKILL 4.1 Compare various features of print and visual media

The wide variety of print and visual media adds both depth and challenge to our lives. As students grapple with interpretation and analysis, they should recognize that communication occurs in many ways.

Print Media: Convenience, Completeness, and Dependability

- The classic foundation of student learning
- Convenient and generally inexpensive
- No need for equipment or electrical power
- No maintenance
- Self-paced (students can skim, read ahead, or re-read as they wish)
- Increases literacy; expands vocabulary
- Not as "snazzy" as electronic or visual media
- Difficult to reach wider audiences
- Requires moderate reading skill and intellectual effort (can be lost on students who lack reading skills)

Examples: Textbooks, literature, magazines, newspapers and worksheets

Visual Media: Simplicity, Impact and Aesthetic Appeal

- Attention-grabbing
- Provides a realistic mental image of a subject or concept that might otherwise not be able to translate mentally
- Promotes the transfer of learning to contexts beyond the confines of the classroom
- Conveys some types of information more effectively
- Communicates data more clearly
- More emotional impact
- Can inhibit grasping the whole picture of a studied subject

Examples: Pictures, charts, videos, maps, slides, and models

SKILL 4.2 Evaluate structure and content of a variety of consumer, workplace, and public documents

Even when faced with non-literary documents, students can still analyze the credibility of the information using literary techniques by examining the form and contents.

Structure:
- Where does the thesis—the point—of the document or speech occur?
    a. At the beginning
    b. In the middle
    c. At the end
    d. Unstated

- Is the reasoning deductive (general to specific) or inductive (specific to general)?

- Is the outline chronological or spatial?

- Are figures of speech used?
    a. Metaphor
    b. Allegory
    c. Simile

Content:
- Thesis—the *point* the document or speech makes.

- Support—the points or examples the writer/speaker uses to establish the thesis.

- Purpose—persuasive, descriptive, expository, or narrative.

- Fallacies:
    a. Ad hominem
    b. Slippery slope
    c. False dilemma
    d. Begging the question
    e. Post hoc ergo propter hoc (false cause)
    f. Red herring
    g. Hasty conclusion

- Coherence—the supporting points move in a logical sequence from first to last and have transitions that establish the relationship to the preceding point.

- Bias—the background or belief system of the speaker/writer and its effect the position taken?

- Value—useful or relevant information

- Ethics
    a. Respect for sensitivities of diverse audience/readership.
    b. Honesty, transparency.

SKILL 4.3   Interpret individual works in their cultural, social, and political contexts

In looking at any piece of writing regardless of genre, readers should think about what was going on in the writer's world at the time the piece was being written. This includes the political milieu, societal mores, the social level of the writer, and cultural influences.

"A writer can only write what he knows" is a statement often heard in discussions about literature. However, Tom Wolfe, a contemporary writer (*Bonfire of the Vanities*) disputes that. He insists that a writer can use exploration and research to write effectively and successfully about topics that he hasn't experienced first-hand. Even so, thinking about the influence of what was going on at the time of the writing of a piece of literature and its impact of the final published work in very important.

A good example is John Steinbeck and his popular novel, *The Grapes of Wrath*. It would certainly be possible to read this book and be moved by it, even to understand the point Steinbeck intended to make, without knowing that it was written during America's Great Depression of the 1930s, but it is much better understood when viewed through that context.

This writer didn't suffer the tribulations that many did during the Depression; his own family was little affected by it. Once he decided that he wanted to write about the people who were being displaced by the political, cultural, and social crisis, he went to Oklahoma and lived with a family who had lost its farm, not only because of the economic disaster but also because of the dust bowl effect in Oklahoma.

Steinbeck obtained information and experience by exploration and research to be sure that he wrote "what he knew." The result is a family that Steinbeck named the Joads, who illustrate and demonstrate in clear, moving, and understandable terms what the Great Depression meant to human lives.

Readers of *Grapes of Wrath* will understand clearly where the lives of the Joads fit into society. The economic well-being of wealthy landowners in California is dependent on these migrants from the Dust Bowl, and the landowners have a vested interest in the status quo.

Check out this detailed lesson plan on
The Grapes of Wrath
http://www.neabigread.org/books/grapesofwrath/

The U.S. president at that time, President Hoover (who had devoted a good part of his life to providing food for hungry people all over the world), found himself in a dilemma: he couldn't meet the needs of the citizens.

Congress opposed his efforts to make organizational changes to avoid such things as the crisis of the migrants that Steinbeck wrote about. Many forces that accounted for this problem were beyond Hoover's control.

Writing that is directly related to political, cultural, and social influences is often the writer's purpose for writing it in the first place. In Steinbeck's case, his purpose was to bring about change. His book is considered a novel of protest, a social document.

Grapes of Wrath is an extreme example of a novel strongly influenced by the political, cultural, and social background of the times in which it was written. Even so, most works whether written or presented via some other medium, reflect the times: the cultural, social, and political atmosphere.

TEACHER CERTIFICATION STUDY GUIDE

DOMAIN II.   **LANGUAGE, LINGUISTICS, AND LITERACY**

Candidates demonstrate knowledge of the foundations and contexts of the language, linguistics, and literacy contained in the *English-Language Arts Content Standards for California Public Schools* (1997) as outlined in *Reading/Language Arts Framework for California Public Schools: Kindergarten through Grade Twelve* (1999) at a post-secondary level of rigor. Candidates have both broad and deep conceptual knowledge of the subject matter.

Many California students, coming from a variety of linguistic and socio-cultural backgrounds, face specific challenges in mastering the English language. The diversity of this population requires the candidate to understand the principles of language acquisition and development. Candidates must become knowledgeable about the nature of human language, language variation, and historical and cultural perspectives on the development of English. In addition, candidates must acquire a complex understanding of the development of English literacy among both native and non-native speakers.

COMPETENCY 5.0   HUMAN LANGUAGE STRUCTURES

SKILL 5.1   Recognize the nature of human language, differences among languages, the universality of linguistic structures, and change across time, locale, and communities

Language, though an innate human ability, must be learned.

Linguists agree that language is first a vocal system of word symbols that enable a human to communicate feelings, thoughts, and desires to other human beings. Language has been instrumental in the development of all cultures and is influenced by the changes in these societies.

Historical influences

English is an Indo-European language that evolved through several periods. The origin of English dates to the settlement of the British Isles in the fifth and sixth centuries by Germanic tribes called the Angles, Saxons, and Jutes. The original Britons spoke a Celtic tongue while the Angles spoke a Germanic dialect.

> Learn more about the
> **History of the English Language**
> http://ebbs.english.vt.edu/hel/hel.html

Modern English derives from the speech of the Anglo-Saxons who imposed not only their language but also their social customs and laws on their new land. From the fifth to the tenth century, Britain's language was the tongue we now refer to as Old English. During the next four centuries, the many French attempts at English conquest introduced many French words to English. However, the grammar and syntax of the language remained Germanic.

ENGLISH

Middle English, most evident in the writings of Geoffrey Chaucer, dates loosely from 1066 to 1509. William Caxton brought the printing press to England in 1474 and increased literacy. Old English words required numerous inflections to indicate noun cases and plurals as well as verb conjugations. Middle English continued the use of many inflections and pronunciations that treated these inflections as separately pronounced syllables. English in 1300 would have been written "Olde Anglishe" with the *e*'s at the ends of the words pronounced as our short *a* vowel. Even adjectives had plural inflections: "long dai" became "longe daies" pronounced "long-a day-as." Spelling was phonetic, thus every vowel had multiple pronunciations, a fact that continues to affect the language.

Modern English dates from the introduction of The Great Vowels Shift because it created guidelines for spelling and pronunciation. Before the printing press, books were copied laboriously by hand; the language was subject to the individual interpretation of the scribes. Printers and subsequently lexicographers including Samuel Johnson and America's Noah Webster influenced the guidelines. As reading matter was mass-produced, the reading public was forced to adopt the speech and writing habits developed by those who wrote and printed books.

Despite many students' insistence to the contrary, Shakespeare's writings are in Modern English. Teachers should stress to students that language, like customs, morals, and other social factors, is constantly subject to change. Immigration, inventions, and cataclysmic events change language as much as any other facet of life is affected by these changes.

The domination of one race or nation over others can change a language significantly. Beginning with the colonization of the New World by England and Spain, English and Spanish became dominant languages in the Western hemisphere.

American English today is somewhat different in pronunciation and sometimes vocabulary from British English. The British call a truck a "lorry," a baby carriage a "pram"--short for "perambulator," and an elevator a "lift." The two languages have very few syntactical differences, and even the tonal qualities that were once so clearly different are converging.

Though Modern English is less complex than Middle English, having lost many unnecessary inflections, it is still considered difficult to learn because of its

> Check out the
> **Learning Resources of the OED**
> hhttp://www.oed.com/learning/

many exceptions to the rules. It has become, however, the world's dominant language by reason of the great political, military, and social power of England from the fifteenth to the nineteenth century and of America in the twentieth century.

Modern inventions--the telephone, phonograph, radio, television, and motion pictures--have especially affected English pronunciation. Regional dialects, once a hindrance to clear understanding, have fewer distinct characteristics. The speakers from different parts of the United States of America can be identified by their accents, but more and more as educators and media personalities stress uniform pronunciations and proper grammar, the differences are diminishing.

The English language has a more extensive vocabulary than any other language. Ours is a language of synonyms, words borrowed from other languages, and coined words, many of them introduced by the rapid expansion of technology.

Students should understand that language is in constant flux. They can demonstrate this when they use language for specific purposes and audiences. Negative criticism of a student's errors in word choice or sentence structures will inhibit creativity. Positive criticism that suggests ways to enhance communication skills will encourage exploration.

Geographical Influences

Dialect differences are mostly in pronunciation. Bostonians say "pahty" for "party" and Southerners blend words like "you all" into "y'all." Besides the dialect differences already mentioned, the biggest geographical factors in American English stem from minor word choice variances. Depending on the region where you live, when you order a carbonated, syrupy beverage most generically called a "soft drink," you might ask for a "soda" in the South, or a "pop" in the Midwest. If you order a soda in New York, then you will get a scoop of ice cream in your soft drink, while in other areas you would have to ask for a "float."

Social Influences

Social influences are mostly those imposed by family, peer groups, and mass media. The economic and educational levels of families determine language use. Exposure to adults who encourage and assist children to speak well enhances readiness for other areas of learning and contributes to their ability to communicate their needs. Historically, children learned language, speech patterns, and grammar from members of the extended family just as they learned the rules of conduct within their family unit and community. In modern times, the mother in a nuclear family became the dominant force in influencing children's development. With increasing social changes, many children are not receiving the proper guidance in all areas of development, especially language.

Those who are fortunate to be in educational day-care programs like Head Start or in certified preschools often develop better language skills than those whose care is entrusted to untrained care providers. Once children enter elementary school, they are also greatly influenced by peer language. This peer influence becomes significant in adolescence as the use of teen jargon gives teenagers a sense of identity within their chosen group(s) and independence from the influence of adults. In some lower socio-economic groups, children use Standard English in school and street language outside the school. Some children of immigrant families become bilingual by necessity if no English is spoken in the home.

Research has shown a strong correlation between socio-economic characteristics and all areas of intellectual development. Traditional measurement instruments rely on verbal ability to establish intelligence. Research findings and test scores reflect that children reared in nuclear families providing cultural experiences and individual attention become more language proficient than those who are denied that security and stimulation.

Personal Influences

The rate of physical development and identifiable language disabilities also influence language development. Nutritional deficiencies, poor eyesight, and conditions such as stuttering or dyslexia can inhibit children's ability to master language. Unless diagnosed early, they can hamper communication into adulthood. These conditions also stymie the development of self-confidence and, therefore, the willingness to learn or to overcome the handicap. Children should receive proper diagnosis and positive corrective instruction.

In adolescence, children's choice of role models and decisions about their future determine the growth of identity. Rapid physical and emotional changes and the stress of coping with the pressure of sexual awareness make concentration on any educational pursuits difficult. The easier the transition from childhood to adulthood, the better the competence will be in all learning areas.

Middle school and junior high school teachers are confronted by a student body ranging from fifth-graders who are still childish to eighth- or ninth-graders who, if not in fact, at least in their minds, are young adults. Teachers must approach language instruction as a social development tool with emphasis on vocabulary acquisition, reading improvement, and speaking/writing skills. High school teachers can deal with the more formalized instruction of grammar, usage, and literature meant for older adolescents whose social development allows them to pay more attention to studies that will improve their chances for a better adult life.

As a tool, language must have relevance to students' real environment. Many high schools have developed practical English classes for business/ vocational students whose specific needs are determined by their desire to enter the workforce upon graduation. More emphasis is placed upon accuracy of mechanics and understanding verbal and written directions because these are skills desired by employers. Writing résumés, completing forms, reading policy and operations manuals, and generating reports are some of the desired skills. Emphasis is placed on higher-level thinking skills, including inferential thinking and literary interpretation, in literature classes for college-bound students.

SKILL 5.2 Demonstrate knowledge of word analysis, including sound patterns (phonology) and inflection, derivation, compounding, roots and affixes (morphology)

Phonological Awareness

Phonological awareness means the ability of the reader to recognize the sound of spoken language. This recognition includes how these sounds can be blended together, segmented (divided up), and manipulated (switched around). This awareness then leads to phonics, a method for teaching students to read. It helps them "sound out words."

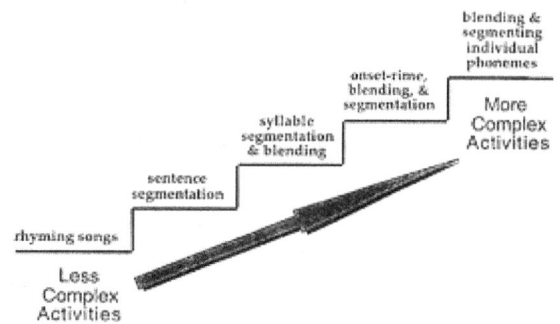

Check out
A Continuum of Complexity
of Phonological Awareness Activities
http://www.ldonline.org/article/6254

Instructional methods to teach phonological awareness may include any or all of the following: auditory games and drills during which students recognize and manipulate the sounds of words, separate or segment the sounds of words, take out sounds, blend sounds, add in new sounds, or take apart sound to recombine them in new formations. These are good ways to foster phonological awareness.

Identification of Common Morphemes, Prefixes, and Suffixes

This aspect of vocabulary development is to help students look for structural elements within words that they can use independently to help them determine meaning.

The terms listed below are generally recognized as the key structural analysis components.

Root Words: A root word is a word from which another word is developed. The second word can be said to have its "root" in the first. This structural component nicely lends itself to the illustration a tree with roots so that students can use a concrete image for an abstract concept.

An example of a root word is "bene" which means "good" or "well." English words from this Latin root include "benefit," "beneficial," "beneficent," and "beneficiary."

Students may also want to construct root words literally by using cardboard trees and/or actual roots from plants to create word family models. This is an effective way to help students own their root words.

Base Words: A base word is a stand-alone linguistic unit which cannot be deconstructed or broken down into smaller words. For example, in the word "re-tell," the base word is "tell."

Contractions: These are shortened forms of two words in which a letter or letters have been deleted. These deleted letters have been replaced by an apostrophe. For example, "hasn't" is the contraction for "has not."

Prefixes: These are beginning units of meaning which can be added (the vocabulary word for this type of structural adding is "affixed") to a base word or root word. They cannot stand-alone. They are also sometimes known as "bound morphemes," meaning that they cannot stand alone as a base word. Some examples of prefixes are "pre," "ex," "trans," and "sub."

Suffixes: These are ending units of meaning that can be "affixed" or added on to the ends of root or base words. Suffixes transform the original meanings of base and root words. Like prefixes, they are also known as "bound morphemes," because they cannot stand alone as words. Some examples of suffixes are "ing," "ful," "ness," and "er."

Inflectional endings: These are types of suffixes that impart a new meaning to the base or root word. These endings in particular change the gender, number, tense, or form of the base or root words. Just like other suffixes, these are also termed "bound morphemes." Some examples are "ette," "es," and "ed."

> Learn more about
> **Word Analysis**
> http://www.orangeusd.k12.ca.us/
> yorba/word_analysis.htm

Compound Words: These occur when two or more base words are connected to form a new word. The meaning of the new word is in some way connected with that of the base word. "Bookkeeper," besides being the only English word with three double letters in a row, is an example of a compound word.

SKILL 5.3 Demonstrate knowledge of sentence structures (syntax), word and sentence meanings (semantics), and language function in communicative context (pragmatics)

To improve the reader's understanding of the ideas, you will want to examine your sentence structure for readability and coherence of ideas.

Sentence Completeness

Avoid fragments and run-on sentences. Recognize the sentence elements necessary to make a complete thought and use independent and dependent clauses properly. (see: *Use correct coordination and subordination*). Proper punctuation will correct such errors.

Sentence Structure

Recognize simple, compound, complex, and compound-complex sentences. Use dependent (subordinate) and independent clauses correctly to create these sentence structures.

Simple	Joyce wrote a letter.
Compound	Joyce wrote a letter, and Dot drew a picture.
Complex	While Joyce wrote a letter, Dot drew a picture.
Compound/Complex	When Mother asked the girls to demonstrate their new-found skills, Joyce wrote a letter, and Dot drew a picture.

Note: Do **not** confuse compound sentence elements with compound sentences.

Simple sentence with compound subject
Joyce and Dot wrote letters.
The girl in row three and the boy next to her were passing notes across the aisle.

Simple sentence with compound predicate
Joyce wrote letters and drew pictures.
The captain of the high school debate team graduated with honors and studied broadcast journalism in college.

Simple sentence with compound object of preposition
Coleen graded the students' essays for style and mechanical accuracy.

TEACHER CERTIFICATION STUDY GUIDE

Parallelism

Recognize parallel structures using phrases (prepositional, gerund, participial, and infinitive) and omissions from sentences that create the lack of parallelism. Parallelism provides balance to the grammar and the ideas.

> Learn more about
> **Parallel Structure vs.
> Faulty Parallelism**
> http://jerz.setonhill.edu/writing/grammar/parallel.html

Prepositional phrase/single modifier
Incorrect: Coleen ate the ice cream with enthusiasm and hurriedly.
Correct: Coleen ate the ice cream with enthusiasm and in a hurry.
Correct: Coleen ate the ice cream enthusiastically and hurriedly.

Participial phrase/infinitive phrase
Incorrect: After hiking for hours and to sweat profusely, Joe sat down to rest and drinking water.
Correct: After hiking for hours and sweating profusely, Joe sat down to rest and drink water.

To improve the reader's understanding of the ideas, you will want to examine your sentence structure for readability and coherence of ideas.

Sentence Completeness

Avoid fragments and run-on sentences. Recognize the sentence elements necessary to make a complete thought and use independent and dependent clauses properly. (See: *Use correct coordination and subordination*). Proper punctuation will correct such errors.

Prepositional phrase/single modifier
Incorrect: Coleen ate the ice cream with enthusiasm and hurriedly.
Correct: Coleen ate the ice cream with enthusiasm and in a hurry.
Correct: Coleen ate the ice cream enthusiastically and hurriedly.

Participial phrase/infinitive phrase
Incorrect: After hiking for hours and to sweat profusely, Joe sat down to rest and drinking water.
Correct: After hiking for hours and sweating profusely, Joe sat down to rest and drink water.

Recognition of Syntactical Redundancy or Omission

These errors occur when superfluous words have been added to a sentence or key words have been omitted from a sentence.

Redundancy

Incorrect: Joyce made sure that when her plane arrived that she retrieved all of her luggage.

Correct: Joyce made sure that when her plane arrived she retrieved all of her luggage.

Incorrect: He was a mere skeleton of his former self.

Correct: He was a skeleton of his former self.

Omission

Incorrect: Dot opened her book, recited her textbook, and answered the teacher's subsequent question.

Correct: Dot opened her book, recited from the textbook, and answered the teacher's subsequent question.

Avoidance of Double Negatives

This error occurs from positioning two negatives that, in fact, cancel each other in meaning.

Incorrect: Harold couldn't care less whether he passes this class.
Correct: Harold could care less whether he passes this class.

Incorrect: Dot didn't have no double negatives in her paper.
Correct: Dot didn't have any double negatives in her paper.

Semantic Connotations

To teach language effectively, we need to understand that as human beings acquire language they realize that words have **denotative** and **connotative** meanings. Generally, denotative words point to things and connotative words deal with mental suggestions that the words convey. The word *skunk* has a denotative meaning if the speaker means the actual animal with a white stripe down its back that lets off a strong odor. *Skunk* has a connotative meaning, too, and calling someone a skunk is not a compliment. Saying that someone "skunked" someone means that a dishonest scheme was underway.

Informative Connotations

Informative connotations are definitions agreed upon by the society in which the learner operates. A *skunk* is "a black and white mammal of the weasel family with a pair of perineal glands which secrete a pungent odor" or as the *Merriam Webster Collegiate Dictionary* says: "an offensive" odor. Identification of the color, species, and glandular characteristics are informative.

Affective Connotations

Affective connotations are the personal feelings a word arouses. A child who has no personal experience with a skunk and its odor or has had a pet skunk will feel differently about the word *skunk* than a child who has smelled the spray or been conditioned to associate offensiveness with the word *skunk*. A toy stuffed skunk could have a very different affective connotation.

> Learn more about **Connotation and Denotation in "Elements of Poetry"**
> http://bcs.bedfordstmartins.com/Virtualit/poetry/denotate_def.html

Using Connotations

In everyday language, we attach affective meanings to words unconsciously; we exercise more conscious control of informative connotations. In the process of language development, the leaner must come not only to grasp the definitions of words but also to become more conscious of the affective connotations and how his listeners process these connotations.

Gaining this conscious control over language makes it possible to use language appropriately in various situations and to evaluate its uses in literature and other forms of communication.

The manipulation of language for a variety of purposes is the goal of language instruction. Advertisers and satirists are especially conscious of the effect word choice has on their audiences. By evoking the proper responses from readers/listeners, we can prompt them to take action.

Choice of the medium through which the message is delivered to the receiver is a significant factor in controlling language. Spoken language relies as much on the gestures, facial expression, and tone of voice of the speaker as on the words that are spoken. Slapstick comics can evoke laughter without speaking a word. Young children use body language overtly and older children more subtly to convey messages. These refinements of body language are paralleled by an ability to recognize and apply the nuances of spoken language. To work strictly with the written work, the writer must use words to imply the body language.

SKILL 5.4   Use appropriate print and electronic sources to research etymologies; recognize conventions of English orthography and changes in word meaning and pronunciation

Just as countries and families have histories, so do words. Knowing and understanding the origin of a word, where and how it has been used through the years, and the history of its meaning as it has changed are important components of the writing and language teacher's toolkit.

Never in the history of the English language--or any other language for that matter--have the forms and meanings of words changed so rapidly. When America was settled originally, immigration from many countries made it a "melting pot." Immigration accelerated rapidly within the first hundred years, resulting in pockets of language throughout the country.

When trains began to make transportation available and affordable, individuals from those various pockets came in contact with each other, shared vocabularies, and attempted to converse. From that time forward, every generation brought the introduction of a technology that made language interchange not only more possible but more important.

> Check out the
> **Learning Resources of the OED**
> hhttp://www.oed.com/learning/

Radio began the trend to standardize dialects. A Bostonian might not be understood by a Houstonian, who might not be interested in turning the dial to hear the news or a drama or the advertisements of the vendors that had a vested interest in being heard and understood. Soap and soup producers knew a gold mine when they saw it and created a market for radio announcers and actors who spoke without a pronounced dialect. In return, listeners began to hear the English language in a dialect very different from the one they spoke. As it settled into their thinking processes, it eventually made its way to their tongues. Consequently, spoken English began to lose some of its local peculiarities.

This change has been a slow process, but most Americans can easily understand other Americans, no matter where they come from. They can even converse with a native of Great Britain or Australia with little difficulty. The introduction of television carried the evolution further as did the explosion of electronic communicating devices over the past fifty years.

An excellent example of the changes that have occurred in English is a comparison of Shakespeare's original works with modern translations. Without help, Americans of the twenty-first century are unable to read the *Folio*. On the other hand, teachers must constantly be mindful of the vocabularies and etymologies of their students, who are on the receiving end of the escalation brought about by technology and increased global influence and contact.

In the past, the *Oxford English Dictionary* has been the most reliable source for etymologies. Some of the collegiate dictionaries are also useful. *Merriam-Webster's 3rd Unabridged Dictionary* is useful in tracing the sources of words in American English. *Merriam-Webster's Unabridged Dictionary* may be out of date, so a teacher should also have a *Merriam-Webster's Collegiate Dictionary*, which is updated regularly.

In addition to etymologies, knowing how and when to label a usage "jargon" or "colloquial" is important. The teacher must be aware of the possibility that a word may now be accepted as standard. To be on top of this, the teacher must continually keep up with the etymological aids that are available, particularly online.

An Internet search for "etymology," or even the word you're unsure of, results in a multitude of sources. The information should be validated by at least three sources. Wikipedia is very useful, but since it can be changed by users, its information should be backed up by other sources. If you go to http://www.etymonline.com/sources.php, you will find a long list of resources on etymology.

Spelling in English is complicated because it is not always phonetic—that is, it is not based on the one-sound/one letter formula used by many other languages. It is based on the Latin alphabet, which originally had twenty letters, consisting of the present English alphabet minus J, K, V, W, Y, and Z. The Romans added K to be used in abbreviations and Y and Z in words that came from the Greek. This 23-letter alphabet was adopted by the English, who developed W as a ligatured doubling of U and later J and V as consonantal variants of I and U. The result was our alphabet of 26 letters with upper case (capital) and lower case forms.

Spelling is based primarily on English from the fifteenth century. The problem is that pronunciation has changed drastically since then, especially long vowels and diphthongs. This Great Vowel Shift affected the seven long vowels.

For a long time, spelling was erratic—there were no standards. As long as the meaning was clear, spelling was not considered very important. Samuel Johnson tackled this problem, and his *Dictionary of the English Language* (1755) brought standards to spelling, so important once printing presses were invented. There have been some changes, of course, through the years, but spelling is still not strictly phonetic.

Despite many attempts to nudge the spelling into a more phonetic representation of the sounds, all have failed for the most part. A good example is Noah Webster's *Spelling Book* (1783), which was a precursor to the first edition (1828) of his *American Dictionary of the English Language*. While there are rules for spelling and it's important that students learn the rules, there are also many exceptions; and memorizing exceptions, and giving plenty of opportunities for practicing them seems the only solution for the teacher of English.

COMPETENCY 6.0 ACQUISITION AND DEVELOPMENT OF LANGUAGE AND LITERACY

SKILL 6.1 Explain the influences of cognitive, affective, and sociocultural factors on language acquisition and development

The way language skills are developed depends on many factors, some internal (the age of the child), some external (immigration). Teachers can use a variety of approaches to accommodate individual differences.

Learning Approach

Early theories of language development were formulated from learning theory research. The assumption was that language development evolved from learning the rules of language structures and applying them through imitation and reinforcement. This approach also assumed that language and cognitive and social developments were independent of each other.

Thus, children were expected to learn language from patterning after adults who spoke and wrote Standard English. No allowance was made for communication through child jargon, idiomatic expressions, or grammatical and mechanical errors resulting from too strict adherence to the rules of inflection ("childs" instead of "children") or conjugation ("runned" instead of "ran"). No association was made between physical and operational development and language mastery.

Linguistic Approach

Studies spearheaded by Noam Chomsky in the 1950s formulated the theory that language ability is innate and develops through natural human maturation as environmental stimuli trigger acquisition of syntactical structures appropriate to each exposure level. The assumption of a hierarchy of syntax downplayed the significance of semantics. Because of the complexity of syntax and the relative speed with which children acquire language, linguists attributed language development to biological rather than cognitive or social influences.

Cognitive Approach

Researchers in the 1970s proposed that language knowledge derives from both syntactic and semantic structures. Drawing on the studies of Piaget and other cognitive learning theorists, supporters of the cognitive approach maintained that children acquire knowledge of linguistic structures after they have acquired the cognitive structures necessary to process language. For example, joining words for specific meaning necessitates sensory motor intelligence.

Children must be able to coordinate movement and recognize objects before they can identify words to name the objects or word groups to describe the actions performed with those objects.

Adolescents must have developed the mental abilities for organizing concepts as well as concrete operations, predicting outcomes, and theorizing before they can assimilate and verbalize complex sentence structures, choose vocabulary for particular nuances of meaning, and examine semantic structures for tone and manipulative effect.

Socio-cognitive Approach

Other theorists in the 1970s proposed that language development results from sociolinguistic competence. Language, cognition, and social knowledge are interactive elements of total human development. Emphasis on verbal communication as the medium for language expression resulted in the inclusion of speech activities in most language arts curricula.

Unlike previous approaches, the sociocognitive approach allowed that determining the appropriateness of language in given situations for specific listeners is as important as understanding semantic and syntactic structures. By engaging in conversation, children at all stages of development have opportunities to test their language skills, receive feedback, and make modifications. As a social activity, conversation is as structured by social order as grammar is structured by the rules of syntax. Conversation satisfies the learner's need to be heard and understood and to influence others. Thus, the choices of vocabulary, tone, and content are dictated by the learner's ability to assess the language knowledge of listeners. The speaker is constantly applying cognitive skills to using language in a social interaction. If the capacity to acquire language is inborn, without an environment in which to practice language, children would not pass beyond grunts and gestures, as did primitive man.

Of course, the varying degrees of environmental stimuli to which children are exposed at all age levels create a slower or faster development of language. Some children are prepared to articulate concepts and recognize symbolism by the time they enter fifth grade because they have been exposed to challenging reading and conversations with well-spoken adults at home or in their social groups. Others are still trying to master the sight recognition skills and are not yet ready to combine words in complex patterns.

Concerns for the Teacher

Because teachers must, by virtue of tradition and the dictates of the curriculum, teach grammar, usage, and writing as well as reading and later literature, the problem becomes when to teach what to whom.

The profusion of approaches to teaching grammar alone is mind-boggling. In the universities, we learn about transformational grammar, stratification grammar, sectoral grammar, and more. But in practice, most teachers, supported by presentations in textbooks and by the methods they learned themselves, keep coming back to the same traditional prescriptive approach—read and imitate—or structural approach—learn the parts of speech, the parts of sentence, punctuation rules, sentence patterns.

After enough of the terminology and rules are stored in the brain, then we learn to write and speak. For some educators, the best solution is the worst—don't teach grammar at all.

The same problems occur in teaching usage. How much can we demand students communicate in only Standard English? Different schools of thought suggest that a study of dialect and idiom and recognition of various jargons is a vital part of language development. Social pressures, especially on students in middle and junior high schools, to be accepted within their peer groups and to speak the non-standard language spoken outside the school make adolescents resistant to the corrective, remedial approach. In many communities where the immigrant populations are high, new words are entering English from other languages even as words and expressions that were common when we were children have become rare or obsolete.

Regardless of differences of opinion concerning language development, language arts teachers will be most effective using the styles and approaches with which they are most comfortable. And, if they subscribe to a student-centered approach, they may find that the students have a lot to teach them and each other.

Moffett and Wagner in the fourth edition of *Student-Centered Language Arts K-12* stress the three I's: individualization, interaction, and integration.

Essentially, they are supporting the socio-cognitive approach to language development. By providing an opportunity for students to select their own activities and resources, their instruction is *individualized*. By centering on and teaching each other, students are *interactive*. Finally, by allowing students to synthesize a variety of knowledge structures, they *integrate* them. The teacher's role becomes that of a facilitator.

> Learn more about
> **Student Centered Learning**
> http://www.wcer.wisc.edu/step/ep301/Fall2000/Tochonites/stu_cen.html

Benefits of the Socio-cognitive Approach

The socio-cognitive approach has tended to guide the whole language movement, currently in fashion. Most basal readers use an integrated, cross-curricular approach to successful grammar, language, and usage. Reinforcement becomes an intradepartmental responsibility. Language incorporates diction and terminology across the curriculum. Standard usage is encouraged and supported by both the core classroom textbooks and current software for technology.

Teachers need to acquaint themselves with the computer capabilities in their school district and at their individual school sites. Advances in new technologies require teachers to familiarize themselves with programs that would serve their students' needs. Students respond enthusiastically to technology.

Several highly effective programs are available in various formats to assist students with initial instruction or remediation. Grammar texts, such as the Warriner's series, employ various methods to reach individual learning styles. The school library media center should become a focal point for individual exploration.

SKILL 6.2   Explain the influence of a first language on second language development

Second Language Learners

Students who are raised in homes where English is not the first language and/or where standard English is not spoken may have difficulty with hearing the difference between similar sounding words like "send" and "sent." Any student who is not in an environment where English phonology operates may have difficulty perceiving and demonstrating the differences between English language phonemes. If students cannot hear the difference between words that sound the same like "grow" and "glow," they will be confused when these words appear in a print context. This confusion will of course, sadly, impact their comprehension.

Considerations for teaching to English Language Learners (ELL) include recognition by the teacher that what works for the English language speaking student from an English language speaking family, does not necessarily work in other languages.

> Visit **Dave's ESL Café**
> http://www.eslcafe.com/

Research recommends that ELL students learn to read initially in their first language. Further, it has been found that a priority for ELL should be learning to speak English before being taught to read English. Research supports oral language development since it lays the foundation for phonological awareness.

SKILL 6.3 Describe methods and techniques for developing academic literacy

Academic literacy encompasses ways of knowing particular content and refers to strategies for 1) understanding, 2) discussing, 3) organizing, and 4) producing texts. This is key to success in school. Students should be able to understand and articulate conceptual relationships within, between, and among disciplines.

Academic literacy also encompasses critical literacy, which is the ability to evaluate the credibility and validity of informational sources.

In a practical sense, when students are academically literate, they should be able to read and understand interdisciplinary texts, to articulate comprehension through expository written pieces, and to further knowledge through sustained and focused research.

Methods and techniques for helping students to develop academic literacy include helping students become "active makers of meaning." Good readers learn critical thinking. Critical thinking involves comparing and contrasting. As students work with texts making meaning, they are enabled to own their ideas. Then they create strategies for remembering and leaning to argue for their ideas.

Developing academic literacy is especially difficult for ELL students who are struggling to acquire and improve the language and critical thinking skills they need to become full members of the academic mainstream community. The needs of these ELL students may be met in through the creation of a functional language learning environment. This environment should engage them in meaningful and authentic language processing through planned, purposeful, and academically-based activities, teaching them how to extract, question, and evaluate the central points and methodology of a range of material, and construct responses using the conventions of academic/expository writing.

Effective academic writing requires that the students be able to choose appropriate patterns of discourse, which in turn involves knowing sociolinguistic conventions relating to audience and purpose. These skills, acquired through students' attempts to process and produce texts, can be refined over time by having students complete a range of assignments of progressive complexity which derive from the sustained and focused study of one or more academic disciplines.

Sustained content area study is more effectively carried out when an extensive body of instructional and informational resources is available. The Internet, through its extensive collection of reading materials and numerous contexts for meaningful written communication and analysis of issues, creates a highly motivating learning environment that encourages ELL students to interact with language in new and varied ways. Used as a resource for focus discipline research, the Internet is highly effective in helping these students develop and refine the academic literacy so necessary for a successful educational experience.

As a tool for sustained content study, the Internet is a powerful resource that offers easier, wider, and more rapid access to interdisciplinary information than traditional libraries. Using the Internet allows ELL students to control the direction of their reading and research, teaches them to think creatively, and increases motivation for learning as students work individually and collaboratively to gather focus discipline information.

By allowing easy access to cross-referenced documents and screens, Internet hypertext encourages students to read widely on interdisciplinary topics. This type of reading presents cognitively demanding language and a wide range of linguistic forms, and enables ELL students to build a wider range of schemata and a broader base of knowledge, which may help them grasp future texts.

Additionally, hypermedia provides the benefit of immediate visual reinforcement through pictures and/or slideshows, facilitating comprehension of the often-abstract concepts presented in academic readings.

Academic research skills are often underdeveloped in the ELL student population making research reports especially frightening and enormously challenging. The research skills students need to complete focus discipline projects are the same skills they need to succeed in classes. Instruction that targets the development of research skills teaches ELL students the rhetorical conventions of term papers, which subsequently leads to better writing and hence improved performance in class. Moreover, the research skills acquired through sustained content study and focus discipline research enable students to manage information more effectively, which serves them throughout their academic years and into the workforce.

TEACHER CERTIFICATION STUDY GUIDE

COMPETENCY 7.0 LITERACY STUDIES

SKILL 7.1 Recognize the written and oral conventions of standard English, and analyze the social implications of mastering them

While defining Standard English is sometimes difficult, the English teacher needs to settle on a definition that is practical in the classes that attempt to teach or promote it. English has become the closest to a universal language that any language has ever attained because of its use in international business and tourism. It also has many more dialects than most languages. Classrooms in California are usually filled with speakers of a variety of these dialects, which presents a special challenge for the teacher of English.

Teachers should remember also that language is very personal. Requiring students from Hispanic families and communities to abandon their own dialect and replace it with the "standard" one may suggest to them that they or their families and communities are personally sub-standard. They will be resistant to accepting the new dialect and will probably resent the implication that they are inherently inferior to other students.

There are many sensitive ways to deal with this situation, and teaching about dialects before attempting to teach Standard English is a good way to proceed. Respect for all dialects on the part of the teacher is important. Many of the variations of speech heard in the ghettos of America are in many ways more efficient in making a point clear and in descriptive elegance than the standard dialect.

Studying important writers such as Oscar Hijuelos and Maya Angelou who have used those features of the dialect in special and endearing ways can be useful in helping students understand how effective dialectal differences can be. This is also a good time to teach the use of dictionaries and encyclopedias to help writers and speakers use words in a way that will be understood by all listeners.

Perhaps the best definition of Standard English is that it is the dialect spoken by successful radio and television announcers and news people. To succeed in the public arena, speakers and writers need to be understood by the greatest number of people possible.

It is also the dialect of the business world. If a student aspires to succeed in a business environment, knowing Standard English is an important building block for success.

In addition, it is the dialect used in most written communications. If a newspaper article were written in a Hispanic dialect of English, many people would not understand it. However, if it is written in Standard English, even the speakers of that dialect will understand it. If a legal brief were written in African-American dialect, it would not make it into the courtroom. Again, if it were written in Standard English, everyone involved, even native speakers of the African-American dialect, will understand it.

So what exactly is Standard English? It is the dialect of the English handbook or textbook that forms the basis for the English classroom curriculum. It is also the dialect of dictionaries and encyclopedias. Guiding students through the English texts and handbooks is a method of teaching Standard English. Marking student papers on the foundation established in the lessons from the textbooks and handbooks is an exercise in teaching Standard English.

SKILL 7.2 Describe and explain cognitive elements of reading and writing processes

Any teacher of high-school students will tell you that the one word that would best characterize those students is *change*. Not only are they changing physically, they are undergoing rapid cognitive development which in turn brings about personality and behavioral changes. The parts of the brain that affect emotions (the limbic system) are growing faster than that in the cerebral cortex. For this reason, emotions are erratic. Because they often feel very insecure with the lack of control they have over what is happening to them, they tend not to want to be the center of attention.

Their thinking is advanced compared to only a short time ago. They are now able to think abstractly and ponder such things as art and beauty. They typically need to be told something only once rather than having concepts repeated, and are able to retain instructions and ideas in their memories and retrieve them more rapidly. They are also more aware of their learning abilities and limitations and are more likely to be able to assume more responsibility for assignments.

The downside is that adolescents tend to be know-it-alls and not so willing to take information or advice from anyone, especially an adult. They doubt that anyone understands their feelings and insecurities. Their thinking also tends to include only two poles—black and white, perfect or worthless, right or wrong. They are not inclined to make nuanced judgments and are judgmental regarding others as well as themselves. On the positive side, they are now able to have passionate feelings even about expressive literature.

How does this translate into classroom planning for the teacher of literature or composition—reading or writing? Remember that for Piaget, the end result of the stages of development should be autonomy, and the teacher of reading and composition has an excellent opportunity to assist students to grow toward that stage. Helping them claim responsibility for their own thoughts, whether private, spoken, or written, should be the ultimate goal of the English curriculum.

Communication should flow back and forth from student to teacher as much as possible. Introducing a poet and feeding relevant information about his/her life and times, then turning students loose to find their own meanings in specific poems can be a very successful exercise for adolescents.

Giving them opportunities to share their own feelings about the poetry with each other, either in a classroom setting or in study/discussion groups sometimes leads a student to a lifetime of poetry reading. Stories about adolescents are useful.

The role of the English teacher in cognitive development is to encourage the students, provide the information they are not able to obtain on their own, and validate their efforts. They come into the classroom fearful that they will be forced into a situation where everyone will be watching them and they will be embarrassed. The teacher must develop a level of trust that relieves that fear. The opportunity to express freely their own emotional and cognitive response to literature will help them to grow cognitively into responsible adults.

Freewriting in the composition classroom can be very useful in introducing students to more structured forms. With some encouragement, students can learn to use freewriting to explore their own feelings and convictions. The teacher needs to be aware that writing is a process that occurs in recursive stages.

The first stage, discovery, can be achieved by building on the freewriting that students have already become comfortable with, to move on to more formalized research to find new information and ideas and explore their own thoughts and feelings about topics or positions. The development of a thesis based on what they have done in the first stage gives them an opportunity to claim responsibility for their convictions.

Once they have settled on a tentative thesis, they are ready to begin to think about development and organization. If they feel free to move backward as well as forward, they will not only feel more comfortable in establishing a conviction about a topic but also will be willing to move forward toward a final essay that makes a point they feel strongly about and are willing to defend. Cognitively, this is an appropriate progression that taps into their stage (or stages) of development and helps them to move toward Piaget's goal of autonomy.

SKILL 7.3 Explain metacognitive strategies for making sense of text

In middle and secondary schools, the emphasis of reading instruction spans the range of comprehension skills: literal, inferential, and critical. Most instruction in grades five and six is based on the skills delineated in basal readers adopted for those grade levels. Reading instruction in grades seven through nine is usually part of the general language arts class instead of being a distinct subject in the curriculum, unless the instruction is remedial. Reading in tenth through twelfth grades is part of the literature curriculum—World, American, and British.

Teachers have many techniques to assure that students understand the text but these techniques vary with student age and ability.

Reading Emphasis in Middle School

Reading for comprehension of factual material—content area textbooks, reference books, and newspapers—is closely related to study strategies in the middle/junior high.

Organized study models teach students to locate main ideas and supporting details, to recognize sequential order, to distinguish fact from opinion, and to determine cause/effect relationships. One such model is the SQ3R method, a technique that enables students to learn the content of even large amounts of text (Survey, Question, Read, Recite, and Review Studying),

Strategies

Teacher-guided activities that require students to organize and to summarize information based on the author's explicit intent are pertinent strategies in middle grades. Evaluation techniques include oral and written responses to standardized or teacher-made worksheets.

Through reading fiction, students can develop skills for inferring meaning. Teachers can identify the skills to be studied, choose the appropriate reading resources, and develop activities to guide students' reading for meaning. To monitor the progress of acquiring these comprehension skills, teachers have at their disposal a variety of printed materials as well as individualized computer software programs.

Older middle school students should be given opportunities for more student-centered activities, such as the individual and collaborative selection of reading choices based on student interest, small group discussions of selected works, and greater written expression. Evaluation techniques include teacher monitoring and observation of discussions and written work samples.

Certain students may begin some fundamental critical interpretation, such as recognizing fallacious reasoning in news media, examining the accuracy of news reports and advertising, or explaining their reasons for preferring one author's writing to another's. Development of these skills may require a more learning-centered approach in which the teacher identifies a number of objectives and suggested resources from which the student may choose a course of study. Teachers can stress self-evaluation through a reading diary or they can encourage teacher and peer evaluation of creative projects resulting from such study.

> Learn more about
> **Monitoring Comprehension**
> http://www.indiana.edu/~l517/monitoring.html

Teachers should encourage one-on-one tutoring or peer-assisted reading instead of evaluating students as they read aloud before the entire class. However, occasional sharing of favored selections by both teachers and willing students is a good oral interpretation basic.

Reading Emphasis in High School

Students in high school literature classes should focus on interpretive and critical reading.

Teachers should guide the study of the elements of inferential (interpretive) reading—drawing conclusions, predicting outcomes, and recognizing examples of specific genre characteristics, for example—and critical reading to judge the quality of the writer's work against recognized standards.

At this level students should understand the skills of language and reading that they are expected to master and be able to evaluate their own progress.

Strategies

The teacher becomes more facilitator than instructor. With the teacher's guidance, students should be able to diagnose their individual strengths and weaknesses, keep a record of progress, and interact with other students and the teacher in practicing skills.

Along with the requisites and prerequisites of most literature courses, teachers need to encourage students to pursue independent study and enrichment reading. Enabling students to be life-long learners is a fundamental goal of teaching.

Teachers should provide ample opportunities for oral interpretation of literature, special projects in creative dramatics, writing for publication in school literary magazines or newspapers, and speech/debate activities. A student portfolio provides for teacher and peer evaluation.

COMPETENCY 8.0 GRAMMATICAL STRUCTURES OF ENGLISH

SKILL 8.1 Identify methods of sentence construction

Students who understand the form and structure of their own language become better communicators. Their writing becomes more purposeful, more exact, and more interesting. They understand that sentence structure can be used to emphasize or de-emphasize a point, and they appreciate that sentence variety is the mark of an efficient and sophisticated style

Correct Use of Coordination and Subordination

Connect independent clauses with the coordinating conjunctions—*and*, *but*, *or*, *for*, or *nor*—when their content is of equal importance. Use subordinating conjunctions—*although, because, before, if, since, though, until, when, whenever, where*—and relative pronouns—*that, who, whom, which*—introduce clauses that express ideas that are subordinate to main ideas expressed in independent clauses.

Be sure to place the conjunctions so that they express the proper relationship between ideas (cause/effect, condition, time, space).

> Incorrect: Because mother scolded me, I was late.
> Correct: Mother scolded me because I was late.
>
> Incorrect: The sun rose after the fog lifted.
> Correct: The fog lifted after the sun rose.

Notice that placement of the conjunction can completely change the meaning of the sentence. Main emphasis is shifted by the change.

> Although Jenny was pleased, the teacher was disappointed.
> The teacher was disappointed although Jenny was pleased.
>
> The boys who had written the essay won the contest.
> The boys who won the contest had written the essay.

Note: While not syntactically incorrect, the second sentence makes it appear that the boys won the contest for something else before they wrote the essay.

TEACHER CERTIFICATION STUDY GUIDE

SKILL 8.2 Analyze parts of speech and their distinctive structures and functions

The longer you teach, the more often you will need to review the basic grammar rules. Experienced teachers swear that you will see words misspelled and used incorrectly so often that you'll get confused. So here's a review

> Check out
> **The Tongue Untied**
> http://grammar.uoregon.edu/case/possnouns.html

Possessives

Make the possessives of singular nouns by adding an apostrophe followed by the letter *s* (*'s*).

>   baby's bottle, father's job, elephant's eye, teacher's desk, sympathizer's protests, week's postponement

Make the possessive of singular nouns ending in *s* by adding either an apostrophe or a s (*'s*) depending upon common usage or sound. When making the possessive causes difficulty, use a prepositional phrase instead. Even with the sibilant ending, with a few exceptions, you should use the *'s* construction.

>   dress's color, species' characteristics or characteristics of the species, James' hat or James's hat, Delores's shirt

Make the possessive of plural nouns ending in *s* by adding the apostrophe after the *s*.

>   horses' coats, jockeys' times, four days' time

Make possessives of plural nouns that do not end in *s* the same as singular nouns by adding *'s*.

>   children's shoes, deer's antlers, cattle's horns

Make possessives of compound nouns by adding the inflection at the end of the word or phrase.

>   the mayor of Los Angeles' campaign, the mailman's new truck, the mailmen's new trucks, my father-in-law's first wife, the keepsakes' values, several daughters-in-law's husbands

ENGLISH

Note: Because a gerund functions as a noun, any noun preceding it and operating as a possessive adjective must reflect the necessary inflection. However, if the gerund following the noun is a participle, no inflection is added.

> The general was perturbed by the private's sleeping on duty. (The word *sleeping* is a gerund, the object of the preposition *by*.

> but

> The general was perturbed to see the private sleeping on duty. (The word *sleeping* is a participle modifying private.)

Use of Pronouns

A pronoun used as a subject of predicate nominative is in nominative case.

> She was the drum majorette. The lead trombonists were Joe and he. The band director accepted whoever could march in step.

A pronoun used as a direct object, indirect object of object of a preposition is in objective case.

> The teacher praised him. She gave him an A on the test. Her praise of him was appreciated. The students whom she did not praise will work harder next time.

Common pronoun errors occur from misuse of reflexive pronouns:

Singular:	*myself, yourself, herself, himself, itself*
Plural:	*ourselves, yourselves, themselves.*
Incorrect:	Jack cut hisself shaving.
Correct:	Jack cut himself shaving.
Incorrect:	They backed theirselves into a corner.
Correct:	They backed themselves into a corner.

Use of Adjectives

An adjective should agree with its antecedent in number.

> Those apples are rotten. This one is ripe. These peaches are hard.

Comparative adjectives end in -er and superlatives in -est, with some exceptions like *worse* and *worst*. *More* and *most* precede some adjectives that cannot easily make comparative inflections.

> Mrs. Carmichael is the better of the two basketball coaches.
>
> That is the hastiest excuse you have ever contrived.
>
> Candy is the most beautiful baby.

Avoid double superlatives.

> Incorrect: This is the worstest headache I ever had.
> Correct: This is the worst headache I ever had.

When comparing one thing to others in a group, exclude the thing under comparison from the rest of the group.

> Incorrect: Joey is larger than any baby I have ever seen. (Since you have seen him, he cannot be larger than himself.)
> Correct: Joey is larger than any other baby I have ever seen.

Include all necessary words to make a comparison clear in meaning.

> I am as tall as my mother. I am as tall as she (is).
> My cats are better behaved than those of my neighbor.

SKILL 8.3 Describe the forms and functions of the English verb system

The varied forms and functions of the English verb system are some of the language's most distinguishing characteristics. While the system can be challenging, it also enables precision of meaning.

Subject-Verb Agreement

A verb agrees in number with its subject. Making them agree relies on the ability to properly identify the subject.

> One of the boys *was playing* too rough.
>
> No one in the class, not the teacher nor the students, was listening to the message from the intercom.
>
> The candidates, including a grandmother and a teenager, are debating some controversial issues.

If two singular subjects are connected by *and* the verb must be plural.

> A *man* and his *dog* were jogging on the beach.

If two singular subjects are connected by *or,* or *nor*, a singular verb is required.

> Neither Dot nor Joyce has missed a day of school this year.
> Either Fran or Paul is missing.

If one singular subject and one plural subject are connected by *or,* or *nor*, the verb agrees with the subject nearest to the verb.

> Neither the coach nor the players were able to sleep on the bus.

If the subject is a collective noun, its sense of number in the sentence determines the verb: singular if the noun represents a group or unit and plural if the noun represents individuals.

> The jury agrees that the defendant is not guilty.
> The jury tell the judge that they are deadlocked on their verdict.

Use of Verbs (Tense)

Present tense is used to express that which is currently happening or is always true.

> Randy is playing the piano.

> Randy plays the piano like a pro.

Past tense is used to express action that occurred in a past time.

> Randy learned to play the piano when he was six years old.

Future tense is used to express action or a condition of future time.

> Randy will probably earn a music scholarship.

Present perfect tense is used to express action or a condition that started in the past and is continued to or completed in the present.

> Randy has practiced piano every day for the last ten years.

> Randy has never been bored with practice.

Past perfect tense expresses action or a condition that occurred as a precedent to some other past action or condition.

> Randy had considered playing clarinet before he discovered the piano.

Future perfect tense expresses action that started in the past or the present and will conclude at some time in the future.

> By the time he goes to college, Randy will have been an accomplished pianist for more than half of his life.

Use of Verbs (Mood)

Indicative mood is used to make unconditional statements; subjunctive mood is used for conditional clauses or wish statements that pose conditions that are untrue. Verbs in subjunctive mood are plural with both singular and plural subjects.

> If I were a bird, I would fly.

> I wish I were as rich as Donald Trump.

Verb Conjugation

The conjugation of verbs follows the patterns used in the discussion of tense above. However, the most frequent problems in verb use stem from the improper formation of past and past participial forms.

> Regular verb: believe, believed, (have) believed

> Irregular verbs: run, ran, run; sit, sat, sat; teach, taught, taught

Other problems stem from the use of verbs that are the same in some tenses but have different forms and different meanings in other tenses.

> I lie on the ground. I lay on the ground yesterday. I have lain down. I lay the blanket on the bed. I laid the blanket there yesterday. I have laid the blanket every night.

> The sun rises. The sun rose. The sun has risen.

> He raises the flag. He raised the flag. He had raised the flag.

> I sit on the porch. I sat on the porch. I have sat in the porch swing.

> I set the plate on the table. I set the plate there yesterday. I had set the table before dinner.

Two other verb problems stem from misusing the preposition *of* for the verb auxiliary *have* and misusing the verb *ought* (now rare).

> Incorrect: I should of gone to bed.
> Correct: I should have gone to bed.

> Incorrect: He hadn't ought to get so angry.
> Correct: He ought not to get so angry.

Resources

Basic teaching texts used by teachers at large and found to be most helpful in teaching structure, grammar and composition:

Warriner's *Composition and Grammar: Fourth - First Course* and *Complete Course*, Orlando, FL: Harcourt, Brace, Jovanovich.
Intermediate to advanced college-bound students and international-ESOL students

Oshima, Alice and Ann Hogue. *Writing Academic English* (Longman Series) *A Writing and Sentence Structure Handbook*. Reading, MA: Addison-Wesley Publications Co., 1991.

Hixon, Mamie W. *The Essentials of English Language*. Piscataway, New Jersey: Research and Education Association, 1995.

English Journal. Urbana, IL: National Council of Teachers of English.

Teachers will find numerous other published local resources in the school library or district resource centers.

DOMAIN III. COMPOSITION AND RHETORIC

Candidates demonstrate knowledge of the foundations and contexts of the composition and rhetoric contained in the *English-Language Arts Content Standards for California Public Schools* (1997) as outlined in the *Reading/Language Arts Framework for California Public Schools: Kindergarten through Grade Twelve* (1999) at a post-secondary level of rigor.

Candidates have both broad and deep conceptual knowledge of the subject matter. Candidates face dynamic challenges in the domains of oral and written communication. They must make appropriate use of current text-production technologies and develop sensitivity to patterns of communication used by different social and cultural groups.

Candidates are competent writers and speakers who are able to communicate appropriately in various rhetorical contexts, using effective text structures, word choice, sentence options, standard usage conventions, and advanced research methods as needed. The subject matter preparation program provides opportunities for candidates to develop skills and confidence in public speaking.

COMPETENCY 9.0 WRITTEN COMPOSING PROCESSES (INDIVIDUAL AND COLLABORATIVE)

SKILL 9.1 Reflect on and describe their own writing processes

Viewing writing as a process allows teachers and students to see the writing classroom as a cooperative workshop where students and teachers encourage and support each other in each writing endeavor. Listed below are some techniques that help teachers facilitate and create a supportive classroom environment.

1. Create peer response/support groups that are working on similar writing assignments. The members help each other in all stages of the writing process - from prewriting, writing, revising, editing, and publishing.

   > Learn more about
   > **Teaching and Managing Peer Review**
   > http://www.utexas.edu/cola/progs/wac/highschool/hspeerreview/

2. Provide several prompts to give students the freedom to write on a topic of their own. Writing should be generated out of personal experience and students should be introduced to in-class journals. One effective way to get into writing is to let them write often and freely about their own lives, without having to worry about grades or evaluation.

3. Respond in the form of a question whenever possible. Teacher/facilitator should respond non-critically and use positive, supportive language.

4. Respond to formal writing acknowledging the student's strengths and focusing on the composition skills demonstrated by the writing. A response should encourage the student by offering praise for what the student has done well. Give the student a focus for revision and demonstrate that the process of revision has applications in many other writing situations.

5. Provide students with readers' checklists so that students can write observational critiques of others' drafts. Then they can revise their own papers at home using the checklists as a guide.

6. Pair students so that they can give and receive responses. Pairing students keeps them aware of the role of an audience in the composing process and in evaluating stylistic effects.

7. Focus critical comments on aspects of the writing that can be observed in the writing. Comments like "I noticed you use the word 'is' frequently" will be more helpful than "Your introduction is dull" and will not demoralize the writer.

8. Provide the group with a series of questions to guide them through the group writing sessions.

SKILL 9.2 Investigate and apply alternative methods of prewriting, drafting, responding, revising, editing, and evaluating

The last twenty years have seen great change in instruction in the English classroom. Gone are the days when Monday is literature day, Wednesday is grammar day, and Friday is writing day. Integrating reading, writing, speaking, listening, and viewing enables students to make connections between each aspect of language development during each class.

Suggestions for Integrating Language Arts

- Use pre-reading activities such as discussion, writing, research, and journals. Use writing to tap into prior knowledge before students read; engage students in class discussions about themes, issues, and ideas explored in journals, predicting the outcome and exploring related information.

- Use prewriting activities such as reading model essays, researching, interviewing others, combining sentences and other prewriting activities. Remember that developing language proficiency is a recursive process and involves practice in reading, writing, thinking, speaking, listening, and viewing.

- Create writing activities that are relevant to students by having them write and share with real audiences.

- Connect correctness—including developing skills of conventional usage, spelling, grammar, and punctuation—to the revision and editing stage of writing. Review of mechanics and punctuation can be done with mini-lessons that use sentences from student papers, sentence combining strategies, and modeling passages of skilled writers.

- Connect reading, writing, listening, speaking, and viewing by using literature read as a springboard for a variety of activities.

Writing is a recursive process. As students engage in the various stages of writing, they develop and improve not only their writing skills but their thinking skills as well.

Prewriting Strategies

Students gather ideas before writing. Prewriting may include clustering, listing, brainstorming, mapping, freewriting, and charting. Providing many ways for a student to develop ideas on a topic will increase his/her chances for success.

Listed below are the most common prewriting strategies students can use to explore, plan, and write on a topic. When teaching these strategies, remember that not all prewriting must eventually produce a finished piece of writing. In fact, in the initial lesson of teaching prewriting strategies, you might have students practice prewriting strategies without the pressure of having to write a finished product.

- Keep an idea book so that they can jot down ideas that come to mind.

- Write in a daily journal.

- Write down whatever comes to mind; this is called freewriting. Students do not stop to make corrections or interrupt the flow of ideas. A variation of this technique is focused freewriting—writing on a specific topic—to prepare for an essay.

- Make a list of all ideas connected with their topic; this is called brainstorming. Make sure students know that this technique works best when they let their mind work freely. After completing the list, students should analyze the list to see if a pattern or way to group the ideas.

- Ask the questions *who, what, when, where, why and how.* Help the writer approach a topic from several perspectives.

- Create a visual map on paper to gather ideas. Cluster circles and lines to show connections between ideas. Students should try to identify the relationship that exists between their ideas. If they cannot see the relationships, have them pair up, exchange papers and have their partners look for some related ideas.

- Observe details of sight, hearing, taste, touch, and taste.

- Visualize by making mental images of something and write down the details in a list.

After they have practiced with each of these prewriting strategies, ask them to pick out the ones they prefer and ask them to discuss how they might use the techniques to help them with future writing assignments. Remind them that they can use more than one prewriting strategy at a time. Also they may find that different writing situations may suggest certain techniques.

These steps are recursive; as a student engages in each aspect of the writing process, he or she may begin with prewriting, write, revise, write, revise, edit, and publish. They do not engage in this process in a lockstep manner; it is more circular.

Teaching the Composing Process

Prewriting Activities

1. Class discussion of the topic.
2. Map out ideas, questions, and graphic organizers on the chalkboard.
3. Break into small groups to discuss different ways of approaching the topic and develop an organizational plan and create a thesis statement.
4. Research the topic if necessary.

Drafting/Revising

1. Students write first draft in class or at home.
2. Students engage in peer response and class discussion.
3. Using checklists or a rubric, students critique each other's writing and make suggestions for revising the writing.
4. Students revise the writing.

Editing and Proofreading

1. Students, working in pairs, analyze sentences for variety.
2. Students work in groups to read papers for punctuation and mechanics.
3. Students perform final edit.

Students need to be trained to become effective at proofreading, revising and editing strategies. Begin by training them using both desk-side and scheduled conferences. Listed below are some strategies to use to guide students through the final stages of the writing process.

- Provide some guide sheets or forms for students to use during peer responses.

- Allow students to work in pairs and limit the agenda.

- Model the use of the guide sheet or form for the entire class.

- Give students a time limit.

- Have the students read their partners' papers and ask at least three who, what, when, why, how questions. The students answer the questions and use them as a place to begin discussing the piece.

- Provide students with a series of questions that will assist them in revising their writing.

    1. Do the details give a clear picture? Add details that appeal to more than just the sense of sight.

    2. How effectively are the details organized? Reorder the details if it is needed.

    3. Are the thoughts and feelings of the writer included? Add personal thoughts and feelings about the subject.

As you discuss revision, you begin with discussing the definition of revise. Also, state that all writing must be revised to improve it. After students have revised their writing, it is time for the final editing and proofreading.

Students should not be taught grammar in isolation, but in context of the writing process. At this point in the writing process a mini-lesson that focuses on some of the problems your students are having would be appropriate. Ask students to read their writing and check for specific errors like using a subordinate clause as a sentence. Provide students with a proofreading checklist to guide them as they edit their work.

When assessing and responding to student writing, teachers should follow these guidelines.

Responding to Non-graded Writing (Formative)

- Avoid using a red pen. Whenever possible use a #2 pencil.
- Explain the criteria that will be used for assessment in advance.
- Read the writing once while asking the question, "Is the student's response appropriate for the assignment?"
- Reread and make note at the end whether the student met the objective of the writing task.
- Responses should be non-critical and use supportive and encouraging language.
- Resist writing on or over the student's writing.
- Highlight the ideas you wish to emphasize, question, or verify.
- Encourage your students to take risks.

Responding to and Evaluating Graded Writing (Summative)

- Ask students to submit prewriting and rough-draft materials including all revisions with their final draft.
- For the first reading, use a holistic method, examining the work as a whole.
- When reading the draft for the second time, assess it using the standards previously established.
- Write your responses in the margin and use supportive language.
- Make sure you address the process as well as the product. It is important that students value the learning process as well as the final product.
- After scanning the piece a third time, write final comments at the end of the draft.

NCTE Beliefs about the Teaching of Writing
by the Writing Study Group of the NCTE Executive Committee
November 2004

1. *Everyone has the capacity to write, writing can be taught, and teachers can help students become better writers.*
2. *People learn to write by writing.*
3. *Writing is a process.*
4. *Writing is a tool for thinking.*
5. *Writing grows out of many different purposes.*
6. *Conventions of finished and edited texts are important to readers and therefore to writers.*
7. *Writing and reading are related.*
8. *Writing has a complex relationship to talk.*
9. *Literate practices are embedded in complicated social relationships.*
10. *Composing occurs in different modalities and technologies.*
11. *Assessment of writing involves complex, informed, human judgment*

SKILL 9.3 **Employ such strategies as graphic organizers, outlines, notes, charts, summaries, or précis to clarify and record meaning**

Teaching students to write is an extremely important part of an English teacher's life. You can help students by showing them that writing is a process accomplished through a series of steps. Here are some techniques for you to follow and incorporate for your students.

Prior to writing, you will need to prewrite for ideas and details and decide how the essay will be organized. In the hour you have to write you should spend no more than 5-10 minutes prewriting and organizing your ideas. As you prewrite, remember that you should have at least three main points and at least two to three details to support your main ideas. You can practice with several types of graphic organizers as you prepare for the essay portion of the test.

Step 1: Practice
Choose one topic from the chart on page and complete the cluster.

Step 2: Prewrite to Explain How or Why
Consider a prompt that asks you to explain how a poet creates tone and mood using imagery and word choice. Then fill out the organizer on the following page that identifies how the poet effectively creates tone and mood. Support with examples from the poem.

VISUAL ORGANIZER: GIVING REASONS

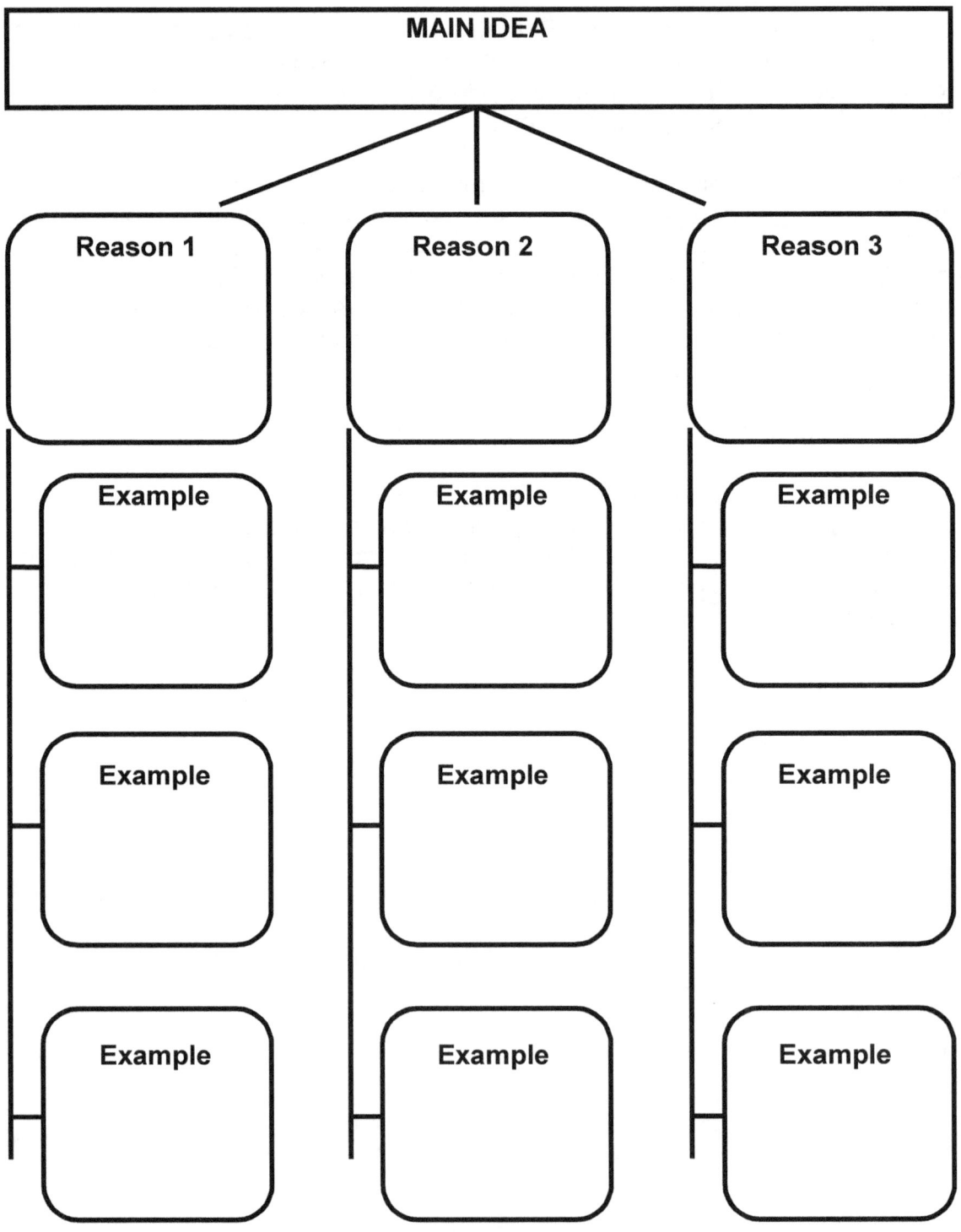

TEACHER CERTIFICATION STUDY GUIDE

Step 3: Prewrite to Organize Ideas
After you have completed a graphic organizer, you need to decide how you will organize your essay. To organize your essay, you might consider one of the following patterns to structure your essay.

1. Examine individual elements such as **plot, setting, theme, character, point of view, tone, mood, or style**. In this case, consider the single element outline.

    Single Element Outline
    Introduction - main idea statement
    Main point 1 with at least two supporting details
    Main point 2 with at least two supporting details
    Main point 3 with at least two supporting details
    Conclusion (restates main ideas and summary of main points)

2. Compare and contrast two elements. You may develop your ideas point-by-point or by block.

POINT-BY-POINT	BLOCK
Introduction Statement of main idea about A and B	Introduction Statement of main idea about A and B
Main Point 1 Discussion of A Discussion of B	Discussion of A Main Point 1 Main Point 2 Main point 3
Main Point 2 Discussion of A Discussion of B	Discussion of B Main Point 1 Main Point 2 Main Point 3
Main Point 3 Discussion of A Discussion of B	Conclusion Restate main idea
Conclusion Restatement or summary of main idea	

PRACTICE:
Using the cluster on the next page, choose an organizing chart and complete for your topic.

VISUAL ORGANIZER: GIVING INFORMATION

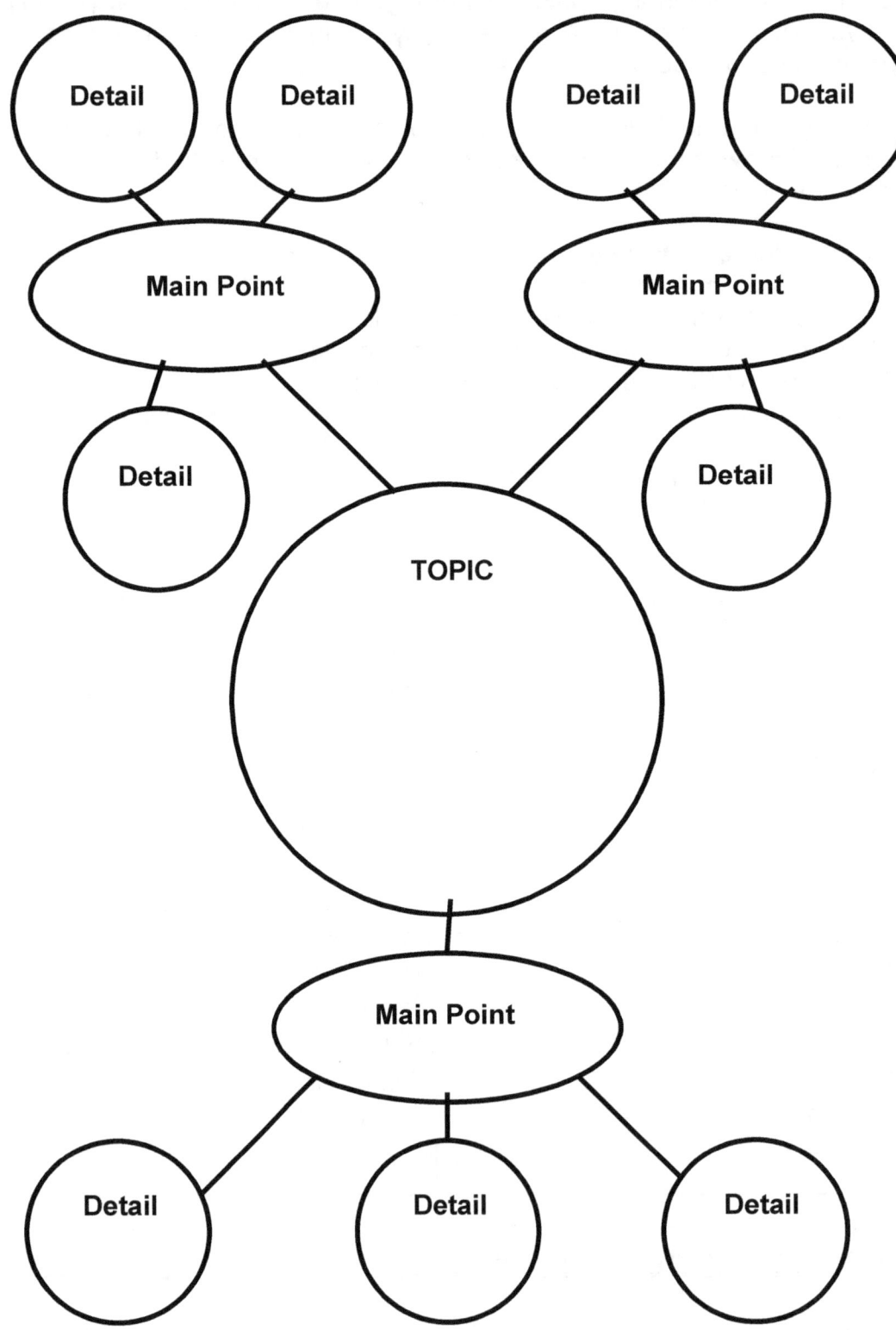

SKILL 9.4 Integrate a variety of software applications to produce print documents and multi-media presentations

The use of technology has broadened and enriched the entire communication process. Teachers and students who learn to use these resources effectively will expand their capabilities inside and outside the classroom.

Multimedia refers to a technology for presenting material in both visual and verbal forms. This format is especially conducive to the classroom, since it reaches both visual and auditory learners.

> Learn more about
> **Incorporating and Using Technology**
> http://al.odu.edu/wts/teachers/technology/

Knowing how to select effective teaching software is the first step in efficient multi-media education. First, decide what you need the software for (creating spreadsheets, making diagrams, or creating slideshows). Consult magazines such as *Popular Computing, PC World, MacWorld,* and *Multimedia World* to learn about the newest programs available. Go to a local computer store and ask a customer service representative to help you find the exact equipment you need. If possible, test the programs you are interested in. Check reviews in magazines such as *Consumer Reports, PCWorld, Electronic Learning* or *Multimedia Schools* to ensure the software's quality.

Software Programs for Producing Teaching Material
- Adobe
- Aldus Freehand
- CorelDRAW!
- DrawPerfect
- Claris Works
- PC Paintbrush
- Harvard Graphics
- Visio
- Microsoft Word
- Microsoft Power Point

Visual media should supplement the presentation, not overwhelm it.

Tips for Creating Visual Media

- Limit your graph to just one idea or concept.
- Keep the content simple and concise (avoid too many lines, words, or pictures).
- Balance substance and visual appeal.
- Make sure the text is large enough for the class to read.
- Match the information to the format that will fit it best.

TEACHER CERTIFICATION STUDY GUIDE

COMPETENCY 10.0 RHETORICAL FEATURES OF LITERARY AND NON-LITERARY, ORAL AND WRITTEN TEXTS

SKILL 10.1 Recognize and use a variety of writing applications

Encourage students to react honestly to literature. Allow them to choose their reading selections; if the choice is their own, their reactions can be more spontaneous and comfortable. With middle school/junior high students, keeping a reading diary may be as much as they can handle. High school students can be encouraged to write analytical reviews but try to keep them informal. Encourage students to read book reviews in current periodicals to see how critics express their responses.

Encourage students to attempt to write in certain genres. Have middle school students compose their own myths. High school students can try their hands at poems, short stories, and one-act plays. By attempting to write in a particular form, the student will gain a greater appreciation of the author's task.

Remember that teaching for appreciation and the encouragement of life-long reading means that instruction must be student centered. If you ever sat through a lecture in a college literature survey class, you can identify with the problems students have with lecturing in secondary schools. Teach the elements of literature and the process of learning through lecture, but avoid lecturing on the meaning of the literature at all costs. If you really want to inspire your students, perform the Lady Macbeth soliloquy or give your own book review - gratis.

Read and write when they do and share your creativity with them. High school students are especially appreciative of teachers who would never ask them to do something the teachers themselves cannot or will not do.

SKILL 10.2 Demonstrate awareness of audience, purpose, and context

In the past, teachers have assigned reports, paragraphs, and essays that focused on the teacher as the audience with the purpose of explaining information. However, for students to be meaningfully engaged in their writing, they must write for a variety of reasons. Writing for different audiences and aims enables students to be more involved in their writing. If they write for the same audience and purpose, they will continue to see writing as just another assignment. Listed below are suggestions that give students an opportunity to write in more creative and critical ways.

- Write letters to the editor, to a college, to a friend, to another student that would be sent to the intended audience.

- Write stories that would be read aloud to a group (the class, another group of students, to a group of elementary school students) or published in a literary magazine or class anthology.

- Write plays that would be performed.

- Have students discuss the parallels between the different speech styles we use and writing styles for different readers or audiences.

- Allow students to write a particular piece for different audiences.

Make sure students consider the following when analyzing the needs of their audience.

- Why is the audience reading my writing? Do they expect to be informed, amused or persuaded?

- What does my audience already know about my topic?

- What does the audience want or need to know? What will interest them?

- What type of language suits my readers?

As part of the prewriting, have students identify the audience. Expose students to writing that is on the same topic but with a different audience and have them identify the variations in sentence structure and style.

Remind your students that it is not necessary to identify all the specifics of the audience in the initial stage of the writing process but that at some point they must make some determinations about audience.

SKILL 10.3 Recognize and use various text structures

Basic expository writing simply gives information not previously known about a topic or is used to explain or define one. Facts, examples, statistics, cause and effect, direct tone, objective rather than subjective delivery, and non-emotional information are presented in a formal manner.

Descriptive writing centers on person, place, or object, using concrete and sensory words to create a mood or impression and arranging details in a chronological or spatial sequence.

Narrative writing is developed using an incident or anecdote or related series of events. Chronology, the 5 Ws, topic sentence, and conclusion are essential ingredients.

Persuasive writing implies the writer's ability to select vocabulary and arrange facts and opinions in such a way as to direct the actions of the listener/reader. Persuasive writing may incorporate exposition and narration as they illustrate the main idea.

Journalistic writing is theoretically free of author bias. It is essential when relaying information about an event, person, or thing that it be factual and objective. Provide students with an opportunity to examine newspapers and create their own. Many newspapers have educational programs that are offered free to schools.

SKILL 10.4 Apply a variety of methods to develop ideas within an essay

Here are some suggested strategies that help students write an essay; however, when you review them, you'll see how they can help you prepare for the essay given during the teacher certification essay as well.

General Strategies for Writing an Essay

- Budget your time. It is important that you write a good first draft.

- Read the question carefully. Make sure you understand what the question is asking you to do.

- Review basic literary terms.

- Take time to pre-write.

- Write a thesis statement by restating the question.

- Keep your purpose in mind as you write your essay.

- Connect the ideas of your essay in a brief conclusion.

- Leave enough time to quickly proofread and edit your essay.

The essay that you are to write must demonstrate the ability to write on a literary topic. As you practice the steps provided to prepare for this test, please keep in mind that this review will not teach you how to analyze literature. Analyzing literature has been the focus of your course of study. The following steps in writing an essay in a timed situation will aid you in preparing to write the essay in the most time efficient manner possible. Keep in mind that a good essay has focus, organization, support, and correct usage.

Step I - Understand the Question

When you receive your question, first you should decide what the question is asking you to do. Look for key words that will establish the purpose of your essay.

For practice, examine the following chart. It identifies some of the key words you might find on an essay test. Please note that for each key word the purpose and an example are illustrated.

KEY WORD	PURPOSE	EXAMPLE
Analyze	To examine the parts of a literary selection	Read a passage and analyze how the author achieves tone using diction and imagery
Compare	To identify the similarities	Read "I Hear America Singing" by Walt Whitman and "Chicago" by Carl Sandburg and compare the similarities in each poet's attitude about America.
Contrast	To identify differences	Read "Thanatopsis" by Bryant and "Do Not Go Gentle Into That Good Night" by Dylan Thomas and contrast how each poet uses imagery to express his distinct views of death.
Discuss	To examine in detail	Read a poem and discuss how the poet establishes the mood using imagery and word choice.
Explain	To provide reasons, examples or clarify the meaning	Read the opening passage of *The Great Gatsby* and explain how the author establishes the tone of the novel.

When writing an essay on literature, consider the following before you begin to pre-write.

Step 2 - Identify the elements for analysis.

If you are asked to examine the tone of poem, you need to look at imagery and word choice, or if you are asked to examine prose and explain how a writer creates mood, you should examine the diction, style, imagery, syntax, structure, and selection of detail.

Step 3 - Decide on your main idea.
Use the question as a guideline. However, do not merely restate the question. Make sure that in restating the topic you have taken a position on how you will answer the prompt. For example, you might be asked to read Whitman's poem "I Hear America Singing" and discuss not only the tone of the poem but also how Whitman creates the tone. To receive a high score on the essay, state your main idea clearly and indicate what the tone is and how it is created.

Step 4 - Write the Thesis Statement
First, you should identify the topic.

> I am going to write about the tone and how it is created in the poem "I Hear America Singing" by Walt Whitman.

Second, state your point of view about the topic.

> The upbeat and optimistic tone of Whitman's poem is created by his word choice, structure and imagery.

Third, summarize the main points you will make in your essay.

> Whitman creates an optimistic tone through his choice of words, parallel structure and images.

Part 5: State the main point of each body paragraph and organize support.

Paragraph	Purpose	Content
1 - Intro	Main Idea Statement	
2 – 1st Body Paragraph	Main Point 1	Quotes or specifics from the text with analysis or explanation of how each detail supports your main point.
3 – 2nd Body Paragraph	Main Point 2	Quotes or specifics from the text with analysis or explanation of how each detail supports your main point.
4 – 3rd Body Paragraph	Main Point 3	Quotes or specifics from the text with analysis or explanation of how each detail supports your main point.
5 - Closing	Summarize Ideas	

Part 6: Consider Audience, Purpose, and Tone.
Keep in mind that as you write this essay, your purpose is to demonstrate literary skill by reading an unfamiliar passage or poem and examining its elements.

Avoid summarizing the piece or writing your personal reaction to the work. Your audience is familiar with the piece and thus does not need to have the work summarized. In fact, the readers of your essay have been trained to look for focus, organization, support and correct usage. Finally, the tone is formal.

SKILL 10.5 Apply critical thinking strategies to evaluate methods of persuasion, including but not limited to:

- **Types of appeal**
- **Types of persuasive speech**
- **Logical fallacies**
- **Advertising techniques**
- **Logical argument**
- **Classical argument**

To achieve a sophisticated level of critical thinking, writers should study various methods of making an argument.

Types of Appeal

Ethos: Refers to the credibility of the speaker. It establishes the speaker as a reliable and trustworthy authority by focusing on the speaker's credentials.

Pathos: Refers to the emotional appeal made by the speaker to the listeners. It emphasizes the fact that the audience responds to ideas with emotion. For example, when the government is trying to persuade citizens to go to war for the sake of "the fatherland," it is using the appeal to *pathos* to target their love of their country.

Logos: Refers to the logic of the speaker's argument. It uses the idea that facts, statistics, and other forms of evidence can convince an audience to accept a speaker's argument. Remember that information can be just as, if not more, persuasive than appeal tactics.

Types of Persuasive Speech

Fact: Similar to an informative speech, a persuasive speech on a question of fact seeks to find an answer where there isn't a clear one. The speaker evaluates evidence and attempts to convince the audience that their conclusion is correct. The challenge is to accept a certain carefully crafted view of the facts presented.

Value: This kind of persuasion tries to convince the audience that a certain thing is good or bad, moral or immoral, valuable or worthless. It focuses less on knowledge and more on beliefs and values.

Policy: This speech is a call to action, arguing that something should be done, improved, or changed. Its goal is action from the audience, but it also seeks passive agreement with the proposition proposed. It appeals to both reason and emotion, and tells listeners what they can do and how to do it.

Logical Fallacies

A fallacy is, essentially, an error in reasoning. In persuasive speech, logical fallacies are instances of reasoning flaws that make an argument invalid. For example, a premature generalization occurs when you form a general rule based on only one or a few specific cases, which do not represent all possible cases. An illustration of this is the statement, "Bob Marley was a Rastafarian singer. Therefore, all Rastafarians sing."

A common fallacy in reasoning is the *post hoc ergo propter hoc* ("after this, therefore because of this") or the false-cause fallacy. These occur in cause/effect reasoning, which may either go from cause to effect or effect to cause.

They happen when an inadequate cause is offered for a particular effect; when the possibility of more than one cause is ignored; and when a connection between a particular cause and a particular effect is not made.

> Learn more about
> **Post Hoc Fallacy**
> http://www.sjsu.edu/depts/itl/graphics/adhom/posthoc.html

An example of a *post hoc*: Our sales shot up thirty-five percent after we ran that television campaign; therefore, the campaign caused the increase in sales.

It might have been a cause, of course, but more evidence is needed to prove it.

Advertising Techniques

Because students are very interested in the types of approaches advertisers use, you can develop high-interest assignments requiring them to analyze commercial messages. What is powerful about Nike's "Just Do It" campaign? What is the appeal of Jessica Simpson's eponymous perfume?

Beauty Appeal: Beauty attracts us; we are drawn to beautiful people, places, and things.

Celebrity Endorsement: This technique associates product use with a well-known person. By purchasing this product we are led to believe that we will attain characteristics similar to the celebrity.

Compliment the Consumer: Advertisers flatter the consumer who is willing to purchase their product. By purchasing the product the consumer is recognized by the advertisers for making a good decision with the selection.

Escape: Getting away from it all is very appealing; you can imagine adventures you cannot have; the idea of escape is pleasurable.

Independence/Individuality: This technique associates product with people who can think and act for themselves. Products are linked to individual decision making.

Intelligence: This technique associates product with smart people who can't be fooled.

Lifestyle: This technique associates product with a particular style of living/way of doing things.

Nurture: Every time you see an animal or a child, the appeal is to your paternal or maternal instincts, so this technique associates products with taking care of someone.

Peer Approval: This technique associates product use with friendship/acceptance. Advertisers can also use this negatively to make you worry that you'll lose friends if you don't use a certain product.

Rebel: This technique associates products with behaviors or lifestyles that oppose society's norms.

Rhetorical Question: This technique poses a question to the consumer that demands a response. A question is asked and the consumer is supposed to answer in such a way that affirms the product's goodness.

Scientific/Statistical Claim: This provides some sort of scientific proof or experiment, very specific numbers, or an impressive sounding mystery ingredient.

Unfinished Comparison/Claim: This technique uses phrases such as "Works better in poor driving conditions!" Works better than what?

Logical Argument

A logical argument consists of three stages. First, **state the premises** of the argument. These are the propositions which are necessary for the argument to continue. They are the evidence or reasons for accepting the argument and its conclusions.

Premises (or assertions) are often indicated by phrases such as "because," "since," "obviously," and so on. (The phrase "obviously" is often viewed with suspicion, as it can be used to intimidate others into accepting suspicious premises. If something doesn't seem obvious to you, don't be afraid to question it. You can always say, "Oh, yes, you're right, it is obvious" when you've heard the explanation.)

Next, **use the premises** to derive further propositions by a process known as inference. In inference, one proposition is arrived at on the basis of one or more other propositions already accepted. There are various forms of valid inference. The propositions arrived at by inference may then be used in further inference. Inference is often denoted by phrases such as "implies that" or "therefore."

Finally, **conclude the argume**nt with the proposition that is affirmed on the basis of the premises and inference. Conclusions are often indicated by phrases such as "therefore," "it follows that," "we conclude" and so on. The conclusion is often stated as the final stage of inference.

Classical Argument

In its simplest form, the classical argument has five main parts:

The **introduction**, which warms up the audience, establishes goodwill and rapport with the readers, and announces the general theme or thesis of the argument.

The **narration**, which summarizes relevant background material, provides any information the audience needs to know about the environment and circumstances that produce the argument, and set up the stakes—what's at risk in this question.

The **confirmation**, lays out in a logical order (usually strongest to weakest or most obvious to most subtle) the claims that support the thesis, providing evidence for each claim.

The **refutation** and concession, which looks at opposing viewpoints to the writer's claims, anticipating objections from the audience, and allowing as much of the opposing viewpoints as possible without weakening the thesis.

The **summation**, which provides a strong conclusion, amplifies the force of the argument and shows the readers that this solution is the best at meeting the circumstances.

COMPETENCY 11.0 RHETORICAL EFFECTS OF GRAMMATICAL ELEMENTS

SKILL 11.1 Employ precise and extensive vocabulary and effective diction to control voice, style, and tone

A planned, effective vocabulary program is not an "extra" but an across-the-curriculum necessity. In this four-step process you should accomplish the following:

1. Evaluate to determine what the students know.

2. Devise a plan to teach the students what they must learn as part of continuum.

3. Determine if students have heard the words to be studied and in what context.

4. Teach vocabulary for mastery.

To reach mastery, set clear-cut objectives and maintain an appropriate pacing since some students will need more practice than others. Building in time for practice, review, and testing is an integral component of a successful program.

Re-teaching words missed on tests or misused in writing is essential until mastery is achieved. The learning of vocabulary through visual, auditory, kinesthetic, and tactical experiences in a systematic order will enhance the learning process.

Methods of presentation for a well-balanced program at all levels include

- Recognizing and using words in context.

- Giving attention to varying definitions of the same word.

- Studying word families (synonyms, antonyms, and homonyms).

- Locating etymologies (word origins).

- Analyzing word parts (roots, prefixes, suffixes).

- Locating phonetic spellings and identifying correct pronunciation.

- Spelling words properly.

- Using words semantically.

Countless enrichment materials are available and include computer software, CD-ROM, board games, flashcards, puzzles, and so on. The more varied the experience, the more easily and quickly students will commit the words to memory and achieve mastery.

The Shostak Vocabulary Series that spans middle school through grade 12, including SAT/ACT preparation, is recommended for use in grades 9-12.

Within the literature series, vocabulary lists and practices are included. Classroom teachers should also review content area texts to add technical and specialized words to the weekly vocabulary study.

SKILL 11.2 Use clause joining techniques to express logical connections between ideas

A basic way to show relationship of ideas in sentences is to use punctuation correctly and effectively. You should be aware of the proper rules and conventions of punctuation, capitalization, and spelling. Competency exams will generally test the ability to apply the more advanced skills; thus, a limited number of more frustrating rules are presented here. Rules should be applied according to the American style of English, i.e., spelling *theater* instead of *theatre* and placing terminal marks of punctuation almost exclusively within other marks of punctuation.

Quotation Marks

The more troublesome punctuation marks involve the use of quotations.

Using Terminal Punctuation in Relation to Quotation Marks: In a quoted statement that is either declarative or imperative, place the period inside the closing quotation marks.

"The airplane crashed on the runway during takeoff."

If the quotation is followed by other words in the sentence, place a comma inside the closing quotations marks and a period at the end of the sentence.

"The airplane crashed on the runway during takeoff," said the announcer.

In most instances in which a quoted title or expression occurs at the end of a sentence, the period is placed before either the single or double quotation marks.

The educator worried, "The middle school readers were unprepared to understand Bryant's poem 'Thanatopsis.'"

Early book-length adventure stories like *Don Quixote* and *The Three Musketeers* are known as "picaresque novels."

There is an instance in which the final quotation mark would precede the period - if the content of the sentence were about a speech or quote so that the understanding of the meaning would be confused by the placement of the period.

The first thing out of his mouth was "Hi, I'm home." *but*
The first line of his speech began "I arrived home to an empty house".

In sentences that are interrogatory or exclamatory, the question mark or exclamation point should be positioned outside the closing quotation marks if the quote itself is a statement or command or cited title.

Who decided to lead us in the recitation of the "Pledge of Allegiance"?

Why was Tillie shaking as she began her recitation, "Once upon a midnight dreary..."?

I was embarrassed when Mrs. White said, "Your slip is showing"!

In sentences that are declarative but the quotation is a question or an exclamation, place the question mark or exclamation point inside the quotation marks.

The hall monitor yelled, "Fire! Fire!"

"Fire! Fire!" yelled the hall monitor.

Cory shrieked, "Is there a mouse in the room?" (In this instance, the question supersedes the exclamation.)

Using Double Quotation Marks with Other Punctuation: Quotations—whether words, phrases, or clauses—should be punctuated according to the rules of the grammatical function they serve in the sentence.

The works of Shakespeare, "the bard of Avon," have been contested as originating with other authors.

"You'll get my money," the old man warned, "when 'Hell freezes over'."

Sheila cited the passage that began "Four score and seven years ago . . . ." (Note the ellipsis followed by an enclosed period.)

"Old Ironsides" inspired the preservation of the *U.S.S. Constitution*.

Use quotation marks to enclose the titles of shorter works: songs, short poems, short stories, essays, and chapters of books. (See "Using Italics" for punctuating longer titles.)

> "The Tell-Tale Heart" - short story
> "Casey at the Bat" - poem
> "America the Beautiful" - song

Using Commas

Separate two or more coordinate adjectives modifying the same word and three or more nouns, phrases, or clauses in a list.

> Maggie's hair was dull, dirty, and lice-ridden.

> Dickens portrayed the Artful Dodger as skillful pickpocket, loyal follower of Fagin, and defendant of Oliver Twist.

> Ellen daydreamed about getting out of the rain, taking a shower, and eating a hot dinner.

> In Elizabethan England, Ben Jonson wrote comedy, Christopher Marlowe wrote tragedies, and William Shakespeare composed both.

Use commas to separate antithetical or complimentary expressions from the rest of the sentence.

> The veterinarian, not his assistant, would perform the delicate surgery.

> The more he knew about her, the less he wished he had known.

> Randy hopes to, and probably will, get an appointment to the Naval Academy.

> His thorough, though esoteric, scientific research could not easily be understood by high school students.

Using Semicolons

Use semicolons to separate independent clauses when the second clause is introduced by a transitional adverb. (These clauses may also be written as separate sentences, preferably by placing the adverb within the second sentence.)

> The Elizabethans modified the rhyme scheme of the sonnet; thus, it was called the English sonnet.
>
> *or*
>
> The Elizabethans modified the rhyme scheme of the sonnet. It thus was called the English sonnet.

Use semicolons to separate items in a series that are long and complex or have internal punctuation.

> The Italian Renaissance produced masters in the fine arts: Dante Alighieri, author of the *Divine Comedy;* Leonardo da Vinci, painter of *The Last Supper;* and Donatello, sculptor of the *Quattro Coronati*, the four saints.
>
> The leading scorers in the WNBA were Haizhaw Zheng, averaging 23.9 points per game; Lisa Leslie, 22; and Cynthia Cooper, 19.5.

Using Colons

Place a colon at the beginning of a list of items. (Note its use in the sentence about Renaissance Italians previously.)

> The teacher directed us to compare Faulkner's three symbolic novels: *Absalom, Absalom; As I Lay Dying;* and *Light in August*.

Do **not** use a comma if the list is preceded by a verb.

> Three of Faulkner's symbolic novels are *Absalom, Absalom; As I Lay Dying,* and *Light in August*.

Using Dashes

Place dashes (called an "em" dash) to denote sudden breaks in thought.

> Some periods in literature—the Romantic Age, for example—spanned different time periods in different countries.

Use dashes instead of commas if commas are already used elsewhere in the sentence for amplification or explanation.

> The Fireside Poets included three Brahmans—James Russell Lowell, Henry David Wadsworth, Oliver Wendell Holmes— and John Greenleaf Whittier.

Using Italics

Use italics to punctuate the titles of long works of literature, names of periodical publications, musical scores, works of art and motion picture television, and radio programs. (When unable to write in italics, you can instruct students to underline in their own writing where italics would be appropriate.)

The Idylls of the King *Hiawatha* *The Sound and the Fury*
Mary Poppins *Newsweek* *The Nutcracker Suite*

SKILL 11.3 Identify and use clausal and phrasal modifiers to control flow, pace, and emphasis

Transitional words and phrases are designed to lead the reader forward and through a piece of writing. Such words as *therefore, however, even so, although* are clues to connections between one part of the writing and another and the nature of the connection. Phrases sometimes substitute for words. Some examples include *as a matter of fact, in the long run, looking back*
You should understand and be able to explain how clauses and phrases can affect the flow, pace, and emphasis within a sentence. Writing will be more clear and concise with the proper understanding and use of effective syntax.

Types of Clauses

Clauses are connected word groups that are composed of *at least* one subject and one verb. (A subject is the doer of an action or the element that is being joined. A verb conveys either the action or the link.)

<u>Students</u> <u>are waiting</u> for the start of the assembly.
Subject   Verb

At the end of the play, <u>students</u> <u>wait</u> for the curtain to come down.
                        Subject   Verb

Clauses can be independent or dependent. Independent clauses can stand alone or can be joined to other clauses.

Comma and coordinating conjunction
Independent clause   , for   Independent clause
                      , and   Independent clause
                      , nor   Independent clause
                      , but   Independent clause
                      , or   Independent clause
                      , yet   Independent clause
                      , so   Independent clause

Semicolon
Independent clause   ;   Independent clause

Subordinating conjunction, dependent clause, and comma
Dependent clause   ,   Independent clause

Independent clause followed by a subordinating conjunction that introduces a dependent clause

Independent clause   Dependent clause

Dependent clauses, by definition, contain at least one subject and one verb. However, they cannot stand alone as a complete sentence. They are structurally dependent on the main clause.

There are two types of dependent clauses: (1) those with a subordinating conjunction, and (2) those with a relative pronoun.

Sample subordinating conjunctions
     Although   When   If   Unless   Because

<u>Unless a cure is discovered</u>, <u>many more people will die of the disease</u>.
     Dependent clause   +   Independent clause

Sample relative pronouns
     Who   Whom   Which   That

<u>The White House has an official website</u>, <u>which</u> <u>contains press releases, news updates, and biographies of the President and Vice President.</u>
(<u>Independent clause</u> + <u>relative pronoun</u> + <u>relative dependent clause</u>)

Misplaced and Dangling Modifiers

Particular phrases that are not placed near the one word they modify often result in misplaced modifiers. Particular phrases that do not relate to the subject being modified result in dangling modifiers.

Error: Weighing the options carefully, a decision was made regarding the punishment of the convicted murderer.

Problem: Who is weighing the options? No one capable of weighing is named in the sentence; thus, the participle phrase weighing the options carefully dangles. This problem can be corrected by adding a subject of the sentence capable of doing the action.

Correction: Weighing the options carefully, the judge made a decision regarding the punishment of the convicted murderer.

Error: Returning to my favorite watering hole brought back many fond memories.

Problem: The person who returned is never indicated, and the participle phrase dangles. This problem can be corrected by creating a dependent clause from the modifying phrase.

Correction: When I returned to my favorite watering hole, many fond memories came back to me.

Error: One damaged house stood only to remind townspeople of the hurricane.

Problem: The placement of the misplaced modifier *only* suggests that the sole reason the house remained was to serve as a reminder. The faulty modifier creates ambiguity.

Correction: Only one damaged house stood, reminding townspeople of the hurricane.

SKILL 11.4 Identifies and uses devices to control focus in sentence and paragraph

Paragraphs are clusters of information that support an author's main points or advance a story's action. They should be clearly focused, well developed, organized, coherent, and neither too long nor too short for easy reading.

> Learn more about
> **Editing and Proofreading Strategies for Revision**
> http://owl.english.purdue.edu/handouts/general/gl_edit.html

Techniques to Maintain Focus

Focus on a main point. The point should be clear to readers, and all sentences in the paragraph should relate to it.

Start the paragraph with a topic sentence. This should be a general, one-sentence summary of the paragraph's main point, relating back to the thesis and forward to the content of the paragraph. (A topic sentence is sometimes unnecessary if the paragraph continues a developing idea clearly introduced in a preceding paragraph, or if the paragraph appears in a narrative of events where generalizations might interrupt the flow of the story.)

Stick to the point. Eliminate sentences that do not support the topic sentence.

Be flexible. If you do not have enough evidence to support the claim of your topic sentence, do not fall into the trap of wandering or introducing new ideas within the paragraph. Either find more evidence, or adjust the topic sentence to corroborate with the evidence that is available.

SKILL 11.5   Maintain coherence through use of cohesive devices

A mark of maturity in writing is the effective use of transitional devices at all levels. For example, a topic sentence can be used to establish continuity, especially if it is positioned at the beginning of a paragraph. The most common use would be to refer to what has preceded, repeat it, or summarize it and then go on to introduce a new topic. An essay by W. H. Hudson uses this device: "Although the potato was very much to me in those early years, it grew to be more when I heard its history." It summarizes what has preceded, makes a comment on the author's interest, and introduces a new topic: the history of the potato.

Another example of a transitional sentence could be, "Not all matters end so happily." This refers to the previous information and prepares for the next paragraph, which will be about matters that do not end happily. This transitional sentence is a little more forthright: "The increase in drug use in our community leads us to another general question."

Another fairly simple and straightforward transitional device is the use of numbers or their approximation: "First, I want to talk about the dangers of immigration; second, I will discuss the enormity of the problem; third, I will propose a reasonable solution."

An entire paragraph may be transitional in purpose and form. In "Darwiniana," Thomas Huxley used a transitional paragraph:

> So much, then, by way of proof that the method of establishing laws in science is exactly the same as that pursued in common life. Let us now turn to another matter (though really it is but another phase of the same question), and that is, the method by which, from the relations of certain phenomena, we prove that some stand in the position of causes toward the others.

The most common transitional device is a single word. Some examples: *and, furthermore, next, moreover, in addition, again, also, likewise, similarly, finally, second*, etc. There are many.

In marking student papers, a teacher can encourage a student to think in terms of moving coherently from one idea to the next by making transitions between the two. If the shift from one thought to another is too abrupt, the student can be asked to provide a transitional paragraph. Lists of possible transitions can be put on a handout and students can be encouraged to have the list at hand when composing essays. These are good tools for nudging students to more mature writing styles.

Common Transitions

Logical Relationship	Transitional Expression
Similarity	also, in the same way, just as ... so too, likewise, similarly
Exception/Contrast	but, however, in spite of, on the one hand ... on the other hand, nevertheless, nonetheless, notwithstanding, in contrast, on the contrary, still, yet, although
Sequence/Order	first, second, third, next, then, finally, until
Time	after, afterward, at last, before, currently, during, earlier, immediately, later, meanwhile, now, presently, recently, simultaneously, since, subsequently, then
Example	for example, for instance, namely, specifically, to illustrate
Emphasis	even, indeed, in fact, of course, truly
Place/Position	above, adjacent, below, beyond, here, in front, in back, nearby, there
Cause and Effect	accordingly, consequently, hence, so, therefore, thus, as a result, because, consequently, hence, if...then, in short
Additional Support or Evidence	additionally, again, also, and, as well, besides, equally important, further, furthermore, in addition, moreover, then
Conclusion/Summary	finally, in a word, in brief, in conclusion, in the end, in the final analysis, on the whole, thus, to conclude, to summarize, in sum, in summary
Statement support	most important, more significant, primarily, most essential
Addition	again, also, and, besides, equally important, finally, furthermore, in addition, last, likewise, moreover, too
Clarification	actually, clearly, evidently, in fact, in other words, obviously, of course, indeed

COMPETENCY 12.0 CONVENTIONS OF ORAL AND WRITTEN LANGUAGE

SKILL 12.1 Apply knowledge of linguistic structure to identify and use the conventions of standard edited English

The knowledge that teachers need to be effective in the multicultural English classroom can be broken into seven broad areas:

1. The nature of human language
2. The components of language
3. The process of language acquisition
4. Language and culture
5. Linguistics and literacy
6. TESOL methodologies
7. Language pathology

Human language is creative in that it allows speakers to form an unlimited number of sentences from the vocabulary and operations base they build when they learn language. Noam Chomsky called language the "human essence" which means that this distinction is, so far as we know, unique to man.

The basics of linguistics are *phonology, morphology, syntax, semantics,* and *pragmatics.* All languages are rule-governed--not the rules we "teach"--but the rules that have become embedded in the brain processes of the user. The rule embedded in the mind of a native speaker of English that the nominative is different from the accusative is well-known to a three-year-old speaker. If he is told that Mommy bit the dog, he will laugh; he will have a quite different response if he is told that the dog bit Mommy.

A native child learning a language will progress through predictable stages. A speaker of another language learning to speak and use English will also go through predictable, though different stages. The age of the learner is significant. Younger children will learn a foreign language much more quickly than older ones. Learning to read is very different from learning to understand and speak the language.

Language is tied to culture and carries with it very strong emotions. The very heated discussions over whether Black English is a different language or a different dialect demonstrate how emotional language can be. It involves not just language usage but also cultural, social, and political matters.

Variations in language are manifested in the phonology, lexicon, morphology, syntax, and semantics of a language and can even be related to gender, ethnicity, social class, geography, and age. Not only are there variations in language, but also all languages change over time, including English.

The English spoken by our parents is not the English that is being spoken today by high-school students. To assume that variations and changes are somehow flaws, wrong, or problematic is to misunderstand the very nature of language.

TESOL—teaching English to speakers of other languages—requires specialized training, knowledge, and experience. While most English teachers are not required to have that training and experience, they do need to understand the needs of students in their classroom who are not native speakers of English. In the same way, teachers should have enough linguistic training to be able to recognize when language or speech production is atypical and when specialists, either speech pathologists or therapists, should be consulted.

SKILL 12.2 Recognize, understand, and use a range of conventions in both spoken and written English, including:
- **Conventions of effective sentence structure (e.g., clear pronoun reference, parallel structure, appropriate verb tense)**
- **Preferred usage (e.g., verb/subject agreement, pronoun agreement, idioms)**
- **Conventions of pronunciation and intonation**
- **Conventional forms of spelling**
- **Capitalization and punctuation**

See 5.3, 8.2 and 8.3

Spelling

Concentration in this section will be on spelling plurals and possessives. If the multiplicity and complexity of spelling rules based on phonics, letter doubling, and exceptions to rules are not mastered by adulthood, writers should use a good dictionary to achieve correctness. As spelling mastery is usually difficult for adolescents, our recommendation for them is the same. Learning the use of a dictionary and thesaurus will be a more rewarding use of time than laboring to master each obscure rule and exception.

Most plurals of nouns that end in hard consonants or hard consonant sounds followed by a silent *e* are made by adding *s*. Some words ending in vowels only add *s*.

    fingers, numerals, banks, bugs, riots, homes, gates, radios, bananas

Nouns that end in soft consonant sounds *s, j, x, z, ch,* and *sh,* add *es*. Some nouns ending in *o* add *es*.

    dresses, waxes, churches, brushes, tomatoes, potatoes

Nouns ending in *y* preceded by a vowel just add *s*.

>boys, alleys

Nouns ending in *y* preceded by a consonant change the *y* to *i* and add *es*.

>babies, corollaries, frugalities, poppies

Some nouns plurals are formed irregularly or remain the same.

>sheep, deer, children, leaves, oxen

Some nouns derived from foreign words, especially Latin, may make their plurals in two different ways - one of them Anglicized. Sometimes, the meanings are the same; other times, the two plurals are used in slightly different contexts. It is always wise to consult the dictionary.

>appendices, appendixes   criterion, criteria
>indexes, indices   crisis, crises

Make the plurals of closed (solid) compound words in the usual way except for words ending in *ful* which make their plurals on the root word.

>timelines, hairpins

Make the plurals of open or hyphenated compounds by adding the change in inflection to the word that changes in number.

>fathers-in-law, courts-martial, masters of art, doctors of medicine

Make the plurals of letters, numbers, and abbreviations by adding *s*.

>fives and tens, IBMs, 1990s, *p*s and *q*s (Note that letters are italicized.)

When in doubt, consult a dictionary.

Capitalization

Capitalize all proper names of persons (including specific organizations or agencies of government); places (countries, states, cities, parks, and specific geographical areas); and things (political parties, structures, historical and cultural terms, and calendar and time designations); and religious terms (any deity, revered person or group, sacred writings).

>Check out this
>**Guide to Grammar and Writing**
>http://grammar.ccc.commnet.edu/grammar/

ENGLISH

Percy Bysshe Shelley, Argentina, Mount Rainier National Park, Grand Canyon, League of Nations, the Sears Tower, Birmingham, Lyric Theater, Americans, Midwesterners, Democrats, Renaissance, Boy Scouts of America, Easter, God, Bible, Dead Sea Scrolls, Koran

Capitalize proper adjectives and titles used with proper names.

California gold rush, President John Adams, French fries, Homeric epic, Romanesque architecture, Senator John Glenn

Note: Some words that represent titles and offices are not capitalized unless used with a proper name.

Capitalized	Not Capitalized
Congressman McKay	the congressman from Florida
Commander Alger	commander of the Pacific Fleet
Queen Elizabeth	the queen of England

Capitalize all main words in titles of works of literature, art, and music.

COMPETENCY 13.0 RESEARCH STRATEGIES

SKILL 13.1 Develop and apply research questions

An easy and effective way of helping students organize information to be used in a work of nonfiction is by asking specific questions that are geared towards a particular mode of presentation. A sample of these questions follows:

What is it? It is the process of thinking up and writing down a set of questions that you want to answer about the research topic you have selected.

Why should I do it? It will keep you from getting lost or off-track when looking for information. You will try to find the answers to these questions when you do your research.

When do I do it? After you have written your statement of purpose and have a focused topic to ask questions about, begin research.

How do I do it? Make two lists of questions. Label one "factual" questions and one "interpretive" questions. The answers to factual questions will give your reader the basic background information they need to understand your topic. The answers to interpretive questions show your creative thinking in your project and can become the basis for your thesis statement.

Ask factual questions: Assume your reader knows nothing about your subject. Make an effort to tell them everything they need to know to understand what you will say in your project.

Make a list of specific questions that ask who, what, when, where, and why.

> **Example**: For a report about President Abraham Lincoln's attitude and policies towards slavery, people will have to know the following: Who was Abraham Lincoln? Where and when was he born? What political party did he belong to? When was he elected president? What were the attitudes and laws about slavery during his lifetime? How did his actions affect slavery?

Asking Interpretive Questions
These kinds of questions are the result of your own original thinking. They can be based on the preliminary research you have done on your chosen topic. Select one or two questions that you will answer in your presentation. They can be the basis of forming a thesis statement.

Learn more about
The Art of Asking Good Questions
http://www.youthlearn.org/learning/teaching/questions.asp

- **Hypothetical**: How would things be different today if something in the past had been different?

    Example: How would our lives be different today if the Confederate (southern) states had won the United States Civil War? What would have happened to the course of World War Two if the atomic bomb hadn't been dropped on Hiroshima and Nagasaki?

- **Prediction:** How will something look or be in the future, based on the way it is now?

    Example: What will happen to sea levels if global warming due to ozone layer depletion continues and the polar caps melt significantly? If the population of China continues to grow at the current rate for the next fifty years, how will that impact its role in world politics?

- **Solution:** What solutions can be offered to a problem that exists today?

    Example: How could global warming be stopped? What can be done to stop the spread of sexually transmitted diseases among teenagers?

- **Comparison or Analogy**: Find the similarities and differences between your main subject and a similar subject, or with another subject in the same time period or place.

    Example: In what ways is the Civil War in the former Yugoslavia similar to (or different from) the United States Civil War? What is the difference in performance between a Porsche and a Lamborghini?

- **Judgment:** Based on the information you find, what can you say as your informed opinion about the subject?

    Example: How does tobacco advertising affect teen cigarette smoking? What are the major causes of eating disorders among young women? How does teen parenthood affect the future lives of young women and men?

SKILL 13.2 Demonstrate methods of inquiry and investigation

Whether researching for your own purposes or teaching students to research, the best place to start research is usually at a library. Not only does it have numerous books, videos, and periodicals to use for references, the librarian is always a valuable resource for information and can help retrieve information. In spite of the abundance of online sources, researchers still need librarians.

Those who declared librarians obsolete when the Internet rage first appeared are now red-faced. We need them more than ever. The Internet is full of 'stuff' but its value and readability is often questionable. 'Stuff' doesn't give you a competitive edge, high-quality related information does.
-Patricia Schroeder, President of the Association of American Publishers

The Internet is a multi-faceted gold mine of information, but you must be careful to discriminate between reliable and unreliable sources. Use sites that are associated with an academic institution, such as a university or a scholarly organization. Typical domain names will end in "edu" or "org."

Keep **content** and **context** in mind when researching. Don't be so wrapped up with how you are going to apply your resource to your project that you miss the author's entire purpose or message. Remember that there are multiple ways to get the information you need. Read an encyclopedia article about your topic to get a general overview, and then focus from there. Note important names of people associated with your subject, time periods, and geographic areas. Make a list of key words and their synonyms to use while searching for information. And finally, don't forget about articles in magazines and newspapers, or even personal interviews with experts related to your field of interest!

SKILL 13.3 Identify and use multiple resources and critically evaluate the quality of the sources

Titles listed in the resource list at the end of this guide are current references with which all language arts teachers should be familiar.

Though the list of literature text publishers is extensive, the following is a tried and true list that meets the needs of students in grades 6-12. Teachers should familiarize themselves with the texts adopted by their own districts and to select those resources that best reflect the district's scope and sequence.

- Heritage Edition Series - Harcourt Brace Jovanovich
- Norton Anthologies
- Bedford Introduction to Literature
- *Sound and Sense - Introduction to Poetry* by Laurence Perrine and R. Arp
- *Sound and Sense - Literature Structure*
- *Literary Cavalcade, Read,* and *Scholastic Magazine* - Scholastic supplemental reading

SKILL 13.4 Interpret and apply findings

While bias cannot be eliminated, writers should carefully examine their resources and their own writings to avoid negative one-sidedness.

When evaluating sources, first go through this checklist to make sure the source is even worth reading:
- Title (How relevant is it to your topic?)
- Date (How current is the source?)
- Organization (What institution is this source coming from?)
- Length (How in depth does it go?)

Check for signs of bias:
- Does the author or publisher have political ties or religious views that could affect their objectivity?

- Is the author or publisher associated with any special-interest groups that might only see one side of an issue, such as Greenpeace or the National Rifle Association?

- How fairly does the author treat opposing views?

- Does the language of the piece show signs of bias?

Keep an open mind while reading, and don't let opposing viewpoints prevent you from absorbing the text. Remember that you are not judging the author's work; you are examining its assumptions, assessing its evidence and weighing its conclusions.

Further, when writing, review carefully to eliminate any conscious bias. Are you so convinced of your own viewpoint that you ignore valid opposing arguments? Have you backed every assertion with credible and reliable information?

Paraphrasing is the art of rewording text. The goal is to maintain the original purpose of the statement while translating it into your own words. Your newly generated sentence can be longer or shorter than the original. Concentrate on the meaning, not on the words. Do not change concept words, special terms, or proper names. There are numerous ways to paraphrase effectively:
- Change the key words' form or part of speech. Example: "American news **coverage** is frequently **biased** in favor of Western views," becomes "When American journalists **cover** events, they often display a Western **bias**."

- Use synonyms of "relationship words." Look for a relationship word, such as **contrast, cause,** or **effect,** and replace it with a word that conveys a similar meaning, thus creating a different structure for your sentence. Example: "**Unlike** many cats, Purrdy can sit on command," becomes "Most cats are not able to be trained, **but** Purrdy can sit on command."

- Use synonyms of phrases and words. Example: "The Beatnik writers were relatively unknown at **the start of the decade**," becomes "**Around the early 1950s**, the Beatnik writers were still relatively unknown."

- Change passive voice to active voice or move phrases and modifiers. Example: "Not to be outdone by the third graders, the fourth grade class added a musical medley to their Christmas performance," becomes "The fourth grade class added a musical medley to their Christmas performance to avoid being showed up by the third graders."

- Use reversals or negatives that do not change the meaning of the sentence. Example: "That burger chain is only found in California," becomes "That burger chain is not found on the East Coast."

SKILL 13.5 Use professional conventions and ethical standards of citation and attribution

Documentation is an important skill in incorporating outside information into a piece of writing. Students must learn that research is more than cut and paste from the Internet and that plagiarism is a serious academic offense.

This skill pertains to recognizing that stealing intellectual property is an academic and, in some cases, a legal crime; because it is so, students need to learn how to give credit where credit is due.

Students need to be aware of the rules that apply to borrowing ideas from various sources. Increasingly, consequences for violations of these rules (plagiarism) are becoming more severe, and students are expected to be aware of how to avoid such problems. Pleading ignorance is less and less of a defense. Such consequences include failing a particular assignment, losing credit for an entire course, expulsion from a learning environment, and civil penalties. Software exists that enables teachers and other interested individuals to determine quickly whether or not a given paper includes plagiarized material. As members of society in the information age, students are expected to recognize the basic justice of intellectual honesty and to conform to the systems meant to ensure it.

There are several style guides for documenting sources. Each guide has its own particular ways of signaling that information has been directly borrowed or paraphrased, and familiarity with at least where to find the relevant details of the major style guides is an essential for students. Many libraries publish overviews of the major style guides for students to consult, most bookstores will carry full guides for the major systems, and relevant information is readily available on the web as well.

Documentation of sources takes two main forms. The first form applies to citing sources in the text of the document or as footnotes or endnotes. In-text documentation is sometimes called parenthetical documentation and requires specific information within parentheses placed immediately after borrowed material. Footnotes or endnotes are placed either at the bottom of relevant pages or at the end of the document.

Beyond citing sources in the text, style guides also require a bibliography, a references section, or a works cited section at the end of the document. Sources for any borrowed material are to be listed according to the rules of the particular guide. In some cases, it may be required to include a works consulted listing even though no material is directly cited or paraphrased to the extent that an in-text citation would be required.

The major style guides to be familiar with include the *Modern Language Association Handbook (MLA)*, the *Manual of the American Psychological Association (APA)*, the *Chicago Manuel of Style*, *Turabian*, and *Scientific Style and Format: the CBE Manual*.

> Learn more about
> **MLA Works Cited Documentation**
> http://www.studyguide.org/MLAdocumentation.htm

Documentation of sources from the Internet is particularly involved and continues to evolve at a pace often requiring visiting the latest online update available for a particular style guide.

Tips for Documentation

- Keep a record of all sources consulted during the research process.

- As you take notes, avoid unintentional plagiarism. Summarize and paraphrase in your own words without the source in front of you. If you use a direct quote, copy it exactly as written and enclose in quotation marks.

- Cite anything that is not common knowledge. This includes direct quotes as well as ideas or statistics.

Within the body of your document follow this blueprint for standard attribution following MLA style.

1. Begin the sentence with, "According to _____,"

2. Proceed with the material being cited, followed by the page number in parentheses.

In-Text Citation Example

According to Steve Mandel, "our average conversational rate of speech is about 125 words per minute" (78).

Once students have mastered this basic approach, they can learn more sophisticated methods such as embedding information.

Each source used within the document will have a complete citation in a bibliography or works cited page.

Works Cited Entry

Mandel, Steve. *Effective Presentation Skills*. Menlo Park, California: Crisp Publications, 1993.

SKILL 13.6 Demonstrate effective presentation methods, including multi-media formats

Now that you have completed your research, you will want to present it so that your audience will understand your results easily. You will find that the very methods you use to present your instruction will adapt very well to other types of presentations.

Principle Methods of Instruction

Lecture Method: This widely used method involves a heavy reliance on telling the students the selected information, with not a lot of opportunity for them to interrupt or ask questions. Sometimes, a question period is allowed at the end of the lecture. The teacher usually uses a detailed set of notes or a brief outline of ideas, along with audio/visual aids (in the form of slides, overhead projections, flip charts, and television). Lectures should be kept relatively short. The lecturer must be credible and qualified.

- Advantages: Large amount of material can be covered, suitable for almost any group size, maximum control over content and sequence of information

- Disadvantages: Only one-way communication, no monitoring of learning or processing of information, little participation from students, attention is hard to maintain over a long period of time

Demonstration Method: This method is used to impart information as well as skill and understanding. It usually involves a procedure of some kind. As the skill is performed in front of the class, the students' attention should be drawn to specific key points but not so much that it detracts from the demonstration as a whole. Stress each key point in its relation to the sequence. Demonstrate the skill slowly, and then repeat it at normal speed, reiterating the main points. Once the demonstration is complete, students should practice the skill for themselves. Carefully supervise and monitor their progress and point out errors to avoid absorption of the wrong sequence. This method is better suited for small groups of students.

- Advantages: Attention-getting form of instruction, relates academic principles to real world skills, flexible pace, and easily altered to fit the needs of students.

- Disadvantages: Requires careful preparation. If the demonstration goes wrong, the effect is lost. Be sure all students can see and hear the instructor; may call for added expense and time.

Discussion Method: This method is particularly popular with both students and teachers. It is student-oriented, and generally participative, informal, and interactive. This method is especially useful for solving problems, exploring issues and making decisions. Make sure that students are effectively prepared and knowledgeable about the discussion topic. Preface the discussion with a short lecture, demonstration, or video clip. Encourage an open-minded and accepting atmosphere, while fostering debate and critical thinking.

- Advantages: Permits everyone to participate, brings together multiple perspectives and experiences, highly stimulating, brings about a more informed and well-rounded group conclusion, and simulates real world situations.

- Disadvantages: Very susceptible to distraction, can be very time-consuming, and can be dominated by highly verbal students.

Lesson Method: Probably the most versatile and useful of all instructional methods, this strategy can be used for teaching both knowledge and skills. The lesson involves the main features of all the above methods. It typically begins with a short lecture and ends with an independent assignment. In between is a great deal of discussion and debate as well as demonstrations and possibly case studies. Constant questioning lets the teacher know whether the students are learning or not.

- Advantages: Extremely flexible, demands and maintains group attention and activity, fosters a cooperative relationship between teacher and students, can be used in small or large groups. No lesson is ever the same.

- Disadvantages: More time-consuming than lectures or demonstrations, not particularly suitable for groups less than five or larger than forty.

TEACHER CERTIFICATION STUDY GUIDE

DOMAIN IV.	COMMUNICATIONS: SPEECH, MEDIA, AND CREATIVE PERFORMANCE

Candidates demonstrate knowledge of the foundations and contexts of the speech, media, and creative performance contained in the *English-Language Arts Content Standards for California Public Schools* (1997) as outlined in the *Reading/Language Arts Framework for California Public Schools: Kindergarten through Grade Twelve* (1999) at a post-secondary level of rigor. Candidates have both broad and deep conceptual knowledge of the subject matter. The *Reading/Language Arts Framework for California Public Schools* (1999) puts consistent emphasis on analysis and evaluation of oral and media communication as well as on effective public speaking and performance.

The candidate must possess the breadth of knowledge needed to integrate journalism, technological media, speech, dramatic performance, and creative writing into the language arts curriculum, including sensitivity to cultural approaches to communication. The subject matter preparation program should include opportunities for candidates to obtain knowledge and experience in these areas. The candidate skillfully applies the artistic and aesthetic tools and sensitivities required for creative expression.

COMPETENCY 14.0 ORAL COMMUNICATION PROCESSES

SKILL 14.1 Identify features of, and deliver oral performance in, a variety of forms

Different Methods of Oral Communication

Different from the basic writing forms of discourse is the art of **debating, discussion, and conversation**. The ability to use language and logic to convince the audience to accept your reasoning and to side with you is an art. This form of writing/speaking is extremely confined or structured, and logically sequenced with supporting reasons and evidence. At its best, it is the highest form of propaganda. A position statement, evidence, reason, evaluation and refutation are integral parts of this writing schema.

> Learn more about
> **Oral Communication Skills**
> http://www.glencoe.com/sec/teachingtoday/weeklytips.phtml/88

Interviewing provides opportunities for students to apply expository and informative communication. It teaches them how to structure questions to evoke fact-filled responses. Compiling the information from an interview into a biographical essay or speech helps students list, sort, and arrange details in an orderly fashion.

ENGLISH 127

Speeches that encourage them to describe persons, places, or events in their own lives or oral interpretations of literature help them sense the creativity and effort used by professional writers.

Additional resources may be found in the library, social studies, economic, debate and journalism textbooks and locally published newspapers.

SKILL 14.2 Demonstrate and evaluate individual performance skills

Instruct your students on the ways that non-verbal communication can affect the way a presentation is understood. You can model these techniques.

Delivery Techniques

Posture: Maintain a straight, but not stiff posture. Instead of shifting weight from hip to hip, point your feet directly at the audience and distribute your weight evenly. Keep shoulders towards the audience. If you have to turn your body to use a visual aid, turn 45 degrees and continue speaking towards the audience.

Movement: Instead of staying glued to one spot or pacing back and forth, stay within four to eight feet of the front row of your audience. Take a step or half-step to the side every once in a while. If you are using a lectern, feel free to move to the front or side of it to engage your audience more. Avoid distancing yourself from the audience; you want them to feel involved and connected.

Gestures: Gestures can maintain a natural atmosphere when speaking publicly. Use them just as you would when speaking to a friend. They shouldn't be exaggerated, but they should be used for added emphasis. Avoid keeping your hands in your pockets or locked behind your back, wringing your hands and fidgeting nervously, or keeping your arms crossed.

Eye Contact: Many people are intimidated by using eye contact when speaking to large groups. Interestingly, eye contact usually *helps* the speaker overcome speech anxiety by connecting with the attentive audience and easing feelings of isolation. Instead of looking at a spot on the back wall or at your notes, scan the room and make eye contact for one to three seconds per person.

In addition to the content of your presentation, you want to use a strong delivery. As with most skills, the key is practice, practice, practice. Record and play back your presentation to hear how you sound.

Voice: Many people fall into one of two traps when speaking: using a monotone or talking too fast. These are both caused by anxiety. A monotone restricts your natural inflection but can be remedied by releasing tension in upper and lower body muscles. Subtle movement will keep you loose and natural.

> Learn more about
> **Using Your Voice**
> http://www.longview.k12.wa.us/mmhs/wyatt/pathway/voice.html

Talking too fast, on the other hand, is not necessarily bad if you are exceptionally articulate. If you are not a strong speaker or if you are talking about very technical items, the audience will easily become lost. When you talk too fast and begin tripping over your words, consciously pause after every sentence you say. Don't be afraid of brief silences. The audience needs time to absorb what you are saying.

Volume: Problems with volume, whether too soft or too loud, can usually be overcome with practice. If you tend to speak too softly, have someone stand in the back of the room and signal you when your volume is strong enough. If possible, have someone in the front of the room as well to make sure you're not overcompensating with excessive volume. Conversely, if you have a problem with speaking too loud, have the person in the front of the room signal you when your voice is soft enough and check with the person in the back to make sure it is still loud enough to be heard. In both cases, note your volume level for future reference. Don't be shy about asking your audience, "Can you hear me in the back?" Suitable volume is beneficial for both you and the audience.

Pitch: Pitch refers to the length, tension, and thickness of your person's vocal bands. As your voice gets higher, the pitch gets higher. In oral performance, pitch reflects the emotional arousal level. More variation in pitch typically corresponds to more emotional arousal, but can also be used to convey sarcasm or highlight specific words.

While these skills are essential for you to be an effective teacher, you want your students to develop these techniques as well. By encouraging the development of proper techniques for oral presentations, you are enabling your students to develop self-confidence for higher levels of communication.

SKILL 14.3 Articulate principles of speaker/audience interrelationship

Because students typically write for their instructor, they have a narrow view of audience. They must learn to adapt their communication to the needs of their audiences. One way to teach this is to have students determine the values, needs, constraints, and demographics of their audience.

Values: What is important to this group of people? What is their background, and how will that affect their perception of your speech?

Needs: Find out in advance what the audience's needs are. Why are they listening to you? Find a way to satisfy their needs.

Constraints: What might hold the audience back from being fully engaged in what you are saying, or agreeing with your point of view, or processing what you are trying to say? These could be political reasons, which make them wary of your presentation's ideology from the start, or knowledge reasons, in which the audience lacks the appropriate background information to grasp your ideas. Avoid this last constraint by staying away from technical terminology, slang, or abbreviations that may be unclear to your audience.

Demographic Information: Take the audience's size into account as well as the location of the presentation. Demographics could include age, gender, education, religion, income level and other such countable characteristics.

Start where the listeners are, and then take them where you want to go!

SKILL 14.4 Identifies and demonstrate collaborative communication skills in a variety of roles

Listening

Communication skills are crucial in a collaborative society. In particular, a person cannot be a successful communicator without being an active listener.

Focus on what others say, rather than planning on what to say next. By listening to everything another person is saying, you may pick up on natural cues that lead to the next conversation move without so much added effort.

> **Reasons to Improve Listening Skills**
> To avoid saying the wrong thing, being tactless
> To dissipate strong feelings
> To learn to accept feelings (yours and others)
> To generate a feeling of caring
> To help people start listening to you
> To increase the other person's confidence in you
> To make the other person feel important and recognized
> To be sure you both are on the same wavelength
> To be sure you both are focused on the same topic
> To check that you are both are on target with one another
> *http://www.coping.org/dialogue/listen.htm*

Facilitating

It is quite acceptable to use standard opening lines to facilitate a conversation. Don't agonize trying to come up with witty "one-liners" as the main obstacle in initiating conversation is just getting the first statement over with. After that, the real substance begins. A useful technique may be to make a comment or ask a question about a shared situation. This may be anything from the weather to the food you are eating to a new policy at work. Use an opener you are comfortable with because your partner in conversation will be comfortable with it as well.

Stimulating Higher Level Critical Thinking Through Inquiry

Many people rely on questions to communicate with others. However, most fall back on simple clarifying questions rather than open-ended inquiries. For example, if you paraphrase a response by asking "Did you mean this…" you may receive merely a "yes" or "no" answer. On open-ended inquiry would ask "What did you mean when you said…?"

Try to ask open-ended, deeper-level questions since those tend to have the greatest reward and lead to a greater understanding. With answers to those questions, you can make more complex connections and achieve more significant information.

COMPETENCY 15.0 MEDIA ANALYSIS AND JOURNALISTIC APPLICATIONS

SKILL 15.1 Analyze the impact on society of a variety of media forms

Media's impact on today's society is immense and ever increasing. Children watch programs on television that are amazingly fast-paced and visually rich. Parents' roles as verbal and moral teachers are diminishing in response to the much more stimulating guidance of the television set. Adolescence, which used to be the time for going out and exploring the world firsthand, is now consumed by the allure of TV, popular music, and video games. Young adults are exposed to uncensored sex and violence.

But media's effect on society is beneficial and progressive at the same time. Its effect on education in particular provides special challenges and opportunities for teachers and students.

> Learn more about
> **Integrating Technology in the Classroom**
> http://www.glencoe.com/sec/teachingtoday/tiparchive.phtml/3

Thanks to satellite technology, urban classrooms and rural villages can receive instructional radio and television programs. CD-ROMs enable students to learn information through a virtual reality experience. The Internet allows instant access to unlimited data and connects people across all cultures through shared interests. Educational media, when used in a productive way, enriches instruction and makes it more individualized, accessible, and economical.

SKILL 15.2 Recognize and evaluate strategies used by the media to inform, persuade, entertain, and transmit culture

More money is spent each year on advertising to children than educating them. Thus, the media's strategies are considerably well thought-out and effective. The media employ large, clear letters, bold colors, simple line drawings, and popular symbols to announce upcoming events, push ideas and advertise products. By using attractive photographs, brightly colored cartoon characters, or instructive messages, they increase sales, win votes, or stimulate learning. The graphics are designed to communicate messages clearly, precisely, and efficiently. Some even target subconscious yearnings for sex and status.

Because so much effort is being spent on influencing students through media tactics, just as much effort should be devoted to educating those students about media awareness. A teacher should explain that artists and what they choose to portray as well as the ways in which they portray them reflect their attitudes and understanding of what they're portraying.

The artistic choices are not entirely based on creative license—they also reflect an imbedded meaning the artist wants to represent. Colors, shapes, and positions are meant to arouse basic instincts for food, sex, and status, and are often used to sell cars, clothing, or liquor.

To stimulate analysis of media strategies, ask students questions such as:

- Where/when do you think this picture was taken/film was shot/piece was written?
- Would you like to have lived at this time in history, or in this place?
- What objects are present?
- What do the people presented look like? Are they happy or sad?
- Who is being targeted?
- What can you learn from this piece of media?
- Is it telling you something is good or bad?
- What message is being broadcasted?
-

> Learn more about
> **Teaching Film, Television, and Media**
> http://www.tc.umn.edu/~rbeach/linksteachingmedia/chapter8/16.htm

SKILL 15.3   Identify aesthetic effects of a media presentation
- **Use of moving pictures and video to document events**
- **Use of sound clips in addition to written text**
- **Use of music/sound effects not printed in text**
- **Links to other web resources and to other archived articles**

As listeners and readers, you and your students are no longer content with one-dimensional messages. Rather than relying only on the written or spoken word, you have become accustomed to an expanded sensory experience. However, sensory overload has become a real problem. Just became we have all the bells and whistles doesn't mean we should use all the bells and whistles. Research studies have determined that basic presentations are more easily remembered than the ones with audio, video, animation combined.

Below are some tips that will help you use these media sources to supplement, rather than substitute for or overwhelm, your presentation

Tips for Using Print Media and Visual Aids

- Use pictures over words whenever possible.
- Present one key point per visual.
- Use no more than 3-4 colors per visual to avoid clutter and confusion.
- Use contrasting colors such as dark blue and bright yellow.
- Use a maximum of 25-35 numbers per visual aid.
- Use bullets instead of paragraphs when possible.

- Make sure it is student-centered, not media-centered. Delivery is just as important as the media presented.

Tips for Using Film and Television

- Study programs in advance.
- Obtain supplementary materials such as printed transcripts of the narrative or study guides.
- Provide your students with background information, explain unfamiliar concepts, and anticipate outcomes.
- Assign outside readings based on their viewing.
- Ask cuing questions.
- Watch along with students.
- Observe students' reactions.
- Follow up viewing with discussions and related activities.

SKILL 15.4 Demonstrate effective and creative application of these strategies and techniques to prepare presentations using a variety of media forms and visual aids

When used correctly, technologies and visual aids can effectively supplement oral presentations. The process that follows can help you use multimedia more effectively.

Multimedia Teaching Model

Step 1. DIAGNOSE
- Figure out what students need to know.
- Assess what students already know.

Step 2. DESIGN
- Design tests of learning achievement.
- Identify effective instructional strategies.
- Select suitable media.
- Sequence learning activities within program.
- Plan introductory activities.
- Plan follow-up activities.

Step 3. PROCURE
- Secure materials at hand.
- Obtain new materials.

Step 4. PRODUCE
- Modify existing materials.
- Craft new materials.

Step 5. REFINE
- Conduct small-scale test of program.
- Evaluate procedures and achievements.
- Revise program accordingly.
- Conduct classroom test of program.
- Evaluate procedures and achievements.
- Revise in anticipation of next school term.

Learn more about
Teaching with Multimedia
http://tep.uoregon.edu/technology/multimedia/multimedia.html

COMPETENCY 16.0 DRAMATIC PERFORMANCE

SKILL 16.1 Describe and use a range of rehearsal strategies to effectively mount a production

As the teacher, you are acting as stage manager for any performance that goes on. This means that you are handling rehearsal schedules, running rehearsals, monitoring action both onstage and backstage, and a number of other activities. To help yourself, appoint an organized and reliable student as an assistant stage manager to hand off smaller tasks to since these duties are difficult to handle simultaneously.

> Check out the resources at
> http://www.highschooldrama.com/

The production cycle of a show breaks down into four major stages:

Preproduction: Before characters are assigned or set building begins, you need to consider many factors. Of course, you must select a play. From there, the questions become more production-oriented. Determine an estimated debut date. Draw up a budget.

Once you have agreed upon the general concepts are agreed upon, appoint a leader for each area of the play (scenery, costumes, lighting, props, audio). Scenery and costume designers create rendering and floor plans, and lighting and sound designers start planning their contributions. Each area presents their plans in a design conference. Once all of this starts moving along, hold the first production meeting; all department heads can share logistical information and work on time, space, and money issues.

Do not let these different meetings melt together into one. Facilitate the discussions and carry out longer discussions in one-on-one conferences. Design conferences and production meetings should not last more than one hour.

Production: Once design is complete and actors are chosen, production begins, and a lot more people are involved. Try to have the department heads handle the scheduling of their respective groups while you concentrate on scheduling rehearsals. Production meetings continue, preferably on a regularly scheduled day of the week, since attendance may dwindle as time progresses. Costume fitting must also be overseen. As opening night gets closer, first get the actors onstage with the scenery, then come the lights, then the costumes, and then the makeup and hair. Each night brings more elements into the mix. Watch the proceedings with an eye for what the audience will see and hear and how they will react.

Run: You have no more artistic responsibilities, just logistical ones. Observe the quality of the show and schedule follow-up rehearsals if needed.

Closing: Compose a plan for striking, or taking apart the stage, when the show is over. Determine what jobs can be done by students (cleaning, transporting, general destruction) and which require skilled technicians and special tools (removing machinery, disassembling complicated scenery, anything involving rigging). Divide students into teams, write out their jobs on separate pieces of paper, and give it to a leader in each team. Confirm that all borrowed props and costumes are returned.

Pat yourself on the back. You survived putting on a student performance!

SKILL 16.2 Employ basic elements of character analysis and approaches to acting, including physical and vocal techniques that reveal character and relationships

Character Analysis

Shifting into a new character calls for an analysis of that character's ways of talking, moving, and relating to others in the world. Everything a student does to give the appearance—both physically and emotionally—of a character involves an interpretation of that character's motivations, intentions and passions. Characterization is the basic decision students make regarding the why and how of their characters. Students may justify their decisions based on details they notice in illustration or word, on the understanding they have about similar characters in real life, and on their own motivations and intentions.

> Learn more about
> **Teaching Literature using Narratives**
> http://www.teachingliterature.org/teachingliterature/chapter7/activities.htm

Use this as a basic frame sentence for character analysis:
"Since my character is _____, then he/she would act like _____."

This may result in students employing a goofy, clumsy shuffle when acting in their role, or addressing everyone as "baby." Each student must evolve from a child into an actor, and finally, into a specific character. Your job is to facilitate this transformation.

Child > Actor > Character

To further the immersion in their role, encourage students to call each other by their characters' names.

Emphasize the "as if" nature of a play, in which the students treat characters as if they were real, with real emotions and motivations driving them to act the way they do. Do not give students your own interpretation of a character's personality. Let them create their own interpretation, and follow along with their reading of the character.

Vocal Techniques

Voice is perhaps the most important tool of interpretation in classroom theater. It can portray anger, sadness, jealousy, happiness, fear, and excitement. Vocal techniques integrate word choice, emphasis, and attitude, accentuating or deemphasizing them as the student sees fit. The voice puts life into the words of the play, with intonation, pitch, loudness, or softness and even accent reflecting or obscuring the intent of the speaker.

Just look at the phrase "It's all right" as an example of the impact of voice and tone. Said with a soothing voice, it implies patience and understanding. Said with a sarcastic, cynical voice, it gives off a dismissive feeling. A host of a party might say the same phrase with suppressed frustration to a guest who has broken a favorite vase. In each case, the vocal choices made either highlight or shadow the inner thoughts of the speaker.

Encourage students to try on different vocal roles. Explain to students that while they must use the words in the script, *how* they say them is up to individual interpretation. A simple explanation is to simply tell them to "read something and then say it in your own way." Have students decide on words they want to stress by highlighting or underlining them in their scripts. Circle words that should be spoken louder and draw a line lightly through words that should be whispered. Allow students to transform vocal inflection to match with their vision of their character. They will soon combine their own attitudes and analyses with attitudinal hints the text supplies to create an effective emotional portrayal.

Physicality in a classroom calls for the performer to embody the emotion of the words into the motion of the character. This can drastically alter the perception of the character's personality, dilemma or situation.

Take a look at the phrase, "No, I don't mind waiting." Said while leaning back in a chair with a casual wave of the hand, the speaker appears easy-going and calm. On the other hand, if the speaker is tapping a foot and constantly checking a watch, the message is very different. Simple gestures, from the raise of an eyebrow to a jump in the air, indicate the speaker's state of mind, supplementing vocal tone and inflection.

Physical techniques can be especially helpful for students that have trouble getting into their character. For young people who naturally gravitate towards physical activity, getting into the physical quality of a character can lead to the emotional quality as well. Ask students to draw on their own experiences to determine what the most natural physical expression would be. Generally, boys are more physically active than girls. They are willing to fall down, hunch over, jump on top of desks and dramatically exaggerate their movements to enhance the performance (or often just to be comical).

> Learn more about
> **Exploring Nonverbal Communications**
> http://nonverbal.ucsc.edu/

Skill 16.3 Demonstrate basic knowledge of the language of visual composition and principles of theatrical design

Students who participate in theater should have a strong foundation in the basics of its composition and principles. One advantage is that if they understand how each of these contributes to the whole, they develop stronger critical thinking skills.

Set: Theater can be performed almost anywhere and is especially useful, although tricky, in a classroom environment. Make sure you have enough space. Avoid distracting sounds (like air conditioning) or noisy areas (next to the cafeteria). Take measurements both vertically and horizontally so you may be sure of how big to build your scenery. Consider storage space, as you will have to store scenery that is not being used and should not be visible to the audience.

Within a classroom setting, desks can be versatile and useful scenery, able to band together to form a wall, be covered with cloth to form a rabbit's hole, or stacked on top of each other to form a tower. Changing booths and prop tables are sometimes needed as well. You must read a script like a set designer, visualizing the number and kinds of spaces the show will require.

Costume: Anything worn by a performer, including clothes, masks and jewelry, is considered a costume. Makeup and wigs are usually grouped into the same category. A costume designer, assisted by a first hand as well as cutters, stitchers, and drapers, is extremely handy. Pay attention to the coherency between the set and the costumers. They should use colors that work well together, and are not too similar but not too different.

Lighting: Lighting discriminates between where the show is happening and where it is not. On a basic level, the audience must be able to see the performers and the scenery clearly. There is a fine line between lighting that is so bright it strains the audience's eyes and lighting that is so dim it puts the audience to sleep. The most attractive lighting angle for actors is forty-five degrees, and a light best illuminates the face on either side of the stage. Use backlight to separate figures from scenery or foot lights to give the scene an old-time theatrical look.

Sound: Sound includes the use of microphones (which can be as cheap as ten dollars), sound effects, and the playback of recorded sound. All sound systems are composed of four pieces:

- Source. This is where the sound comes from, whether it is a naturally occurring sound captured by a microphone or a recorded sound coming from a CD player.

- Routing. The sound must be sent to the proper place at the proper volume. This is done by a mixer, does the same thing you do at home when you choose "tape" or "CD" on your stereo, but does it more quietly and with more options. On a mixer, you may play input from several different sources simultaneously, and set different volumes for each sound.

- Amplification. For the sound to be loud enough for a theatrical production, you need an amplifier. This is usually a unit that takes the output from the mixer and pumps it up to a strong enough level for the speakers.

- Output. Output is the way the sound gets out of the system so people can hear it. Essentially, speakers are the output.

When using microphones, remember these guidelines:
- Do not run mics next to power cords, video cables or lighting equipment.
- Do not blow into the mic. It may damage the diaphragm. Instead, tap the mic gently to check if it is turned on.
- When speaking into the mic, put your mouth about a hand's distance away and keep it at a constant distance.
- Do not point the mic at a speaker. This creates feedback that is an unpleasant noise to say the least.

Props: Anything that is carried by an actor, or could be carried by an actor within the context of the play, is considered a prop. Therefore, a picture on the wall is labeled a prop while a fireplace is deemed scenery. Prop work can be a great job for shyer students or those with artistic tendencies. Make a list of all the props the show will need. *Set props* are pre-set on the stage and generally left there. This includes furniture, lamps, rugs, phones, etc. Actors carry personal props, such as pens, documents, and money onstage. Set dressing is the lowest priority since it has no effect on the action of the play. Items like paintings on the wall, drapes, and vases are there simply to set the scene.

Buying a prop saves time and labor but is limited by availability and budget.

Building a prop is usually cheaper than buying, but necessary skill is needed.

Borrowing a prop saves time and money but is completely dependent on availability.

Pulling a prop from stock is always the best option but availability is limited.

SKILL 16.4 Apply fundamentals of stage directing, including conceptualization, blocking (movement patterns), tempo, and dramatic arc (rising and falling action)

Conceptualization

Directors have two basic duties: (1) to implement a unified vision within the finished production, and (2) to lead others toward its ultimate actualization. To meet these charges, the directors must organize the realization of vision. They must decide upon the interpretation of the play; work with the playwright (if possible), designers, and technicians in planning the production, cast and rehearse the actors; and coordinate all elements into the finished production.

To decide upon interpretation, directors must analyze the script to discover the play's structure and meanings. Without understanding, they cannot make choices. They seek to know what the play is about and to understand each character in terms of both the script and the demands that character places upon the actor. Directors must be able to envision the play's atmosphere or mood and know how to actualize in terms of design and theatrical space. And, finally, the directors must be able to see the play in terms of both physical and verbal action.

Blocking

Stage blocking is one of the most basic and technical elements of play direction but should never be taken lightly by the directors. Indeed, few other elements of a play are more exciting and glamorous; blocking provides the backbone and structure needed to make those other elements a reality.

Blocking is the choreography of actors' movements throughout the entire play. If a character needs to exit the scene, for example, the actor must be able to move naturally towards the exit. The director's goal is to come up with a plausible means of getting that actor across the stage and through the door, window, transporter beam, or whatever. The same holds true for a character delivering a monologue—should that character break away from the other actors or deliver the speech in the middle of a crowd? Other blocking considerations may include entrances of a character, or places for actors to go when their character has no function in the scene.

Consider these hints when blocking your actors in a play:

1. Let the script do most of the work for you. As a director, you may have plenty of ideas on changing the setting or the costumes or the dialogue but leave the basic stage direction as intact as possible. You aren't trying to reinvent the wheel, just making sure your actors know where to stand and when to cross. Most scripts already contain enough staging information to allow you to form a rough idea of blocking. You should know when the characters are supposed to enter and exit, and what obstacles are in their way during their dialogue. Trust the script notes to paint the broadest strokes you will need to do basic blocking.

2. Avoid clutter by keeping the audience in mind. A stage should be viewed as a living painting. No artist would dare place all of his painting's elements on one side of the painting. Balance the stage movements so that the audience has a feeling of aesthetics. If a character has no interaction with others in the scene, move them to the opposite side of the stage for balance. If you have furniture on stage, avoid piling every actor on the couch center stage. You might set up more furniture on both sides of the stage to keep your actors from crowding each other. You might also consider building various levels to keep all actors in plain view.

   Build up different parts of the set, and when one actor moves to a different 'level,' move another actor to replace them. If done subtly, the audience should not notice the continuous shift.

3. Allow the actors to improvise and contribute to the blocking process. During the rehearsal process, a director must be a benevolent dictator and democratic leader at the same time. Some blocking directions, such as exits, dramatic crosses and entrances, should be seen as final. These movements need to be fixed and unchanged, so that lighting directors and other technical people can get a proper fix on actor positions.

   But some elements of blocking, such as internal monologues and staged arguments, can be modified through improvisation and actor input. You should listen carefully to your actors' ideas, even if you still veto them. Actors can get a feel for where their characters would want to move during a scene, so their input can be very useful indeed. During a conflict scene, you may feel that the couple would naturally move away from each other to get some emotional distance whereas the actors involved may feel like moving in closer to increase the tension between them. Both actions seem reasonable, so see which movements improve the scene. Be prepared to adjust your original ideas accordingly—move other actors out of the scene or change the stage layout.

4. Never let the props or set do the acting. If your set has a lot of furniture or levels or props, keep their presence to a minimum. Make sure your actors' movements upstage the furniture, rather than risk the furniture upstaging the actors. Unless the stage directions call for it, do not allow actors to perform entire scenes behind a prop or furniture. Keep the actors visible and clutter-free. If a prop is misplaced or a set piece is in the way of an actor's path, tell your actors to get it out of the way by any means necessary. No one should feel obligated to tiptoe around a piece of misplaced scenery.

Tempo

Interpretation of dialogue must be connected to motivation and detail. During this time, the director is also concerned with pace and seeks a variation of tempo. If the overall pace is too slow, then the action becomes dull and dragging. If the overall pace is too fast, then the audience will not be able to understand what is going on, for they are being hit with too much information to process.

Dramatic Arc

Good drama is built on conflict of some kind—an opposition of forces or desires that must be resolved by the end of the story. The conflict can be internal, involving emotional and psychological pressures, or it can be external, drawing the characters into tumultuous events. These themes are presented to the audience in a narrative arc that looks roughly like this:

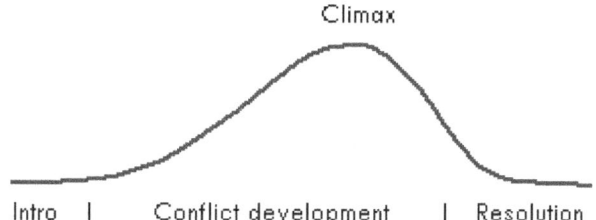

Following the Arc

Although any performance may have a series of rising and falling levels of intensity, in general the opening should set in motion the events which will generate an emotional high toward the middle or end of the story. Then, regardless of whether the ending is happy, sad, bittersweet, or despairing, the resolution eases the audience down from those heights and establishes some sense of closure. Reaching the climax too soon undermines the dramatic impact of the remaining portion of the performance whereas reaching it too late rushes the ending and creates a jarringly abrupt end to events.

SKILL 16.5 Demonstrate facility in a variety of oral performance traditions

Epic Poetry

Epic, long narrative poems, deal with legendary or historical events of national or universal significance. Epic poems are not merely entertaining stories of legendary or historical heroes; they summarize and express the nature or ideals of an entire nation at a significant or crucial period of its history.

They were originally handed down through the oral tradition so they had undergone much embellishment and permutations before being finally written down.

Typically, an epic includes several features: the introduction of supernatural forces that shape the action; conflict in the form of battles or other physical combat; and stylistic conventions such as an invocation to the Muse, a formal statement of the theme, long lists of the protagonists involved, and set speeches spoken in elevated language. Commonplace details of everyday life may appear, but they serve as background for the story and are described in the same lofty style as the rest of the poem.

Examples include the ancient Greek epics by the poet Homer, the *Iliad* and the *Odyssey*. The characteristics of the hero of an epic are national rather than individual, and the exercise of those traits in heroic deeds serves to gratify a sense of national pride. At other times epics may synthesize the ideals of a great religious or cultural movement. *The Divine Comedy* (1307-1321) by the Italian poet Dante Alighieri expresses the faith of medieval Christianity. *The Faerie Queene* (1590-1609) by the English poet Edmund Spenser represents the spirit of the Renaissance in England and like *Paradise Lost* (1667) by the English poet John Milton, represents the ideals of Christian humanism.

Recitation

The memorization and recitation of poetry allow students a level of familiarity and a deeper comprehension of a poem than is available upon simply reading or studying the words. The act of recitation involves projecting yourself into the poet's position, fully personifying the emotions and ideas of the poem as conveyed through language. To fully convey the meaning of a poem in recitation, students learn to make important decisions regarding style, tone of voice, projection, speed or slowness, emotional tenor, and character.

Public speaking skills are enhanced through recitation as students who memorize and recite poetry become cognizant of the power of words, which has relevance in many different walks of life. Students also become aware of the connections between traditional poetic forms and contemporary ones, such as hip-hop, slam, song lyrics, and performance poetry, making palpable a connection between historical periods and the current moment. Memorization of "classics" of poetry is an excellent way for students to study elements of prosody (rhyme, meter, conventions of open and closed form) in an activated context, rather than just in a book, supplying them a wide range of techniques and tools for their own future writing and reading.

Storytelling Techniques

One way to improve oral skills is to practice storytelling. Here are some tips for both teachers and students.

- Be sure you have complete silence before you begin so that the listeners are concentrating and focused on the story and the person reading it. Turn off any background music.
- Make eye contact with everyone. At least you should be able to see all the students from where you are sitting or standing. Move them around if necessary.

- Make sure no distractions are behind you, so stand in front of a wall, not an interesting bookshelf or a window.

- Think about yourself telling a favorite anecdote to your friends. "Did I tell you about the time when I . . . . " How do you tell it? What gestures and effects do you use? At what points are you sure of getting a laugh? What are you doing with your body language and how are you telling the story? Is there a particular pause before the punch line that works wonders?

- Apply your style to the story you're telling.

TEACHER CERTIFICATION STUDY GUIDE

COMPETENCY 17.0 CREATIVE WRITING

Skill 17.1 Demonstrate facility in creative composition in a variety of genres

One way students can come to appreciate great literature and writing is to model various creative techniques themselves. By trying to mimic a certain style or genre, students will recognize the inherent challenges.

Any of the activities listed below can be used to promote creative literary response and analysis:

- Have students take a particular passage from a story and retell it from another character's perspective.

- Challenge students to suggest a sequel or a prequel (what happened before) to any given story they have read.

- Ask the students to recast a story in which the key characters are male into one where the key characters are female (or vice versa). Have them explain how these changes alter the narrative, plot, or outcomes.

- Have the students produce a newspaper, as the characters of a given story would have reported the news in their community.

- Transform the story into a ballad poem or a picture book version for younger peers.

SKILL 17.2 Understand and apply processes and techniques that enhance the impact of the creative writing product

An example of an integrated creative writing lesson plan might begin with a discussion about lessons nature can teach us.

- Begin by exploring in a journal a lesson the students have learned from nature. (Writing/pre-reading/prior knowledge)

> **Teaching Creative Writing**
> http://teacher2b.com/creative/createwr.htm

- Create a brainstorming chart/ cluster on the board from students' responses.

- Students would begin reading selections from "Nature" by Ralph Emerson. (Reading)

- Discuss in class the connections. (Speaking/listening)

- Read aloud models of reflective essays on nature's lessons. Next students would go outside and, using a series of guided questions, observe an object in nature. (Writing/viewing)

- Use observations to allow students to write their own reflective essay on an object in nature (writing). Use of peer response and editing would encourage students to share and improve their writing. (Writing/reading/speaking/listening)

- Read final pieces aloud to the class or publish them on a bulletin board.

SKILL 17.3 Demonstrate skill in composing creative and aesthetically compelling responses to literature

Before responding to a literary piece, be it short story, novel, or poetry, there must be analysis. For fiction, the first step is to identify the protagonist, the conflicts, and the pattern of action. Are the conflicts resolved? Do they remain unresolved? If so, what is the redeeming quality of the plot? Remember that readers like resolution, which is the reason many people read and can often be the compelling reason that a work becomes a best seller or endures for generations.

For the resolution to be satisfying, the conflicts must be particularly engaging. For example, in Mitch Albom's *The Five People You Meet in Heaven* (which remained at the top of best-seller lists for months), the conflicts were between a skillfully-created protagonist and a hostile world, including an abusive father. The resolution of those conflicts involves a twist at the end, where it is revealed to the character that his life has, in fact, been lived meaningfully to protect and save children even though he had been denied parenthood. This story strikes a chord with readers because of the depth of satisfaction that comes with the resolution of intense and engaging conflicts.

An analysis of characterization may be appropriate in writing about a piece of fiction. The devices a writer uses to reveal character may be uniquely artistic and worth writing about. Students can analyze characters by examining what the characters say, what others say about the character, and what the author writes about the character.

Setting is often an important device for adding depth and meaning to a story. Albom's story is set in a seaside recreation park, and it plays an important role in the development of the story--particularly in the long ending where the purpose of the protagonist's life is revealed. Setting itself may play a role as a character in a story.

The writer's life and times may add interest to a story. Albom's story is set in World War II and the years following, but the long ending reaches into the past in order to add depth and meaning to the resolution.

A writer's use of language may be unique. Ernest Hemingway established new approaches to dialogue and description with his spare and economically pared-down use of words.

When writing about **poetry**, many of the same factors may be useful. What is the statement the poet wishes to make? Why is it relevant or meaningful? What is unique about the use of words, particularly descriptive ones? How does the form chosen by this poet add strength and meaning to this particular poem? Or is there dissonance? Does the form contradict the theme? Does the sound of the words create cacophony? Remember that poetry is meant to be read aloud, so sounds should be uppermost when analyzing a poem.

RESOURCES

Abrams, M. H. ed. *The Norton Anthology of English Literature*. 6th ed. 2 vols. New York: Norton, 1979.

A comprehensive reference for English literature, containing selected works from *Beowulf* through the twentieth century and information about literary criticism.

Beach, Richard. "Strategic Teaching in Literature." *Strategic Teaching and Learning: Cognitive Instruction in the Content Areas*. Edited by Beau Fly Jones and others. ASCD Publications, 1987: 135-159.

A chapter dealing with a definition of and strategic teaching strategies for literature studies.

Brown, A. C. and others. *Grammar and Composition* 3rd Course. Boston: Houghton Mifflin, 1984.

A standard ninth-grade grammar text covering spelling, vocabulary, reading, listening, and writing skills.

Burmeister, L. E. *Reading Strategies for Middle and Secondary School Teachers*. Reading, MA: Addison-Wesley, 1978.

A resource for developing classroom strategies for reading and content area classes, using library references, and adapting reading materials to all levels of students.

Carrier, W. and B. Neumann, eds. *Literature from the World*. New York: Scribner, 1981.

A comprehensive world literature text for high school students, with a section on mythology and folklore.

Cline, R. K. J. and W. G. McBride. *A Guide to Literature for Young Adults: Background, Selection, and Use*. Glenview, IL: Scott Foresman, 1983.

A literature reference containing sample readings and an overview of adolescent literature and the developmental changes that affect reading.

Coater, R.B., Jr., ed. "Reading Research and Instruction." *Journal of the College Research Association*. Pittsburgh, PA: 1995.

A reference tool for reading and language arts teachers, covering the latest research and instructional techniques.

Corcoran, B. and E. Evans, eds. *Readers, Texts, Teachers*. Upper Montclair, NJ: Boynton/Cook, 1987.

A collection of essays concerning reader response theory, including activities that help students interpret literature and help the teacher integrate literature into the course study.

Cutting, Brian. *Moving on in Whole Language: The Complete Guide for Every Teacher.* Bothell, WA: Wright Group, 1992.

A resource of practical knowledge in whole language instruction.

Damrosch, L. and others. *Adventures in English Literature.* Orlando, FL: Harcourt, Brace, Jovanovich, 1985.

One of many standard high school English literature textbooks with a solid section on the development of the English language.

Davidson, A. *Literacy 2000 Teacher's Resource. Emergent Stages 1 & 2.* 1990.

Devine, T. G. *Teaching Study Skills: A Guide for Teachers.* Boston: Allyn and Bacon, 1981.

Duffy, G. G. and others. *Comprehension Instruction: Perspectives and Suggestions.* New York: Longman, 1984.

Written by researchers at the Institute of Research on Teaching and the Center for the Study of Reading, this reference includes a variety of instructional techniques for different levels.

Fleming, M. ed. *Teaching the Epic.* Urbana, IL: NCTE, 1974.

Methods, materials, and projects for the teaching of epics with examples of Greek, religious, national, and American epics.

Flood, J. Ed. *Understanding Reading Comprehension: Cognition, Language, and the Structure of Prose.* Newark, DE: IRA, 1984.

Essays by preeminent scholars dealing with comprehension for learners of all levels and abilities.

Fry, E. B. and others. *The Reading Teacher's Book of Lists.* Edgewood Cliffs, NJ: Prentice-Hall, 1984.

A comprehensive list of book lists for students of various reading levels.

Garnica, Olga K. and Martha L. King. *Language, Children, and Society.* New York: Pergamon Press, 1981.

Gere, A. R. and E. Smith. *Attitude, Language and Change.* Urbana, IL: NCTE, 1979.

A discussion of the relationship between standard English and grammar and the vernacular usage, including various approaches to language instruction.

Hayakawa, S. I. *Language in Thought and Action.* 4th ed. Orlando, Fl: Harcourt, Brace, Jovanovich, 1979.

Hook, J. N. and others. *What Every English Teacher Should Know*. Champaign, IL: NCTE, 1970.

Research-based text that summarizes methodologies and specific application for use with students.

Johnson, D. D. and P. D. Pearson. *Teaching Reading Vocabulary*. 2nd ed. New York: Holt, Rinehart, and Winston, 1984.

A student text that stresses using vocabulary study in improving reading comprehension, with chapters on instructional components in the reading and content areas.

Kaywell, I. F. Ed. *Adolescent Literature as a Complement to the Classics*. Norwood, MA: Christopher-Gordon Pub., 1993.

A correlation of modern adolescent literature to classics of similar themes.

Mack, M. Ed. *World Masterpieces*. 3rd ed. 2 vols. New York: Norton, 1973.

A standard world literature survey, with useful introductory material on a critical approach to literature study.

McLuhan, M. *Understanding Media: The Extensions of Man*. New York: Signet, 1964.

The most classic work on the effect media has on the public and the power of the media to influence thinking.

McMichael, G. ed. *Concise Anthology of American Literature*. New York: Macmillan, 1974.

A standard survey of American literature text.

Moffett, J. *Teaching the Universe of Discourse*. Boston: Houghton Mifflin, 1983.

A significant reference text that proposes the outline for a total language arts program, emphasizing the reinforcement of each element of the language arts curriculum to the other elements.

Moffett, James and Betty Jane Wagner. *Student-Centered Language Arts K-12*. 4th ed. Boston: Houghton Mifflin, 1992.

Nelms, B. F., ed. *Literature in the Classroom: Readers, Texts, and Contexts*. Urbana, IL: NCTE, 1988.

Essays on adolescent and multicultural literature, social aspects of literature, and approaches to literature interpretation.

Nilsen, A. P. and K. L. Donelson. *Literature for Today's Young Adults*. 2nd ed. Glenview, IL: Scott, Foresman, and Co., 1985.

An excellent overview of young adult literature - its history, terminologies, bibliographies, and book reviews.

Perrine, L. *Literature: Structure, Sound, and Sense.* 5th ed. Orlando, FL: Harcourt, Brace, Jovanovich, 1988.

A much revised text for teaching literature elements, genres, and interpretation.

Piercey, Dorothy. *Reading Activities in Content Areas: An Ideabook for Middle and Secondary Schools.* 2nd ed. Boston: Allyn and Bacon, 1982.

Pooley, R. C. *The Teaching of English Usage.* Urbana, IL: NCTE, 1974.

A revision of the important 1946 text, which discusses the attitudes toward English usage through history and recommends specific techniques for usage instruction.

Probst, R. E. *Response and Analysis: Teaching Literature in Junior and Senior High School.* Upper Montclair, NJ: Boynton/Cook, 1988.

A resource that explores reader response theory and discusses student-centered methods for interpreting literature. Contains a section on the progress of adolescent literature.

Pyles, T. and J. Alges. *The Origin and Development of the English Language*. 3rd ed. Orlando, FL: Harcourt, Brace, Jovanovich, 1982.

A history of the English language; sections on social, personal, historical, and geographical influences on language usage.

Readence, J. E. and others. *Content Area Reading: An Integrated Approach*. 2nd ed. Dubuque, IA: Kendall/Hunt, 1985.

A practical instruction guide for teaching reading in the content areas.

Robinson, H. Alan. *Teaching Reading and Study Strategies: The Content Areas*. Boston: Allyn and Bacon, 1978.

Roe, B. D. and others. *Secondary School Reading Instruction: The Content Areas*. 3rd ed. Boston: Houghton Mifflin, 1987.

A resource of strategies for the teaching of reading for language arts teachers with little reading instruction background.

Rosenberg, D. *World Mythology: An Anthology of the Great Myths and Epics*. Lincolnwood, IL: National Textbook, 1986.

Presents selections of main myths from which literary allusions are drawn. Thorough literary analysis of each selection.

Rosenblatt, L. M. *The Reader, the Text, the Poem. The Transactional Theory of the Literary Work*. Southern Illinois University Press, 1978.

A discussion of reader-response theory and reader-centered methods for analyzing literature.

Santeusanio, Richard P. *A Practical Approach to Content Area Reading*. Reading, MA.: Addison-Wesley Publishing Co., 1983.

Strickland, D. S. and others. *Using Computers in the Teaching of Reading*. New York: Teachers College Press, 1987.

Resource for strategies for teaching and learning language and reading with computers and recommendations for software for all grades.

Sutherland, Zena and others. *Children and Books*. 6th ed. Glenview, IL: Scott, Foresman, and Co., 1981.

Thorough study of children's literature, with sections on language development theory and chapters on specific genres with synopses of specific classic works for child/adolescent readers.

Tchudi, S. and D. Mitchell. *Explorations in the Teaching of English*. 3rd ed. New York: Harper Row, 1989.

A thorough source of strategies for creating a more student-centered involvement in learning.

Tompkins, Gail E. *Teaching Writing: Balancing Process and Product*. 2nd ed. New York: Macmillan, 1994.

A tool to aid teachers in integrating recent research and theory about the writing process, writing reading connections, collaborative learning, and across the curriculum writing with practices in the fourth through eighth grade classrooms.

Warriners, J. E. *English Composition and Grammar*. Benchmark ed. Orlando, FL: Harcourt, Brace, Jovanovich, 1988.

Standard grammar and composition textbook, with a six-book series for seventh through twelfth grades; includes vocabulary study, language history, and diverse approaches to writing process.

Sample Test

Section I: Essay Test

You will respond to several prompts intended to gauge your competence in a variety of writing skills. In most testing situations, you will have 30 minutes to respond to these prompts. Some tests may allow 60 minutes for the essay in order to incorporate more than one question or to allow for greater preparation and editing time. Read the directions carefully and organize your time wisely.

Section II: Multiple-choice Test

This section contains 125 questions. In most testing situations, you would be expected to answer 35-40 questions in about 30 minutes. If you time yourself on the entire battery, try to finish it in about 90 minutes.

Section III: Answer Key

Section I: Essay Prompts

Prompt A

Write an expository essay discussing effective teaching strategies for helping a heterogeneous class of ninth graders to appreciate literature. Select any appropriate piece(s) of world literature to use as examples in the discussion.

Prompt B

After reading the following passage from Alduous Huxley's *Brave New World,* discuss the types of reader responses possible with a group of eight graders.

> "He hated them all - all the men who came to visit Linda. One afternoon, when he had been playing with the other children - it was cold, he remembered, and there was snow on the mountains - he came back to the house and heard angry voices in the bedroom. They were women's voices, and they were words he didn't understand; but he knew they were dreadful words. Then suddenly, crash! something was upset; he heard people moving about quickly, and there was another crash and then a noise like hitting a mule, only not so bony; then Linda screamed. 'Oh, don't, don't, don't!' she said. He ran in. There were three women in dark blankets. Linda was on the bed. One of the women was holding her wrists. Another was lying across her legs, so she couldn't kick. The third was hitting her with a whip. Once, twice, three times; and each time Linda screamed."

Prompt C

Write a persuasive letter to the editor on any contemporary topic of special interest. Employ whatever forms of discourse, stylistic devices, and audience-appeal techniques that seem appropriate to the topic.

Section II: Writing and Language Skills

Part A

Directions: Sentences 1-15 each contain four underlined words or phrases. If you determine that any underlined word or phrase has an error in grammar, usage, or mechanics, circle the letter underneath that underlined word or phrase. If there are no errors, circle the letter E at the end of the sentence. There is no more than one error in any sentence.

1. When the <u>school district</u> privatized the school cafeteria, <u>us</u> students <u>were</u>
        A   B   C
   thrilled to purchase more than soggy <u>French fries</u> E
                 D

   Skill 8.2, Easy

2. We <u>were</u> dismayed at <u>them</u> failing the <u>fitness</u> exam on <u>their</u> second attempt.
      A   B   C   D
   E

   Skill 8.2, Rigorous

3. She, not her sister, <u>is</u> the one <u>who</u> the librarian <u>has questioned</u> about the
            A   B   C
   missing books, <u>*Butterfly's*</u> *Ball* and *The Bear's House* E
          D

   Skill 8.2, Rigorous

4. If Cullen was to think up the practical joke,, then he <u>must</u> suffer the
   <u>consequences</u>
           A B   C   D
   E

   Skill 8.3, Rigorous

5. Jack told a <u>credulous</u> story about his trip <u>up the beanstalk</u> because each
             A   B
   child in the room <u>was convinced</u> by his <u>reasoning</u>   E
                          C   D

   Skill 11.1, Average Rigor

6. Walter said <u>that</u> his calculator <u>has been missing</u> <u>since</u> last Monday
                  A   B   C
   <u>responding</u> to my question   E
        D

   Skill 11.2, Average Rigor

7. The volcanic eruption in Montserrat displaced residents of Plymouth <u>which</u>
                                                                          A
   felt that the <u>English government</u> <u>was</u> responsible for <u>their</u> evacuation   E
                        B   C   D

   Skill 11.3, Easy

8. The future <u>will be</u> <u>because</u> of the past: <u>by changing the past</u> <u>would alter</u>
                  A   B   C   D
   the future.   E

   Skill 11.4, Average Rigor

9. <u>Although she was nervous</u> on her first day, the new employee, <u>hired to</u>
              A
   <u>replace the retired secretary,</u> grew <u>more comfortable</u> as she was told
              B   C
   <u>where she should park her car</u>, her schedule, and her duties.   E
              D

   Skill 11.5, Rigorous.

10. Martha <u>had considered</u> <u>playing drums</u> <u>before</u> <u>she discovers</u> the piano
               A   B   C   D   E

   Skill 8.3, Easy

11. Mr. Thomas' daughter-in-law encouraged her husband's boss to host a
        A   B
    fund-raiser for the United Way, a charity that Mr. Thomas supports. E
                  C   D

Skill 12.1, Easy

12. The homecoming Queen and King were chosen by the student body for
                A   B   C
    their popularity   E
    D

Skill 12.2, Easy

13. There are fewer students in school this year despite the principal's
        A B   C
    prediction of increasing enrollment   E
    D

Skill 12.2, Easy

14. My mother is a Methodist. She married a Southern Baptist and took us
                  A   B   C
    children to the First Baptist church in Stuart   E
    D

Skill 12.2, Average Rigor

15. When we moved from Jacksonville, Florida, to Little Rock, Arkansas, my
                                     A   B
    Dad was promoted to store manager.   E
    C   D

Skill 12.2, Average Rigor

16. Miriam decided to remain stationery since to move would startle the
                                      A   B   C
    horses, one of which might bolt.   E
    D

Skill 12.2 Rigorous

Part B

Each underlined portion of sentences 16-25 contains one or more errors in grammar, usage, mechanics, or sentence structure. Circle the choice which best corrects the error without changing the meaning of the original sentence.

17. Joe didn't hardly know his cousin Fred who'd had a rhinoplasty. (Skill 5.3, Easy)

    A. hardly did know his cousin Fred

    B. didn't know his cousin Fred hardly

    C. hardly knew his cousin Fred

    D. didn't know his cousin Fred

    E. didn't hardly know his cousin Fred

18. **Mixing the batter for cookies,** the cat licked the Crisco from the cookie sheet. (Skill 5.3, Average Rigor)

    A. While mixing the batter for cookies

    B. While the batter for cookies was mixing

    C. While I mixed the batter for cookies

    D. While I mixed the cookies

    E. Mixing the batter for cookies

19. Walt Whitman was famous for his composition, *Leaves of Grass*, serving as a nurse during the Civil War, and a devoted son (Skill 5.3, Rigorous)

    A. *Leaves of Grass*, his service as a nurse during the Civil War, and a devoted son

    B. composing **Leaves of Grass**, serving as a nurse during the Civil War, and being a devoted son

    C. his composition, *Leaves of Grass*, his nursing during the Civil War, and his devotion as a son

    D. his composition, *Leaves of Grass*, serving as a nurse during the Civil War, and a devoted son

    E. his composition, *Leaves of Grass*, serving as a nurse during the Civil War, and a devoted son

20. The coach offered her assistance but the athletes wanted to practice on their own. (Skill 11.2, Rigorous)

   A. The coach offered her assistance, however, the athletes wanted to practice on their own.

   B. The coach offered her assistance: furthermore, the athletes wanted to practice on their own.

   C. Having offered her assistance, the athletes wanted to practice on their own.

   D. The coach offered her assistance; however, the athletes wanted to practice on their own.

   E. The coach offered her assistance, and the athletes wanted to practice on their own.

21. A teacher must know not only her subject matter but also the strategies of content teaching. (Skill 11.3, Rigorous)

   A. must not only know her subject matter but also the strategies of content teaching

   B. not only must know her subject matter but also the strategies of content teaching

   C. must not know only her subject matter but also the strategies of content teaching

   D. must know not only her subject matter but also the strategies of content teaching

22. Mr. Smith respectfully submitted his resignation and had a new job. (Skill 11.4, Average Rigor)

    A. respectfully submitted his resignation and has

    B. respectfully submitted his resignation before accepting

    C. respectfully submitted his resignation because of

    D. respectfully submitted his resignation and had

23. The Taj Mahal has been designated one of the Seven Wonders of the World, and people know it for its unique architecture. (Skill 11.4, Rigorous)

    A. The Taj Mahal has been designated one of the Seven Wonders of the World, and it is known for its unique architecture.

    B. People know the Taj Mahal for its unique architecture, and it has been designated one of the Seven Wonders of the World.

    C. People have known the Taj Mahal for its unique architecture, and it has been designated of the Seven Wonders of the World.

    D. The Taj Mahal has designated itself one of the Seven Wonders of the World.

24. There were fewer pieces of evidence presented during the second trial (Skill 12.2, Easy)

    A. fewer peaces

    B. less peaces

    C. less pieces

    D. fewer pieces

25. The teacher implied from our angry words that there was conflict between you and me. (Skill 12.2, Average Rigor)

    A. Implied... between you and I

    B. Inferred... between you and I

    C. Inferred... between you and me

    D. Implied... between you and me

26. Wally groaned, "Why do I have to do an oral interpretation of "The Raven." (Skill 12.2, Average Rigor)

    A. groaned "Why... of 'The Raven'?"

    B. groaned "Why... of "The Raven"?

    C. groaned ", Why... of "The Raven?"

    D. groaned, "Why... of "The Raven."

Part C Multiple Choice

Select the letter for the most correct response.

27. A traditional, anonymous story, ostensibly having a historical basis, usually explaining some phenomenon of nature or aspect of creation, defines a (Skill 1.1, Easy)

  A. proverb.

  B. idyll.

  C. myth.

  D. epic.

28. The tendency to emphasize and value the qualities and peculiarities of life in a particular geographic area exemplifies (Skill 1.1, Easy)

  A. pragmatism.

  B. regionalism.

  C. pantheism.

  D. abstractionism.

29. Which of the following writers did not win a Nobel Prize for literature? (Skill 1.1, Average Rigor)

  A. Gabriel Garcia-Marquez of Colombia

  B. Nadine Gordimer of South Africa

  C. Pablo Neruda of Chile

  D. Alice Walker of the United States

30. The writing of Russian naturalists is (Skill 1.1, Average Rigor)

  A. optimistic.

  B. pessimistic.

  C. satirical.

  D. whimsical.

31. Which of the following is not a theme of Native American writing? (Skill 1.1, Average Rigor)

   A. Emphasis on the hardiness of the human body and soul

   B. The strength of multi-cultural assimilation

   C. Contrition for the genocide of native peoples

   D. Remorse for the love of the Indian way of life

32. Which sonnet form describes the following? (Skill 1.1, Rigorous)

My galley charg'd with
   forgetfulness,
Through sharp seas, in
   winter night doth pass
'Tween rock and rock; and
   eke mine enemy, alas,
That is my lord steereth with
   cruelness.
And every oar a thought with
   readiness,
As though that death were
   light in such a case.
An endless wind doth tear
   the sail apace
Or forc'ed sighs and trusty
   fearfulness.

A rain of tears, a cloud of dark
   disdain,
Hath done the wearied
   cords great hinderance,
Wreathed with error and eke
   with ignorance.
The stars be hid that led me
   to this pain
Drowned is reason that
   should me consort,
And I remain despairing
   of the poet

   A. Petrarchan or Italian sonnet

   B. Shakespearian or Elizabethan sonnet

   C. Romantic sonnet

   D. Spenserian sonnet

33. Children's literature became established in the (Skill 1.2, Average Rigor)

    A. seventeenth century

    B. eighteenth century

    C. nineteenth century

    D. twentieth century

34. Latin words that entered the English language during the Elizabethan Age include (Skill 1.2, Average Rigor)

    A. allusion, education, and esteem

    B. vogue and mustache

    C. canoe and cannibal

    D. alligator, cocoa, and armadillo

35. American colonial writers were primarily (Skill 1.2, Average Rigor)

    A. Romanticists.

    B. Naturalists.

    C. Realists.

    D. Neo-classicists.

36. Which is the best definition of Imagism? (Skill 1.2, Rigorous)

    A. A doctrine which teaches that comfort is the only goal of value in life.

    B. A movement in modern poetry (c. 1910-1918) characterized by precise, concrete images, free verse, and suggestion rather than complete statement.

    C. The belief that people are motivated only by self-centeredness.

    D. The doctrine that the human mind cannot know where there is a God or an ultimate cause, or anything beyond material phenomenon.

37. Which choice below best defines naturalism? (Skill 1.2, Rigorous)

    A. A belief that the writer or artist should apply scientific objectivity in his/her observation and treatment of life without imposing value judgments.

    B. The doctrine that teaches that the existing world is the best to be hoped for.

    C. The doctrine which teaches that God is not a personality, but that all laws, forces and manifestations of the universe are God-related.

    D. A philosophical doctrine which professes that the truth of all knowledge must always be in question.

38. Among junior-high school students with low-to-average readability levels, which work would most likely stir reading interest? (Skill 1.3, Easy)

    A. *Elmer Gantry*, Sinclair Lewis

    B. *Smiley's People*, John Le Carre

    C. *The Outsiders*, S.E. Hinton

    D. *And Then There Were None*, Agatha Christie.

39. Written on the sixth-grade reading level, most of S. E. Hinton's novels (for instance, *The Outsiders*) have the greatest reader appeal with (Skill 1.3, Average Rigor)

    A. sixth-graders.

    B. ninth-graders.

    C. twelfth-graders.

    D. adults.

40. In the hierarchy of needs for adolescents who are becoming more team-oriented in their approach to learning, which need do they exhibit most? (Skill 1.3, Average Rigor)

    A. Need for competence

    B. Need for love/acceptance

    C. Need to know

    D. Need to belong

ENGLISH

41. Piaget's learning theory asserts that adolescents in the formal operations period (Skill 1.3, Rigorous)

    A. behave properly from fear of punishment rather than from a conscious decision to take a certain action.

    B. see the past more realistically and can relate to people from the past more than preadolescents.

    C. are less self-conscious and thus more willing to project their own identities into those of fictional characters.

    D. have not yet developed a symbolic imagination.

42. Which poet was a major figure in the Harlem Renaissance? (Skill 1.4, Easy)

    A. E. E. Cummings

    B. Rita Dove

    C. Margaret Atwood

    D. Langston Hughes

43. Which of the writers below is a renowned black poet? (Skill 1.4, Average Rigor)

    A. Maya Angelou

    B. Sandra Cisneros

    C. Richard Wilbur

    D. Richard Wright

44. Which of the following titles is known for its scathingly condemning tone? (Skill 1.4, Average Rigor)

    A. Boris Pasternak's *Dr Zhivago*

    B. Albert Camus' *The Stranger*

    C. Henry David Thoreau's "On the Duty of Civil Disobedience"

    D. Benjamin Franklin's "Rules by Which a Great Empire May Be Reduced to a Small One"

45. Charles Dickens, Robert Browning, and Robert Louis Stevenson were (Skill 1.4, Average Rigor)

    A. Victorians.

    B. Medievalists.

    C. Elizabethans.

    D. Absurdists.

46. Arthur Miller wrote *The Crucible* as a parallel to what twentieth century event? (Skill 1.4, Average Rigor)

    A. Sen. McCarthy's House un-American Activities Committee Hearing

    B. The Cold War

    C. The fall of the Berlin wall

    D. The Persian Gulf War

47. Which author did not write satire? (Skill 1.4, Rigorous)

    A. Joseph Addison

    B. Richard Steele

    C. Alexander Pope

    D. John Bunyan

48. Which of the following is the best definition of existentialism? (Skill 1.4, Rigorous)

    A. The philosophical doctrine that matter is the only reality and that everything in the world, including thought, will and feeling, can be explained only in terms of matter.

    B. Philosophy which views things as they should be or as one would wish them to be.

    C. A philosophical and literary movement, variously religious and atheistic, stemming from Kierkegaard and represented by Sartre.

    D. The belief that all events are determined by fate and are hence inevitable.

49. Which of the following is not a characteristic of a fable? (Skill 2.1, Easy)

    A. Animals that feel and talk like humans.

    B. Happy solutions to human dilemmas.

    C. Teaches a moral or standard for behavior.

    D. Illustrates specific people or groups without directly naming them.

50. "Everyone must pass through Vanity Fair to get to the celestial city" is an allusion from a (Skill 2.1, Rigorous)

   A. Chinese folk tale.

   B. Norse saga.

   C. British allegory.

   D. German fairy tale.

51. Which definition is the best for defining diction? (Skill 2.2, Easy)

   A. The specific word choices of an author to create a particular mood or feeling in the reader.

   B. Writing which explains something thoroughly.

   C. The background, or exposition, for a short story or drama.

   D. Word choices which help teach a truth or moral.

52. The literary device of personification is used in which example below? (Skill 2.2, Easy)

   A. "Beg me no beggary by soul or parents, whining dog!"

   B. "Happiness sped through the halls cajoling as it went."

   C. "O wind thy horn, thou proud fellow."

   D. "And that one talent which is death to hide."

53. In the following quotation, addressing the dead body of Caesar as though he were still a living being is to employ an (Skill 2.2, Average Rigor)

   O, pardon me, though

   Bleeding piece of earth

   That I am meek and gentle with

   These butchers.

      -Marc Antony from Julius Caesar

   A. apostrophe

   B. allusion

   C. antithesis

   D. anachronism

54. Which is the best definition of free verse, or *vers libre*? (Skill 2.2, Average Rigor)

A. Poetry which consists of an unaccented syllable followed by an unaccented sound.

B. Short lyrical poetry written to entertain but with an instructive purpose.

C. Poetry which does not have a uniform pattern of rhythm.

D. A poem which tells the story and has a plot

55. Which is not a Biblical allusion? (Skill 2.2, Rigorous)

A. The patience of Job

B. Thirty pieces of silver

C. "Man proposes; God disposes"

D. "Suffer not yourself to be betrayed by a kiss"

56. What is the salient literary feature of this excerpt from an epic? (Skill 2.2, Rigorous)

Hither the heroes and the nymphs
resorts,
To taste awhile the pleasures
of a court;
In various talk th'instructive
hours they passed,
Who gave the ball, or paid the
visit last;
One speaks the glory of the
English Queen,
And another describes a
charming Indian screen;
A third interprets motion, looks
and eyes;
At every word a reputation dies.

A. Sprung rhythm

B. Onomatopoeia

C. Heroic couplets

D. Motif

57. What syntactic device is most evident from Abraham Lincoln's "Gettysburg Address? (Skill 2.2, Rigorous)

It is rather for us to be here dedicated to the great task remaining before us—that from these honored dead we take increased devotion to that cause for which they gave the last full measure of devotion—that we here highly resolve that these dead shall not have died in vain—that this nation, under God, shall have a new birth of freedom—and that government of the people, by the people, for the people, shall not perish from the earth.

A. Affective connotation

B. Informative denotations

C. Allusion

D. Parallelism

58. Which term best describes the form of the following poetic excerpt? (Skill 2.2, Rigorous)

And more to lulle him in his slumber soft,
A trickling streake from high rock
tumbling downe,
And ever-drizzling raine upon
the loft.
Mixt with a murmuring winde,
much like a swowne
No other noyse, nor peoples troubles cryes.
As still we wont t'annoy the walle'd towne,
Might there be heard: but careless Quiet lyes,
Wrapt in eternall silence farre
from enemyes.

A. Ballad

B. Elegy

D. Spenserian stanza

D. Octava rima

59. In the phrase "The Cabinet conferred with the President," Cabinet is an example of a/an (Skill 2.2, Rigorous)

    A. metonym

    B. synecdoche

    C. metaphor

    D. allusion

60. Which of the following definitions best describes a parable? (Skill 2.3, Average Rigor)

    A. A short entertaining account of some happening, usually using talking animals as characters.

    B. A slow, sad song or poem, or prose work expressing lamentation.

    C. An extensive narrative work expressing universal truths concerning domestic life.

    D. A short, simple story of an occurrence of a familiar kind, from which a moral or religious lesson may be drawn.

61. Most children's literature prior to the development of popular literature was intended to be didactic. Which of the following would not be considered didactic? (Skill 2.3, Average Rigor)

    A. "A Visit from St. Nicholas" by Clement Moore

    B. McGuffy's Reader

    C. Any version of Cinderella

    D. Parables from the Bible

62. Which of the following is a characteristic of blank verse? (Skill 2.3, Average Rigor)

    A. Meter in iambic pentameter

    B. Clearly specified rhyme scheme

    C. Lack of figurative language

    D. Unspecified rhythm

63. The following lines from Robert Browning's poem "My Last Duchess" is an example of what form of dramatic literature? (Skill 2.3, Rigorous)

> That's my last Duchess painted on the wall,
>
> Looking as if she were alive. I call
>
> That piece a wonder, now: Frà Pandolf's hands
>
> Worked busily a day, and there she stands.
>
> Will 't please you sit and look at her?

A. Tragedy

B. Comic opera

C. Dramatis personae

D. Dramatic monologue

64. Which is an untrue statement about a theme in literature? (Skill 2.4, Average Rigor)

A. The theme is always stated directly somewhere in the text.

B. The theme is the central idea in a literary work.

C. All parts of the work (plot, setting, mood) should contribute to the theme in some way.

D. By analyzing the various elements of the work, the reader should be able to arrive at an indirectly stated theme.

65. In literature, evoking feelings of pity or compassion is to create (Skill 2.4, Average Rigor)

A. colloquy.

B. irony.

C. pathos.

D. paradox

66. The students in Mrs. Cline's seventh-grade language arts class were invited to attend a performance of *Romeo and Juliet* presented by the drama class at the high school. To best prepare, they should (Skill 3.2, Average Rigor)

   A. read the play as a homework exercise.

   B. read a synopsis of the plot and a biographical sketch of the author.

   C. examine a few main selections from the play to become familiar with the language and style of the author.

   D. read a condensed version of the story and practice attentive listening skills.

67. Which of the following is an example of the post hoc fallacy? (Skill 4.2, Rigorous)

   A. When the new principal was hired, student reading scores improved; therefore, the principal caused the increase in scores.

   B. Why are we spending money on the space program when our students don't have current textbooks?

   C. You can't give your class a 10-minute break. Once you do that, we'll all have to give our students a 10-minute break.

   D. You can never believe anything he says because he's not from the same country as we are.

68. Mr. Phillips is creating a unit to study *To Kill a Mockingbird* and wants to familiarize his high school freshmen with the attitudes and issues of the historical period. Which activity would familiarize students with the attitudes and issues of the Depression-era South? (Skill 4.3, Rigorous)

   A. Create a detailed timeline of 15-20 social, cultural, and political events that focus on race relations in the 1930s.

   B. Research and report on the life of its author Harper Lee. Compare her background with the events in the book.

   C. Watch the movie version and note language and dress.

   D. Write a research report on the stock market crash of 1929 and its effects.

69. The Elizabethans wrote in (Skill 5.1, Easy)

   A. Celtic

   B. Old English

   C. Middle English

   D. Modern English

70. The synonyms "gyro," "hero," and "submarine" reflect which influence on language usage? (Skill 5.1, Average Rigor)

   A. Social

   B. Geographical

   C. Historical

   D. Personal

71. Which event triggered the beginning of Modern English? (Skill 5.1, Average Rigor)

   A. Conquest of England by the Normans in 1066

   B. Introduction of the printing press to the British Isles

   C. Publication of Samuel Johnson's lexicon.

   D. American Revolution

72. Which of the following is not true about the English language? (Skill 5.1, Average Rigor)

A. English is the easiest language to learn.

B. English is the least inflected language.

C. English has the most extensive vocabulary of any language.

D. English originated as a Germanic tongue.

73. Which aspect of language is innate? (Skill 5.1, Rigorous)

A. Biological capability to articulate sounds understood by other humans

B. Cognitive ability to create syntactical structures

C. Capacity for using semantics to convey meaning in a social environment

D. Ability to vary inflections and accents

74. Which word in the following sentence is a bound morpheme: "The quick brown fox jumped over the lazy dog"? (Skill 5.2, Rigorous)

A. The

B. fox

C. lazy

D. jumped

75. The substitution of "went to his rest" for "died" is an example of a/an (Skill 5.3, Easy)

A. bowdlerism.

B. jargon.

C. euphemism.

D. malapropism.

76. A punctuation mark indicating omission, interrupted thought, or an incomplete statement is a/an (Skill 5.3, Easy)

A. ellipsis.

B. anachronism.

C. colloquy.

D. idiom.

77. The arrangement and relationship of words in sentences or sentence structures best describes (Skill 5.3, Rigorous)

   A. style.

   B. discourse.

   C. thesis.

   D. syntax.

78. To understand the origins of a word, one must study the (Skill 5.4, Easy)

   A. synonyms

   B. inflections

   C. phonetics

   D. etymology

79. What was responsible for the standardizing of dialects across America in the 20th century? (Skill 5.4, Rigorous)

   A. With the immigrant influx, American became a melting pot of languages and cultures.

   B. Trains enabled people to meet other people of different languages and cultures.

   C. Radio, and later, television, used actors and announcers who spoke without pronounced dialects.

   D. Newspapers and libraries developed programs to teach people to speak English with an agreed-upon common dialect.

80. After watching a movie of a train derailment, a child exclaims, "Wow, look how many cars fell off the tracks. There's junk everywhere. The engineer must have really been asleep." Using the facts that the child is impressed by the wreckage and assigns blame to the engineer, a follower of Piaget's theories would estimate the child to be about (Skill 6.1, Rigorous)

    A. ten years old.

    B. twelve years old.

    C. fourteen years old.

    D. sixteen years old.

81. In a class of non-native speakers of English, which type of activity will help students the most? (Skill 6.2, Rigorous)

    A. Have students make oral presentations so that they can develop a phonological awareness of sounds.

    B. Provide students more writing opportunities to develop their written communication skills.

    C. Encourage students to listen to the new language on television and radio.

    D. Provide a variety of methods to develop speaking, writing, and reading skills.

82. Which of the following is a formal reading-level assessment? (Skill 6.3, Average Rigor)

    A. A standardized reading test

    B. A teacher-made reading test

    C. An interview

    D. A reading diary

83. Middle and high school students are more receptive to studying grammar and syntax (Skill 6.3, Average Rigor)

    A. through worksheets and end of lessons practices in textbooks.

    B. through independent, homework assignment.

    C. through analytical examination of the writings of famous authors.

    D. through application to their own writing.

84. For their research paper on the effects of the Civil War on American literature, students have brainstormed a list of potential online sources and are seeking your authorization. Which of these represent the strongest source? (Skill 6.3, Rigorous)

    A. http://www.wikipedia.org/

    B. http://www.google.com

    C. http://www.nytimes.com

    D. http://docsouth.unc.edu/southlit/civilwar.html

85. If a student has a poor vocabulary, the teacher should recommend first that (Skill 7.2, Average Rigor)

    A. the student read newspapers, magazines and books on a regular basis.

    B. the student enroll in a Latin class.

    C. the student write the words repetitively after looking them up in the dictionary.

    D. the student use a thesaurus to locate synonyms and incorporate them into his/her vocabulary

86. Which of the following would be the most significant factor in teaching Homer's *Iliad* and *Odyssey* to any particular group of students? (Skill 7.2, Average Rigor)

   A. Identifying a translation on the appropriate reading level

   B. Determining the students' interest level

   C. Selecting an appropriate evaluative technique

   D. Determining the scope and delivery methods of background study

87. Which of the following responses to literature typically give middle school students the most problems? (Skill 7.2, Average Rigor)

   A. Interpretive

   B. Evaluative

   C. Critical

   D. Emotional

88. The most significant drawback to applying learning theory research to classroom practice is that (Skill 7.2, Rigorous)

   A. today's students do not acquire reading skills with the same alacrity as when greater emphasis was placed on reading classical literature.

   B. development rates are complicated by geographical and cultural differences that are difficult to overcome.

   C. homogeneous grouping has contributed to faster development of some age groups.

   D. social and environmental conditions have contributed to an escalated maturity level than research done twenty of more years ago would seem to indicate.

89. Which teaching method would best engage underachievers in the required senior English class? (Skill 7.3, Average Rigor)

   A. Assign use of glossary work and extensively footnoted excerpts of great works.

   B. Have students take turns reading aloud the anthology selection

   C. Let students choose which readings they'll study and write about.

   D. Use a chronologically arranged, traditional text, but assigning group work, panel presentations, and portfolio management

90. What is the best course of action when a child refuses to complete a reading/literature assignment on the grounds that it is morally objectionable? (Skill 7.3, Average Rigor)

   A. Speak with the parents and explain the necessity of studying this work

   B. Encourage the child to sample some of the text before making a judgment

   C. Place the child in another teacher's class where they are studying an acceptable work

   D. Provide the student with alternative selections that cover the same performance standards that the rest of the class is learning.

91. Overcrowded classes prevent the individual attention needed to facilitate language development. This drawback can be best overcome by (Skill 7.3, Average Rigor)

   A. dividing the class into independent study groups.

   B. assigning more study time at home.

   C. using more drill practice in class.

   D. team teaching.

92. Based on the excerpt below from Kate Chopin's short story "The Story of an Hour," what can students infer about the main character? (Skill 7.3, Rigorous)

   She did not stop to ask if it were or were not a monstrous joy that held her. A clear and exalted perception enabled her to dismiss the suggestion as trivial. She knew that she would weep again when she saw the kind, tender hands folded in death; the face that had never looked save with love upon her, fixed and gray and dead. But she saw beyond that bitter moment a long procession of years to come that would belong to her absolutely. And she opened and spread her arms out to them in welcome.

   A. She dreaded her life as a widow.

   B. Although she loved her husband, she was glad that he was dead for he had never loved her.

   C. She worried that she was too indifferent to her husband's death.

   D. Although they had both loved each other, she was beginning to appreciate that opportunities had opened because of his death.

93. In preparing a speech for a contest, your student has encountered problems with gender specific language. Not wishing to offend either women or men, he seeks your guidance. Which of the following is not an effective strategy? (Skill 8.2, Rigorous)

   A. Use the generic "he" and explain that people will understand and accept the male pronoun as all-inclusive.

   B. Switch to plural nouns and use "they" as the gender neutral pronoun.

   C. Use passive voice so that the subject is not required.

   D. Use male pronouns for one part of the speech and then use female pronouns for the other part of the speech.

94. Which of the following sentences contains a subject-verb agreement error? (Skill 8.3, Average Rigor)

   A. Both mother and her two sisters were married in a triple ceremony.

   B. Neither the hen nor the rooster is likely to be served for dinner.

   C. My boss, as well as the company's two personnel directors, have been to Spain.

   D. Amanda and the twins are late again.

95. Writing ideas quickly without interruption of the flow of thoughts or attention to conventions is called (Skill 9.2, Easy)

   A. brainstorming.

   B. mapping.

   C. listing.

   D. freewriting.

96. Reading a piece of student writing to assess the overall impression of the product is (Skill 9.2, Easy)

   A. holistic evaluation.

   B. portfolio assessment.

   C. analytical evaluation.

   D. using a performance system.

97. Which of the following is the least effective procedure for promoting consciousness of audience? (Skill 9.2, Average Rigor)

   A. Pairing students during the writing process

   B. Reading all rough drafts before the students write the final copies

   C. Having students compose stories or articles for publication in school literary magazines or newspapers

   D. Writing letters to friends or relatives

98. Modeling is a practice that requires students to (Skill 9.2, Average Rigor)

   A. create a style unique to their own language capabilities.

   B. emulate the writing of professionals.

   C. paraphrase passages from good literature.

   D. peer evaluate the writings of other students.

99. A formative evaluation of student writing (Skill 9.2, Rigorous)

   A. requires thorough markings of mechanical errors with a pencil or pen.

   B. making comments on the appropriateness of the student's interpretation of the prompt and the degree to which the objective was met.

   C. should require that the student hand in all the materials produced during the process of writing.

   D. several careful readings of the text for content, mechanics, spelling, and usage.

100. In this paragraph from a student essay, identify the sentence that provides a detail. (Skill 9.3 Rigorous)

(1) The poem concerns two different personality types and the human relation between them. (2) Their approach to life is totally different. (3) The neighbor is a very conservative person who follows routines. (4) He follows the traditional wisdom of his father and his father's father. (5) The purpose in fixing the wall and keeping their relationship separate is only because it is all he knows.

A. Sentence 1

B. Sentence 3

C. Sentence 4

D. Sentence 5

101. In general, the most serious drawback of using a computer in writing is that (Skill 9.4, Average Rigor)

A. the copy looks so good that students tend to overlook major mistakes.

B. the spell check and grammar programs discourage students from learning proper spelling and mechanics.

C. the speed with which corrections can be made detracts from the exploration and contemplation of composing.

D. the writer loses focus by concentrating on the final product rather than the details.

102. Which of the following is most true of expository writing? (Skill 10.1, Easy)

   A. It is mutually exclusive of other forms of discourse.

   B. It can incorporate other forms of discourse in the process of providing supporting details.

   B. It should never employ informal expression.

   D. It should only be scored with a summative evaluation.

103. Which of the following is not one of the four forms of discourse? (Skill 10.1, Average Rigor)

   A. Exposition

   B. Description

   C. Rhetoric

   D. Persuasion

104. If a student uses slang and expletives, what is the best course of action to take in order to improve the student's formal communication skills? (Skill 10.2, Average Rigor)

   A. Ask the student to paraphrase their writing, that is, translate it into language appropriate for the school principal to read.

   B. Refuse to read the student's papers until he conforms to a more literate style.

   C. Ask the student to read his work aloud to the class for peer evaluation.

   D. Rewrite the flagrant passages to show the student the right form of expression.

105. Which of the following should not be included in the opening paragraph of an informative essay? (Skill 10.3, Easy)

   A. Thesis sentence

   B. Details and examples supporting the main idea

   C. Broad general introduction to the topic

   D. A style and tone that grabs the reader's attention

106. Explanatory or informative discourse is (Skill 10.3, Average Rigor)

    A. exposition.

    B. narration.

    C. persuasion.

    D. description.

107. Oral debate is most closely associated with which form of discourse? (Skill 10.5, Average Rigor)

    A. Description

    B. Exposition

    C. Narration

    D. Persuasion

108. Which of the following is not a fallacy in logic? (Skill 10.5 Rigorous)

    A. All students in Ms. Suarez's fourth period class are bilingual. Beth is in Ms. Suarez's fourth period. Beth is bilingual.

    B. All bilingual students are in Ms. Suarez's class. Beth is in Ms. Suarez's fourth period. Beth is bilingual.

    C. Beth is bilingual. Beth is in Ms. Suarez's fourth period. All students in Ms. Suarez's fourth period are bilingual.

    D. If Beth is bilingual, then she speaks Spanish. Beth speaks French. Beth is not bilingual.

109. Which part of a classical argument is illustrated in this excerpt from the essay "What Should Be Done About Rock Lyrics?" (Skill 10.5, Rigorous)

> But violence against women is greeted by silence. It shouldn't be.
>
> This does not mean censorship, or book (or record) burning. In a society that protects free expression, we understand a lot of stuff will float up out of the sewer. Usually, we recognize the ugly stuff that advocates violence against any group as the garbage it is, and we consider its purveyors as moral lepers. We hold our nose and tolerate it, but we speak out against the values it proffers.
>
> --"What Should Be Done About Rock Lyrics?" Caryl Rivers

A. Narration

B. Confirmation

C. Refutation and concession

D. Summation

110. Identify the type of appeal used by Molly Ivins in this excerpt from her essay "Get a Knife, Get a Dog, But Get Rid of Guns." (Skill 10.5, Rigorous)

As a civil libertarian, I, of course, support the Second Amendment. And I believe it means exactly what it says:

> *A well regulated militia being necessary to the security of a free state, the right of the people to keep and bear arms shall not be infringed.*

A. Ethos

B. Pathos

C. Logos

D. Mythos

111. Which sentence below best minimizes the impact of bad news? (Skill 11.3, Rigorous)

   A. We have denied you permission to attend the event.

   B. Although permission to attend the event cannot be given, you are encouraged to buy the video.

   C. Although you cannot attend the event, we encourage you to buy the video.

   D. Although attending the event is not possible, watching the video is an option.

112. Which of the following sentences is properly punctuated? (Skill 12.2, Easy)

   A. The more you eat; the more you want.

   B. The authors—John Steinbeck, Ernest Hemingway, and William Faulkner—are staples of modern writing in American literature textbooks.

   C. Handling a wild horse, takes a great deal of skill and patience.

   D. The man, who replaced our teacher, is a comedian.

113. Which of the following sentences contains a capitalization error? (Skill 12.2, Average Rigor)

   A. The commander of the English navy was Admiral Nelson

   B. Napoleon was the president of the French First Republic

   C. Queen Elizabeth II is the Monarch of the British Empire

   D. William the Conqueror led the Normans to victory over the British

114. Students have been asked to write a research paper on automobiles and have brainstormed a number of questions they will answer based on their research findings. Which of the following is not an interpretive question to guide research? (Skill 13.1, Rigorous)

   A. Who were the first ten automotive manufacturers in the United States?

   B. What types of vehicles will be used fifty years from now?

   C. How do automobiles manufactured in the United States compare and contrast with each other?

   D. What do you think is the best solution for the fuel shortage?

115. In preparing a report about William Shakespeare, students are asked to develop a set of interpretive questions to guide their research. Which of the following would not be classified as an interpretive question? (Skill 13.1, Rigorous)

   A. What would be different today if Shakespeare had not written his plays?

   B. How will the plays of Shakespeare affect future generations?

   C. How does the Shakespeare view nature in A Midsummer's Night Dream and Much Ado About Nothing?

   D. During the Elizabethan age, what roles did young boys take in dramatizing Shakespeare's plays?

116. To determine the credibility of information, researchers should do all of the following except (Skill 13.4, Rigorous)

   A. Establish the authority of the document.

   B. Disregard documents with bias.

   C. Evaluate the currency and reputation of the source.

   D. Use a variety of research sources and methods.

117. Which of the following type of question will not stimulate higher-level critical thinking? (Skill 14.4, Rigorous)

   A. A hypothetical question

   B. An open-ended question

   C. A close-ended question

   D. A judgment question

118. Mr. Ledbetter has instructed his students to prepare a slide presentation that illustrates an event in history. Students are to include pictures, graphics, media clips and links to resources. What competencies will students exhibit at the completion of this project? Skill 15.4, Rigorous)

   A. Analyze the impact of society on media.

   B. Recognize the media's strategies to inform and persuade.

   C. Demonstrate strategies and creative techniques to prepare presentations using a variety of media.

   D. Identify the aesthetic effects of a media presentation.

119. For students to prepare for their roles in a dramatic performance, (Skill 16.3, Average Rigor)

   A. they should analyze their characters to develop a deeper understanding of the character's attitudes and motivations.

   B. they should attend local plays to study settings and stage design

   C. they should read articles and books on acting methodology

   D. they should practice the way other actors have performed in these roles.

120. The new teaching intern is developing a unit on creative writing and is trying to encourage her freshman high school students to write poetry. Which of the following would not be an effective technique? (Skill 17.2, Average Rigor)

   A. In groups, students will draw pictures to illustrate "The Love Song of J. Alfred Prufrock" by T.S. Eliot.

   B. Either individually or in groups, students will compose a song, writing lyrics that try to use poetic devices.

   C. Students will bring to class the lyrics of a popular song and discuss the imagery and figurative language.

   D. Students will read aloud their favorite poems and share their opinions of and responses to the poems.

Answer Key

1. B	26. A	51. A	76. A	101. C
2. B	27. C	52. B	77. D	102. B
3. B	28. B	53. A	78. D	103. C
4. A	29. D	54. C	79. C	104. A
5.	30. B	55. C	80. A	105. B
6. D	31. B	56. C	81. A	106. A
7. A	32. A	57. D	82. A	107. D
8. C	33. A	58. D	83. D	108. A
9. D	34. A	59. B	84. D	109. C
10. D	35. D	60. D	85. A	110. A
11. E	36. B	61. A	86. A	111. B
12. A	37. A	62. A	87. B	112. B
13. E	38. C	63. D	88. D	113. C
14. D	39. B	64. A	89. C	114. A
15. C	40. B	65. C	90. D	115. D
16. A	41. B	66. D	91. A	116. B
17. C	42. D	67. A	92. D	117. C
18. C	43. A	69. D	93. B	118. B
19. B	44. D	70. B	94. C	119. A
20. D	45. A	71. B	95. D	120. A
21. D	46. A	72. A	96. A	
22. C	47. D	73. A	97. B	
23. A	48. C	74. D	98. B	
24. D	49. D	75. C	99. B	
25. C	50. C		100. C	

Rigor Table

	Easy %20	Average Rigor %40	Rigorous %40
Question #	1, 6, 10, 11, 12, 16, 23, 26, 27, 38, 42, 50, 52, 53, 70, 76, 77, 79, 96, 97, 103, 106, 113	5, 7, 13, 14, 17, 21, 24, 25, 28, 29, 30, 32, 33, 34, 39, 42, 43, 44, 45, 52, 53, 59, 60, 61, 63, 64, 65, 70, 71, 72, 82, 83, 85, 86, 87, 89, 90, 91, 94, 95, 97, 98, 101, 103, 104, 106, 107, 113, 119, 120	2, 3, 4, 15, 18, 19, 20, 22, 31, 36, 37, 41, 48, 49, 51, 56, 57, 59, 60, 64, 68, 69, 74, 75, 78, 80, 81, 82, 85, 89, 93, 94, 99, 100, 108, 109, 110, 111, 114, 115, 116, 117, 118

Easy: The majority of test takers would get this question correct. It is a simple understanding of the facts and/or the subject matter is part of the basics of an education for teaching English.

Average Rigor: This question represents a test item that most people would pass. It requires a level of analysis or reasoning and/or the subject matter exceeds the basics of an education for teaching English.

Rigor: The majority of test takers would have difficulty answering this question. It involves critical thinking skills such as a very high level of abstract thought, analysis or reasoning, and it would require a very deep and broad education for teaching English.

Rationales for Sample Questions

Directions: Sentences 1-15 each contain four underlined words or phrases. If you determine that any underlined word or phrase has an error in grammar, usage, or mechanics, circle the letter underneath that underlined word or phrase. If there are no errors, circle the letter E at the end of the sentence. There is no more than one error in any sentence.

1. When the <u>school district</u> privatized the school cafeteria, <u>us</u> students <u>were</u>
                  A   B   C
   thrilled to purchase more than soggy <u>French fries</u> E
                                           D

   The error is B: "us" is an object pronoun, not the needed subject pronoun. "We" is the right pronoun. **Skill 8.2, Easy**

2. We <u>were</u> dismayed at <u>them</u> failing the <u>fitness</u> exam on <u>their</u> second attempt.
        A   B   C   D
   E

   The error is B: the possessive form of the adjective precedes a gerund (an "ing" participle), so it should read "…"their failing…" **Skill 8.2, Rigorous**

3. She, not her sister, <u>is</u> the one <u>who</u> the librarian <u>has questioned</u> about the
                              A   B   C
   missing books, <u>*Butterfly's*</u> Ball and *The Bear's House* E
                        D

   The error is B: the relative pronoun "who" is a subject pronoun, but the sentence requires the object form at this point, "whom." **Skill 8.2, Rigorous**

4. <u>If</u> Cullen was to think up the practical joke, then he <u>must</u> suffer the <u>consequences</u>
                       A B   C   D
   E

   The error is A: in a sentence beginning with "If" and expressing a condition, it is necessary to use the correct subjunctive forms: "If I were, if you were, if he/she/it were, if we were, if you were, if they were". The sentence here should read: "If Cullen were to think up the practical joke…" **Skill 8.3, Rigorous**

5. Jack told a <u>credulous</u> story about his trip <u>up the beanstalk</u> because each
                            A   B

    child in the room <u>was convinced</u> by his <u>reasoning</u>   E
                            C   D

6. Walter said <u>that</u> his calculator <u>has been missing</u> <u>since</u> last Monday
                       A   B   C

    <u>responding to my question</u>   E
             D

The error is D: the participle phrase ("responding to my question") modifies Walter, not "Monday." The sentence should read: "Walter, responding to my question, said that his calculator has been missing since last Monday." **Skill 11.2, Average Rigor**

7. The volcanic eruption in Montserrat displaced residents of Plymouth <u>which</u>
                                                                         A

    felt that the <u>English government</u> <u>was</u> responsible for <u>their</u> evacuation   E
                          B   C   D

The error is A: "which" is a relative pronoun whose antecedent is "residents of Plymouth." This antecedent represents persons, not things. If the antecedent were a thing or things, then "which" would be correct. "Who" is the correct pronoun. **Skill 11.3, Easy**

8. The future <u>will be</u> <u>because</u> of the past: <u>by changing the past</u> <u>would alter</u>
                       A   B   C   D

    the future.   E

The answer is C: including "by" is incorrect here. The sentence should read: "... because of the past: changing the past would alter the future." **Skill 11.4, Average Rigor**

9. Although she was nervous on her first day, the new employee, hired to
             A
   replace the retired secretary, grew more comfortable as she was told
             B   C
   where she should park her car, her schedule, and her duties. E
             D

   The error is D: "where to park her car" is a dependent clause and not grammatically parallel to the other nouns in the group. It should be a noun phrase like the other direct objects "schedule" and "duties." **Skill 11.5 Rigorous.**

10. Martha had considered playing drums before she discovers the piano
              A   B   C   D   E

   Skill 8.3, Easy

   The answer is D. It should be discovered. Discovers is the wrong tense. **Skill 8.3, Easy.**

11. Mr. Thomas' daughter-in-law encouraged her husband's boss to host a
    A   B
    fund-raiser for the United Way, a charity that Mr. Thomas supports.   E
                    C   D

   The answer is E: there are no errors in this sentence. **Skill 12.1, Easy**

12. The homecoming Queen and King were chosen by the student body for
                   A   B   C
    their popularity   E
    D

   The error is A: "Queen and King" are used as common nouns here, and not as proper nouns naming a real sovereign such as Queen Elizabeth. Since the words "king and queen" are common nouns, they are not capitalized. **Skill 12.2, Easy**

TEACHER CERTIFICATION STUDY GUIDE

13. There <u>are</u> <u>fewer</u> students in school this year despite the <u>principal's</u> prediction
     A   B   C

    of <u>increasing</u> enrollment   E
            D

The answer is E: there are no grammatical or syntactical errors in this sentence. **Skill 12.2, Easy**

14. My mother is a <u>Methodist</u>. She married a <u>Southern Baptist</u> and took <u>us</u>
                       A   B   C

    children to the <u>First Baptist church</u> in Stuart   E
                             D

The error is D: the name of the church should be completely capitalized. It should read: "… the First Baptist Church." **Skill 12.2, Average Rigor**

15. When we moved from <u>Jacksonville, Florida,</u> to Little Ro<u>ck,</u> Arkansas, my
                                 A   B

    <u>Dad</u> <u>was promoted</u> to store manager.   E
    C   D

The error is C: in this sentence, "dad" is a common noun, which is indicated by the possessive "my". "Dad" used as an actual name gets capitalized. **Skill 12.2, Average Rigor**

16. Miriam decided to remain <u>stationery</u> <u>since</u> <u>to move</u> would startle the
                                       A   B   C

    horses, one of <u>which</u> might bolt.   E
                   D

The error is A: "stationery" is not an adjective, but it refers to writing paper materials. Motionless" would be a viable correction. **Skill 12.2 Rigorous**

ENGLISH

Part B

Each underlined portion of sentences 16-25 contains one or more errors in grammar, usage, mechanics, or sentence structure. Circle the choice which best corrects the error without changing the meaning of the original sentence.

17. **Joe didn't hardly know his cousin Fred who'd had a rhinoplasty. (Skill 5.3, Easy)**

    A. hardly did know his cousin Fred

    B. didn't know his cousin Fred hardly

    C. hardly knew his cousin Fred

    D. didn't know his cousin Fred

    E. didn't hardly know his cousin Fred

    The answer is C: using the adverb "hardly" to modify the verb creates a negative, and adding "not" creates the dreaded double negative.

18. **Mixing the batter for cookies, the cat licked the Crisco from the cookie sheet. (Skill 5.3, Average Rigor)**

    A. While mixing the batter for cookies

    B. While the batter for cookies was mixing

    C. While I mixed the batter for cookies

    D. While I mixed the cookies

    E. Mixing the batter for cookies

    The answer is C: A and E give the impression that the cat was mixing the batter (it is a dangling modifier), B that the batter was mixing itself, and D lacks precision: it is the batter that was being mixed, not the cookies themselves.

19. **Walt Whitman was famous for his composition, *Leaves of Grass*, serving as a nurse during the Civil War, and a devoted son (Skill 5.3, Rigorous)**

    A. *Leaves of Grass*, his service as a nurse during the Civil War, and a devoted son

    B. composing *Leaves of Grass*, serving as a nurse during the Civil War, and being a devoted son

    C. his composition, *Leaves of Grass*, his nursing during the Civil War, and his devotion as a son

    D. his composition, *Leaves of Grass*, serving as a nurse during the Civil War, and a devoted son

    E. his composition, *Leaves of Grass*, serving as a nurse during the Civil War, and a devoted son

    The answer is B: in order to be parallel, the sentence needs three gerunds. The other sentences use both gerunds and nouns, which is a lack of parallelism.

TEACHER CERTIFICATION STUDY GUIDE

20. **The coach offered her assistance but the athletes wanted to practice on their own. (Skill 11.2, Rigorous)**

    A. The coach offered her assistance, however, the athletes wanted to practice on their own.

    B. The coach offered her assistance: furthermore, the athletes wanted to practice on their own.

    C. Having offered her assistance, the athletes wanted to practice on their own.

    D. The coach offered her assistance; however, the athletes wanted to practice on their own.

    E. The coach offered her assistance, and the athletes wanted to practice on their own.

The answer is D: a semicolon precedes a transitional adverb that introduces an independent clause. A is a comma splice. In B, the colon is used incorrectly since the second clause does not explain the first. In C, the opening clause confuses the meaning of the sentence. In D, the conjunction "and" is weak since the two ideas show contrast rather than an additional thought.

21. **A teacher must know not only her subject matter but also the strategies of content teaching. (Skill 11.3, Rigorous)**

    A. must not only know her subject matter but also the strategies of content teaching

    B. not only must know her subject matter but also the strategies of content teaching

    C. must not know only her subject matter but also the strategies of content teaching

    D. must know not only her subject matter but also the strategies of content teaching

The answer is D: "not only" must come directly after "know" because the intent is to create the clearest meaning link with the "but also" predicate section later in the sentence.

ENGLISH

22. **Mr. Smith respectfully submitted his resignation and had a new job. (Skill 11.4, Average Rigor)**

    A.   respectfully submitted his resignation and has

    B.   respectfully submitted his resignation before accepting

    C.   respectfully submitted his resignation because of

    D.   respectfully submitted his resignation and had

    The answer is C. A eliminates any relationship of causality between submitting the resignation and having the new job. B just changes the sentence and does not indicate the fact that Mr. Smith had a new job before submitting his resignation. D means that Mr. Smith first submitted his resignation, and then got a new job.

23. **The Taj Mahal has been designated one of the Seven Wonders of the World, and people know it for its unique architecture. (Skill 11.4, Rigorous)**

    A.   The Taj Mahal has been designated one of the Seven Wonders of the World, and it is known for its unique architecture.

    B.   People know the Taj Mahal for its unique architecture, and it has been designated one of the Seven Wonders of the World.

    C.   People have known the Taj Mahal for its unique architecture, and it has been designated of the Seven Wonders of the World.

    D.   The Taj Mahal has designated itself one of the Seven Wonders of the World.

    The answer is A. In the original sentence, the first clause is passive voice and the second clause is active voice, causing a voice shift. B merely switches the clauses but does not correct the voice shift. In C, only the verb tense in the first clause has been changed but it still active voice. Sentence D changes the meaning. In A, both clauses are passive voice.

24. **There were fewer pieces of evidence presented during the second trial (Skill 12.2, Easy)**

    A. fewer peaces

    B. less peaces

    C. less pieces

    D. fewer pieces

    The answer is D. Use "fewer" for countable items; use "less" for amounts and quantities, such as fewer minutes but less time. "Peace" is the opposite of war, not a "piece" of evidence.

25. **The teacher implied from our angry words that there was conflict between you and me. (Skill 12.2, Average Rigor)**

    A. Implied... between you and I

    B. Inferred... between you and I

    C. Inferred... between you and me

    D. Implied... between you and me

    The answer is C: the difference between the verb "to imply" and the verb "to infer" is that implying is directing an interpretation toward other people; to infer is to deduce an interpretation from someone else's discourse. Moreover, "between you and I" is grammatically incorrect: after the preposition "between," the object (or 'disjunctive' with this particular preposition) pronoun form, "me," is needed.

26. **Wally groaned, "Why do I have to do an oral interpretation of "The Raven." (Skill 12.2, Average Rigor)**

    A. groaned "Why... of 'The Raven'?"

    B. groaned "Why... of "The Raven"?

    C. groaned ", Why... of "The Raven?"

    D. groaned, "Why... of "The Raven."

The answer is A. The question mark in a quotation that is an interrogation should be within the quotation marks. Also, when quoting a work of literature within another quotation, one should use single quotation marks ('...') for the title of this work, and they should close before the final quotation mark.

Part C Multiple Choice

Select the letter for the most correct response.

27. **A traditional, anonymous story, ostensibly having a historical basis, usually explaining some phenomenon of nature or aspect of creation, defines a (Skill 1.1, Easy)**

    A. proverb.

    B. idyll.

    C. myth.

    D. epic.

The answer is C. A myth is usually traditional and anonymous and e plains natural and supernatural phenomena. Myths are usually about creation, divinity, the significance of life and death, and natural phenomena.

28. The tendency to emphasize and value the qualities and peculiarities of life in a particular geographic area exemplifies (Skill 1.1, Easy)

    A. pragmatism.

    B. regionalism.

    C. pantheism.

    D. abstractionism.

The answer is B. regionalism. Pragmatism is a philosophical doctrine according to which there is no absolute truth. All truths change their trueness as their practical utility increases or decreases. The main representative of this movement is William James who in 1907 published *Pragmatism: A New Way for Some Old Ways of Thinking*. Pantheism is a philosophy according to which God is omnipresent in the world, everything is God and God is everything. The great representative of this sensibility is Spinoza. Also, the works of writers such as Wordsworth, Shelly and Emerson illustrate this doctrine. Abstract Expressionism is one of the most important movements in American art. It began in the 1940s with artists such as Willem de Kooning, Mark Rothko and Arshile Gorky. The paintings are usually large and nonrepresentational.

29. Which of the following writers did not win a Nobel Prize for literature? (Skill 1.1, Average Rigor)

    A. Gabriel Garcia-Marquez of Colombia

    B. Nadine Gordimer of South Africa

    C. Pablo Neruda of Chile

    D. Alice Walker of the United States

The answer is D. Even though Alice Walker received the Pulitzer Price and the American Book Award for her best-known novel, The Color Purple, and is the author of six novels and three collections of short stories that have received wide critical acclaim, she has not yet received the Nobel Prize.

30. **The writing of Russian naturalists is (Skill 1.1, Average Rigor)**

    A.   optimistic.

    B.   pessimistic.

    C.   satirical.

    D.   whimsical.

    The answer is B. Although the movement, which originated with the critic Vissarion Belinsky, was particularly strong in the 1840's, it can be said that the works of Dostoevsky, Tolstoy, Chekov, Turgenev and Pushkin owe much to it. These authors' works are among the best in international literature, yet are shrouded in stark pessimism. Tolstoy's *Anna Karenina* or Dostoevsky's *Crime and Punishment* are good examples of this dark outlook.

31. **Which of the following is not a theme of Native American writing? (Skill 1.1, Average Rigor)**

    A.   Emphasis on the hardiness of the human body and soul

    B.   The strength of multi-cultural assimilation

    C.   Contrition for the genocide of native peoples

    D.   Remorse for the love of the Indian way of life

    The answer is B. Native American literature was first a vast body of oral traditions from as early as before the fifteenth century. The characteristics include reverence for and awe of nature and the interconnectedness of the elements in the life cycle. The themes often reflect the hardiness of body and soul, remorse for the destruction of the Native American way of life, and the genocide of many tribes by the encroaching settlements of European Americans. These themes are still present in today's contemporary Native American literature, such as in the works of Duane Niatum, Gunn Allen, Louise Erdrich and N. Scott Momaday.

32. Which sonnet form describes the following? (Skill 1.1, Rigorous)

My galley chargèd with forgetfulness
Through sharp seas in winter nights doth pass
'Twene rock and rock; and eke mine enemy, alas,
That is my lord, steereth with cruelness.
And every oar a thought in readiness
As though that death were light in such a case;
An endless wind doth tear the sail apace
Of forcèd sighs and trusty fearfulness.
A rain of tears, a cloud of dark disdain
Hath done the wearied cords great hindrance,
Wreathèd with error and eke with ignorance.
The stars be hid that led me to this pain,
Drownèd is reason that should me comfort,
And I remain despairing of the port.

A. Petrarchan or Italian sonnet

B. Shakespearian or Elizabethan sonnet

C. Romantic sonnet

D. Spenserian sonnet

The answer is A. The Petrarchan sonnet, also known as Italian sonnet, is named after the Italian poet Petrarch (1304-74). It is divided into an octave rhyming abbaabba and a sestet normally rhyming cdecde.

33. **Children's literature became established in the (Skill 1.2, Average Rigor)**

    A. seventeenth century

    B. eighteenth century

    C. nineteenth century

    D. twentieth century

    The answer is A. In the seventeenth century, authors such as Jean de La Fontaine and his fables, Pierre Perreault's tales, Mme d'Aulnoye's novels based on old folktales and Mme de Beaumont's "Beauty and the Beast" all created a children's literature genre. In England, Perreault was translated and a work allegedly written by Oliver Smith, *The Renowned History of Little Goody Two Shoes*, also helped to establish children's literature in England.

34. **Latin words that entered the English language during the Elizabethan age include (Skill 1.2, Average Rigor)**

    A. allusion, education, and esteem

    B. vogue and mustache

    C. canoe and cannibal

    D. alligator, cocoa, and armadillo

    The answer is A. These words reflect the Renaissance interest in the classical world and the study of ideas. The words in B are French derivation, and the words in C and D are more modern with younger etymologies.

35. American colonial writers were primarily (Skill 1.2, Average Rigor)

A. Romanticists.

B. Naturalists.

C. Realists.

D. Neo-classicists.

The answer is D. The early colonists had been schooled in England, and even though their writing became quite American in content, their emphasis on clarity and balance in their language remained British. This literature reflects the lives of the early colonists, such as William Bradford's excerpts from *The Mayflower Compact*, Anne Bradstreet's poetry and William Byrd's journal, *A History of the Dividing Line*.

36. Which is the best definition of Imagism? (Skill 1.2, Rigorous)

A. A doctrine which teaches that comfort is the only goal of value in life.

B. A movement in modern poetry (c. 1910-1918) characterized by precise, concrete images, free verse, and suggestion rather than complete statement.

C. The belief that people are motivated in all their [sic] only by self-centeredness.

D. The doctrine that the human mind cannot know where there is a God or an ultimate cause, or anything beyond material phenomenon.

The answer is B. The group was led by Ezra Pound at first, but he left for Vorticism and was replaced by Amy Lowell. They rejected 19th century poetry and were looking for clarity and exactness. Their poems were usually short and built around a single image. Other writers representative of the movement are Richard Addington, "H.D." (Hilda Doolittle), F.S. Flint, D.H. Lawrence, Ford Madox Ford, and William Carlos Williams.

37. **Which choice below best defines naturalism? (Skill 1.2, Rigorous)**

   A. A belief that the writer or artist should apply scientific objectivity in his/her observation and treatment of life without imposing value judgments.

   B. The doctrine that teaches that the existing world is the best to be hoped for.

   C. The doctrine which teaches that God is not a personality, but that all laws, forces and manifestations of the universe are God-related.

   D. A philosophical doctrine which professes that the truth of all knowledge must always be in question.

   The answer is A. Naturalism is a movement that was started by French writers Jules and Edmond de Goncourt with their novel *Germinie Lacerteux* (1865), but its real leader is Emile Zola, who wanted to bring "a slice of life" to his readers. His saga, *Les Rougon Macquart*, consists in twenty-two novels depicting various aspects of social life. English writing authors representative of this movement include George Moore and George Gissing in England, but the most important naturalist novel in English is Theodore Dreiser's *Sister Carrie*.

38. **Among junior-high school students with low-to-average readability levels, which work would most likely stir reading interest? (Skill 1.3, Easy)**

   A. *Elmer Gantry*, Sinclair Lewis

   B. *Smiley's People*, John Le Carre

   C. *The Outsiders,* S.E. Hinton

   D. *And Then There Were None*, Agatha Christie.

   The answer is C. The students can easily identify with the characters and the gangs in the book. S.E. Hinton has actually said about this book: "*The Outsiders* is definitely my best-selling book; but what I like most about it is how it has taught a lot of kids to enjoy reading."

TEACHER CERTIFICATION STUDY GUIDE

39. Written on the sixth-grade reading level, most of S. E. Hinton's novels (for instance, *The Outsiders*) have the greatest reader appeal with (Skill 1.3, Average Rigor)

   A. sixth-graders.

   B. ninth-graders.

   C. twelfth-graders.

   D. adults.

   The answer is B. Adolescents are concerned with their changing bodies, their relationships with each other and adults, and their place in society. Reading The Outsiders makes them confront different problems that they are only now beginning to experience as teenagers, such as gangs and social identity. Hinton's book *The Outsiders* is universal in its appeal to adolescents.

40. In the hierarchy of needs for adolescents who are becoming more team-oriented in their approach to learning, which need do they exhibit most? (Skill 1.3, Average Rigor)

   A. Need for competence

   B. Need for love/acceptance

   C. Need to know

   D. Need to belong

   The answer is B. In Abraham's Maslow's *Theory of Humanistic Development*, there is a hierarchy of needs, from basic physiological needs to the need for self-actualization. The need for love presupposes that every human being needs to love and be loved. With young children this reciprocal need is directed at and received from family members, pets, and friends. In older children and adolescents, this need does not disappear. On the contrary, it extends to new recipients such as peers and romantic partners.

TEACHER CERTIFICATION STUDY GUIDE

41. **Piaget's learning theory asserts that adolescents in the formal operations period (Skill 1.3, Rigorous)**

    A. behave properly from fear of punishment rather than from a conscious decision to take a certain action.

    B. see the past more realistically and can relate to people from the past more than preadolescents.

    C. are less self-conscious and thus more willing to project their own identities into those of fictional characters.

    D. have not yet developed a symbolic imagination.

    The answer is B, since according to Piaget, adolescents 12-15 years old begin thinking beyond the immediate and obvious, and theorize. Their assessment of events shifts from considering an action as "right" or "wrong" to considering the intent and behavior in which the action was performed. Fairy tale or other kinds of unreal characters have ceased to satisfy them and they are able to recognize the difference between pure history and historical fiction.

42. **Which poet was a major figure in the Harlem Renaissance? (Skill 1.4, Easy)**

    A. E. E. Cummings

    B. Rita Dove

    C. Margaret Atwood

    D. Langston Hughes

    The answer is D. Hughes' collection of verse includes *The Weary Blues* (1926), *Shakespeare in Harlem* (1942), and *The Panther and the Lash* (1967). E. E. Cummings referred the lower case in the spelling of his name until the 1930's. He is also a celebrated poet, but is not a part of the Harlem Renaissance. Rita Dove is a very famous African American poet, but she was born in 1952 and therefore is not a part of the Harlem Renaissance. Margaret Atwood is a Canadian novelist.

ENGLISH

TEACHER CERTIFICATION STUDY GUIDE

43. **Which of the writers below is a renowned black poet? (Skill 1.4, Average Rigor)**

    A. Maya Angelou

    B. Sandra Cisneros

    C. Richard Wilbur

    D. Richard Wright

    The answer is A. Among her most famous work are *I Know Why the Caged Bird Sings* (1970), *And Still I Rise* (1978), and *All God's Children Need Traveling Shoes* (1986). Richard Wilbur is a poet and a translator of French dramatists Racine et Moliere, but he is not African American. Richard Wright is a very important African American author of novels such as *Native Son* and *Black Boy*. However, he was not a poet. Sandra Cisneros is a Latina author who is very important in developing Latina women's literature.

44. **Which of the following titles is known for its scathingly condemning tone? (Skill 1.4, Average Rigor)**

    A. Boris Pasternak's *Dr Zhivago*

    B. Albert Camus' *The Stranger*

    C. Henry David Thoreau's "On the Duty of Civil Disobedience"

    D. Benjamin Franklin's "Rules by Which a Great Empire May Be Reduced to a Small One"

    The answer is D. In this work, Benjamin Franklin adopts a scathingly ironic tone to warn the British about the probable outcome in their colonies if they persist with their policies. These are discussed one by one in the text, and the absurdity of each is condemned.

45. **Charles Dickens, Robert Browning, and Robert Louis Stevenson were (Skill 1.4, Average Rigor)**

    A. Victorians.

    B. Medievalists.

    C. Elizabethans.

    D. Absurdists.

    The answer is A. The Victorian Period is remarkable for the diversity and quality of its literature. Robert Browning wrote chilling monologues such as "My Last Duchess," and long poetic narratives such as *The Pied Piper of Hamlin*. Robert Louis Stevenson wrote his works partly for young adults, whose imaginations were quite taken by his *Treasure Island* and *The Case of Dr. Jekyll and Mr. Hyde*. Charles Dickens tells of the misery of the time and the complexities of Victorian society in novels such as *Oliver Twist* or *Great Expectations*.

46. **Arthur Miller wrote *The Crucible* as a parallel to what twentieth century event? (Skill 1.4, Average Rigor)**

    A. Sen. McCarthy's House un-American Activities Committee Hearing

    B. The Cold War

    C. The fall of the Berlin wall

    D. The Persian Gulf War

    The answer is A. The episode of the seventeenth century witch hunt in Salem, Mass., gave Miller a storyline that was very comparable to what was happening to persons suspected of communist beliefs in the 1950's.

47. Which author did not write satire? (Skill 1.4, Rigorous)

   A. Joseph Addison

   B. Richard Steele

   C. Alexander Pope

   D. John Bunyan

The answer is D. John Bunyan was a religious writer, known for his autobiography, *Grace Abounding to the Chief of Sinners,* as well as other books, all religious in their inspiration, such as *The Holy City, or the New Jerusalem* (1665), *A Confession of my Faith, and a Reason of My Practice* (1672), or *The Holy War* (1682).

48. Which of the following is the best definition of existentialism? (Skill 1.4, Rigorous)

   A. The philosophical doctrine that matter is the only reality and that everything in the world, including thought, will, and feeling, can be explained only in terms of matter.

   B. Philosophy which views things as they should be or as one would wish them to be.

   C. A philosophical and literary movement, variously religious and atheistic, stemming from Kierkegaard and represented by Sartre.

   D. The belief that all events are determined by fate and are hence inevitable.

The answer is C. Even though there are other very important thinkers in the movement known as Existentialism, such as Camus and Merleau-Ponty, Sartre remains the main figure in this movement.

49. Which of the following is not a characteristic of a fable? (Skill 2.1, Easy)

    A. Animals that feel and talk like humans.

    B. Happy solutions to human dilemmas.

    C. Teaches a moral or standard for behavior.

    D. Illustrates specific people or groups without directly naming them.

    The answer is D. A fable is a short tale with animals, humans, gods, or even inanimate objects as characters. Fables often conclude with a moral, delivered in the form of an epigram (a short, witty, and ingenious statement in verse). Fables are among the oldest forms of writing in human history: it appears in Egyptian papyri of c1500 BC. The most famous fables are those of Aesop, a Greek slave living in about 600 BC. In India, the *Pantchatantra* appeared in the third century. The most famous modern fables are those of seventeenth century French poet Jean de La Fontaine.

50. "Everyone must pass through Vanity Fair to get to the celestial city" is an allusion from a (Skill 2.1, Rigorous)

    A. Chinese folk tale.

    B. Norse saga.

    C. British allegory.

    D. German fairy tale.

    The answer is C. This is a reference to John Bunyan's *Pilgrim's Progress* from *This World to That Which Is to Come* (Part I, 1678; Part II, 1684), in which the hero, Christian, flees the City of Destruction and must undergo different trials and tests to get to the Celestial City.

TEACHER CERTIFICATION STUDY GUIDE

51. **Which definition is the best for defining diction? (Skill 2.2, Easy)**

    A. The specific word choices of an author to create a particular mood or feeling in the reader.

    B. Writing which explains something thoroughly.

    C. The background, or exposition, for a short story or drama.

    D. Word choices which help teach a truth or moral.

    The answer is A. Diction refers to an author's choice of words, expressions and style to convey his/her meaning.

52. **The literary device of personification is used in which example below? (Skill 2.2, Easy)**

    A. "Beg me no beggary by soul or parents, whining dog!"

    B. "Happiness sped through the halls cajoling as it went."

    C. "O wind thy horn, thou proud fellow."

    D. "And that one talent which is death to hide."

    The answer is B. "Happiness," an abstract concept, is described as if it were a person.

53. **In the following quotation, addressing the dead body of Caesar as though he were still a living being is to employ an (Skill 2.2, Average Rigor)**

   O, pardon me, though
   Bleeding piece of earth
   That I am meek and gentle with
   These butchers.
      -Marc Antony from Julius Caesar

   A. apostrophe

   B. allusion

   C. antithesis

   D. anachronism

   The answer is A. This rhetorical figure addresses personified things, absent people or gods. An allusion, on the other hand, is a quick reference to a character or event known to the public. An antithesis is a contrast between two opposing viewpoints, ideas, or presentation of characters. An anachronism is the placing of an object or person out of its time with the time of the text. The best-known example is the clock in Shakespeare's *Julius Caesar*.

54. **Which is the best definition of free verse, or vers libre? (Skill 2.2, Average Rigor)**

   A. Poetry which consists of an unaccented syllable followed by an unaccented sound.

   B. Short lyrical poetry written to entertain but with an instructive purpose.

   C. Poetry which does not have a uniform pattern of rhythm.

   D. A poem which tells the story and has a plot

   The answer is C. Free verse has lines of irregular length (but it does not run on like prose).

55. Which is not a biblical allusion? (Skill 2.2, Rigorous)

    A. The patience of Job

    B. Thirty pieces of silver

    C. "Man proposes; God disposes"

    D. "Suffer not yourself to be betrayed by a kiss"

The answer is C. This saying is attributed to Thomas à Kempis (1379-1471) in his *Imitation of Christ*, Book 1, Chapter 19. Anyone who exhibits the patience of Job is being compared to the Old Testament biblical figure who retained his faith despite being beset by a series of misfortunes. "Thirty pieces of silver" refers to the amount of money paid to Judas to identify Jesus. Used by Patrick Henry, the quote in D is a biblical reference to Judas' betrayal of Judas by a kiss.

56. What is the salient literary feature of this excerpt from an epic? (Skill 2.2, Rigorous)

> Hither the heroes and the nymphs resort,
> To taste awhile the pleasures of a court;
> In various talk th' instructive hours they passed,
> Who gave the ball, or paid the visit last;
> One speaks the glory of the British Queen,
> And one describes a charming Indian screen;
> A third interprets motions, looks, and eyes;
> At every word a reputation dies.

A. Sprung rhythm

B. Onomatopoeia

C. Heroic couplets

D. Motif

The answer is C. A couplet is a pair of rhyming verse lines, usually of the same length. It is one of the most widely used verse-forms in European poetry. Chaucer established the use of couplets in English, notably in the *Canterbury Tales,* using rhymed iambic pentameters (a metrical unit of verse having one unstressed syllable followed by one stressed syllable) later known as heroic couplets. Other authors who used heroic couplets include Ben Jonson, Dryden, and especially Alexander Pope, who became the master of them.

57. What syntactic device is most evident from Abraham Lincoln's "Gettysburg Address? (Skill 2.2, Rigorous)

It is rather for us to be here dedicated to the great task remaining before us—that from these honored dead we take increased devotion to that cause for which they gave the last full measure of devotion—that we here highly resolve that these dead shall not have died in vain—that this nation, under God, shall have a new birth of freedom—and that government of the people, by the people, for the people, shall not perish from the earth.

A. Affective connotation

B. Informative denotations

C. Allusion

D. Parallelism

The answer is D. Parallelism is the repetition of grammatical structure. In speeches such as this as well as speeches of Martin Luther King, Jr., parallel structure creates a rhythm and balance of related ideas. Lincoln's repetition of clauses beginning with "that" ties four examples back "to the great task." Connotation is the emotional attachment of words; denotation is the literal meaning of words. Allusion is a reference to a historic event, person, or place.

58. Which term best describes the form of the following poetic excerpt? (Skill 2.2, Rigorous)

   And more, to lulle him in his slumber soft,
     A trickling streame from high rocke tumbling downe
     And euer-drizling raine vpon the loft,
     Mixt with a murmuring winde, much like the sowne
     Of swarming Bees, did cast him in a swowne:
     No other noyse, nor peoples troublous cryes,
     As still are wont t'annoy the walled towne,
     Might there be heard: but carelesse Quiet lyes,
Wrapt in eternall silence farre from enemyes..

   A. Ballad

   B. Elegy

   D. Spenserian stanza

   D. Octava rima

The answer is D. The octava rima is a specific eight-line stanza whose rhyme scheme is abababcc.

59. **In the phrase "The Cabinet conferred with the President," Cabinet is an example of a/an (Skill 2.2, Rigorous)**

    A. metonym

    B. synecdoche

    C. metaphor

    D. allusion

    The answer is B. In a synecdoche, a whole is referred to by naming a part of it. Also, a synecdoche can stand for a whole of which it is a part: for example, the Cabinet for the government. Skill 2.2, Rigorous

60. **Which of the following definitions best describes a parable? (Skill 2.3, Average Rigor)**

    A. A short entertaining account of some happening, usually using talking animals as characters.

    B. A slow, sad song or poem, or prose work expressing lamentation.

    C. An extensive narrative work expressing universal truths concerning domestic life.

    D. A short, simple story of an occurrence of a familiar kind, from which a moral or religious lesson may be drawn.

    The answer is D. A parable is usually brief, and should be interpreted as an allegory teaching a moral lesson. Jesus' forty parables are the model of the genre, but modern, secular examples exist such as Wilfred Owen's "The Parable of The Young Man" and "The Young" (1920), or John Steinbeck's prose work *The Pearl* (1948).

61. Most children's literature prior to the development of popular literature was intended to be didactic. Which of the following would not be considered didactic? (Skill 2.3, Average Rigor)

    A. "A Visit from St. Nicholas" by Clement Moore

    B. McGuffy's Reader

    C. Any version of Cinderella

    D. Parables from the Bible

    The answer is A. "A Visit from St. Nicholas" is a cheery, non-threatening child's view of "The Night before Christmas." Didactic means intended to teach some lesson.

62. Which of the following is a characteristic of blank verse? (Skill 2.3, Average Rigor)

    A. Meter in iambic pentameter

    B. Clearly specified rhyme scheme

    C. Lack of figurative language

    D. Unspecified rhythm

    The answer is A. An iamb is a metrical unit of verse having one unstressed syllable followed by one stressed syllable. This is the most commonly used metrical verse in English and American poetry. An iambic pentameter is a ten-syllable verse made of five of these metrical units, either rhymed as in sonnets, or unrhymed as in free —or blank verse.

63. **The following lines from Robert Browning's poem "My Last Duchess" is an example of what form of dramatic literature? (Skill 2.3, Rigorous)**

> That's my last Duchess painted on the wall,
>
> Looking as if she were alive. I call
>
> That piece a wonder, now: Frà Pandolf's hands
>
> Worked busily a day, and there she stands.
>
> Will 't please you sit and look at her?

   A. Tragedy

   B. Comic opera

   C. Dramatis personae

   D. Dramatic monologue

The answer is D. A dramatic monologue is a speech given by a character or narrator that reveals characteristics of the character or narrator. This form was first made popular by Robert Browning, a Victorian poet. Tragedy is a form of literature in which the protagonist is overwhelmed by opposing forces. Comic opera is a form of sung music based on a light or happy plot. *Dramatis personae* is the Latin phrase for the cast of a play.

64. **Which is an untrue statement about a theme in literature? (Skill 2.4, Average Rigor)**

   A. The theme is always stated directly somewhere in the text.

   B. The theme is the central idea in a literary work.

   C. All parts of the work (plot, setting, and mood) should contribute to the theme in some way.

   D. By analyzing the various elements of the work, the reader should be able to arrive at an indirectly stated theme.

The answer is A. The theme may be stated directly, but it can also be implicit in various aspects of the work, such as the interaction between characters, symbolism, or description.

65. In literature, evoking feelings of pity or compassion is to create (Skill 2.4, Average Rigor)

   A. colloquy.

   B. irony.

   C. pathos.

   D. paradox

   The answer is C. A very well-known example of pathos is Desdemona's death in *Othello*, but there are many other examples of pathos.

66. The students in Mrs. Cline's seventh-grade language arts class were invited to attend a performance of *Romeo and Juliet* presented by the drama class at the high school. To best prepare, they should (Skill 3.2, Average Rigor)

   A. read the play as a homework exercise.

   B. read a synopsis of the plot and a biographical sketch of the author.

   C. examine a few main selections from the play to become familiar with the language and style of the author.

   D. read a condensed version of the story and practice attentive listening skills.

   The answer is D. By reading a condensed version of the story, students will know the plot and therefore be able to follow the play on stage. It is also important for them to practice listening techniques such as one one-to-one tutoring and peer-assisted reading.

67. **Which of the following is an example of the post hoc fallacy? (Skill 4.2, Rigorous)**

    A. When the new principal was hired, student reading scores improved; therefore, the principal caused the increase in scores.

    B. Why are we spending money on the space program when our students don't have current textbooks?

    C. You can't give your class a 10-minute break. Once you do that, we'll all have to give our students a 10-minute break.

    D. You can never believe anything he says because he's not from the same country as we are.

The correct answer is A. A post hoc fallacy assumes that because one event preceded another, the first event caused the second event. In this case, student scores could have increased for other reasons. B is a red herring fallacy in which one raises an irrelevant topic to side track from the first topic. In this case, the space budget and the textbook budget have little effect on each other. Response C is an example of a slippery slope, in which one event is followed precipitously by another event. Response D is an ad hominem ("to the man") fallacy in which a person is attacked rather than the concept or interpretation.

68. Mr. Phillips is creating a unit to study *To Kill a Mockingbird* and wants to familiarize his high school freshmen with the attitudes and issues of the historical period. Which activity would familiarize students with the attitudes and issues of the Depression-era South? (Skill 4.3, Rigorous)

   A. Create a detailed timeline of 15-20 social, cultural, and political events that focus on race relations in the 1930s.

   B. Research and report on the life of its author Harper Lee. Compare her background with the events in the book.

   C. Watch the movie version and note language and dress.

   D. Write a research report on the stock market crash of 1929 and its effects.

The answer is A. By identifying the social, cultural, and political events of the 1930s, students will better understand the attitudes and values of America during the time of the novel. While researching the author's life could add depth to their understanding of the novel, it is unnecessary to the appreciation of the novel by itself. The movie version is an accurate depiction of the novel's setting but it focuses on the events in the novel, not the external factors that fostered the conflict. The stock market crash and the subsequent Great Depression would be important to note on the timeline but students would be distracted from themes of the book by narrowing their focus to only these two events.

69. **The Elizabethans wrote in (Skill 5.1, Easy)**

   A. Celtic

   B. Old English

   C. Middle English

   D. Modern English

   The answer is D. There is no document written in Celtic in England, and a work such as *Beowulf* is representative of Old English in the eighth century. It is also the earliest Teutonic-written document. Before the fourteenth century, little literature is known to have appeared in Middle English, which had absorbed many words from the Norman French spoken by the ruling class, but at the and of the fourteenth century there appeared the works of Chaucer, John Gower, and the novel *Sir Gawain and The Green King*. The Elizabethans wrote in modern English and their legacy is very important: they imported the Petrarchan, or Italian, sonnet, which Sir Thomas Wyatt and Sir Philip Sydney illustrated in their works. Sir Edmund Spencer invented his own version of the Italian sonnet and wrote *The Faerie Queene*. Other literature of the time includes the hugely important works of Shakespeare and Marlowe.

70. **The synonyms "gyro," "hero," and "submarine" reflect which influence on language usage? (Skill 5.1, Average Rigor)**

   A. Social

   B. Geographical

   C. Historical

   D. Personal

   The answer is B. They are interchangeable but their use depends on the region of the United States, not on the social class of the speaker. Nor is there any historical context around any of them. The usage can be personal, but will most often vary with the region.

71. **Which event triggered the beginning of Modern English? (Skill 5.1, Average Rigor)**

    A. Conquest of England by the Normans in 1066

    B. Introduction of the printing press to the British Isles

    C. Publication of Samuel Johnson's lexicon.

    D. American Revolution

    The answer is B. With the arrival of the written word, reading matter became mass produced, so the public tended to adopt the speech and writing habits printed in books and the language became more stable.

72. **Which of the following is not true about the English language? (Skill 5.1, Average Rigor)**

    A. English is the easiest language to learn.

    B. English is the least inflected language.

    C. English has the most extensive vocabulary of any language.

    D. English originated as a Germanic tongue.

    The answer is A. Just like any other language, English has inherent difficulties which make it difficult to learn, even though English has no declensions such as those found in Latin, Greek, or contemporary Russian, or a tonal system such Chinese.

73. **Which aspect of language is innate? (Skill 5.1, Rigorous)**

    A. Biological capability to articulate sounds understood by other humans

    B. Cognitive ability to create syntactical structures

    C. Capacity for using semantics to convey meaning in a social environment

    D. Ability to vary inflections and accents

    The answer is A. Language ability is innate and the biological capability to produce sounds lets children learn semantics and syntactical structures through trial and error. Linguists agree that language is first a vocal system of word symbols that enable a human to communicate his/her feelings, thoughts, and desires to other human beings.

74. **Which word in the following sentence is a bound morpheme: "The quick brown fox jumped over the lazy dog"? (Skill 5.2, Rigorous)**

    A. The

    B. fox

    C. lazy

    D. jumped

    The answer is D. The suffix –ed is an affix that cannot stand alone as a unit of meaning. Thus it is bound to the free morpheme "jump." "The" is always an unbound morpheme since no suffix or prefix can alter its meaning. As written, "fox" and "lazy" are unbound but their meaning is changed with affixes, such as "foxes" or "laziness."

75. The substitution of "went to his rest" for "died" is an example of a/an (Skill 5.3, Easy)

    A. bowdlerism.

    B. jargon.

    C. euphemism.

    D. malapropism.

    The answer is C. A euphemism replaces an unpleasant or offensive word or expression by a more agreeable one. It also alludes to distasteful things in a pleasant manner, and it can even paraphrase offensive texts.

76. A punctuation mark indicating omission, interrupted thought, or an incomplete statement is a/an (Skill 5.3, Easy)

    A. ellipsis.

    B. anachronism.

    C. colloquy.

    D. idiom.

    The answer is A. In an ellipsis, word or words that would clarify the sentence's message are missing, yet it is still possible to understand them from the context.

TEACHER CERTIFICATION STUDY GUIDE

77. **The arrangement and relationship of words in sentences or sentence structures best describes (Skill 5.3, Rigorous)**

    A. style.

    B. discourse.

    C. thesis.

    D. syntax.

    The answer is D. Syntax is the grammatical structure of sentences. Style refers to the way something is written. Discourse, broadly, means communication. A thesis is the main idea that holds an essay together.

78. **To understand the origins of a word, one must study the (Skill 5.4, Easy)**

    A. synonyms

    B. inflections

    C. phonetics

    D. etymology

    The answer is D. Etymology is the study of word origins. A synonym is an equivalent of another word and can substitute for it in certain contexts. Inflection is a modification of words according to their grammatical functions, usually by employing variant word-endings to indicate such qualities as tense, gender, case, and number. Phonetics are the science devoted to the physical analysis of the sounds of human speech, including their production, transmission, and perception.

79. **What was responsible for the standardizing of dialects across America in the 20th century? (Skill 5.4, Rigorous)**

    A. With the immigrant influx, American became a melting pot of languages and cultures.

    B. Trains enabled people to meet other people of different languages and cultures.

    C. Radio, and later, television, used actors and announcers who spoke without pronounced dialects.

    D. Newspapers and libraries developed programs to teach people to speak English with an agreed-upon common dialect.

The answer is C. The growth of immigration in the early part of the twentieth century created pockets of language throughout the country. Coupled with regional differences already in place, the number of dialects grew. Transportation enabled people to move to different regions where languages and dialects continued to merge. With the growth of radio and television, however, people were introduced to a standardized dialect through actors and announcers who spoke so that anyone across American could understand them. Newspapers and libraries never developed programs to standardize spoken English.

80. After watching a movie of a train derailment, a child exclaims, "Wow, look how many cars fell off the tracks. There's junk everywhere. The engineer must have really been asleep." Using the facts that the child is impressed by the wreckage and assigns blame to the engineer, a follower of Piaget's theories would estimate the child to be about (Skill 6.1, Rigorous)

    A.   ten years old.

    B.   twelve years old.

    C.   fourteen years old.

    D.   sixteen years old.

    The answer is A. According to Piaget's theory, children seven to eleven years old begin to apply logic to concrete things and experiences. They can combine performance and reasoning to solve problems. They have internalized moral values and are willing to confront rules and adult authority.

81. In a class of non-native speakers of English, which type of activity will help students the most? (Skill 6.2, Rigorous)

    A.   Have students make oral presentations so that they can develop a phonological awareness of sounds.

    B.   Provide students more writing opportunities to develop their written communication skills.

    C.   Encourage students to listen to the new language on television and radio.

    D.   Provide a variety of methods to develop speaking, writing, and reading skills.

    The answer is A. Research indicates that non-native speakers of English develop stronger second language skills by understanding the phonological differences in spoken words.

82. Which of the following is a formal reading-level assessment? (Skill 6.3, Average Rigor)

    A. A standardized reading test

    B. A teacher-made reading test

    C. An interview

    D. A reading diary

    The answer is A. If assessment is standardized, it has to be objective, whereas B, C and D are all subjective assessments.

83. Middle and high school students are more receptive to studying grammar and syntax (Skill 6.3, Average Rigor)

    A. through worksheets and end of lessons practices in textbooks.

    B. through independent, homework assignment.

    C. through analytical examination of the writings of famous authors.

    D. through application to their own writing.

    The answer is D. At this age, students learn grammatical concepts best through practical application in their own writing.

TEACHER CERTIFICATION STUDY GUIDE

88. **The most significant drawback to applying learning theory research to classroom practice is that (Skill 7.2, Rigorous)**

    A. today's students do not acquire reading skills with the same alacrity as when greater emphasis was placed on reading classical literature.

    B. development rates are complicated by geographical and cultural differences that are difficult to overcome.

    C. homogeneous grouping has contributed to faster development of some age groups.

    D. social and environmental conditions have contributed to an escalated maturity level than research done twenty of more years ago would seem to indicate.

    The answer is D. Because of the rapid social changes, topics which did not use to interest younger readers are now topics of books for even younger readers. There are many books dealing with difficult topics, and it is difficult for the teacher to steer students toward books which they are ready for and to try to keep them away from books whose content, although well written, is not yet appropriate for their level of cognitive and social development. There is a fine line between this and censorship.

89. **Which teaching method would best engage underachievers in the required senior English class? (Skill 7.3, Average Rigor)**

    A. Assign use of glossary work and extensively footnoted excerpts of great works.

    B. Have students take turns reading aloud the anthology selection

    C. Let students choose which readings they'll study and write about.

    D. Use a chronologically arranged, traditional text, but assigning group work, panel presentations, and portfolio management

    The answer is C. It will encourage students to react honestly to literature. Students should take notes on what they're reading so they will be able to discuss the material. They should not only react to literature, but also experience it. Small-group work is a good way to encourage them. The other answers are not fit for junior high or high school students. They should be encouraged, however, to read critics of works in order to understand criteria work.

90. **What is the best course of action when a child refuses to complete a reading/ literature assignment on the grounds that it is morally objectionable? (Skill 7.3, Average Rigor)**

    A. Speak with the parents and explain the necessity of studying this work

    B. Encourage the child to sample some of the text before making a judgment

    C. Place the child in another teacher's class where they are studying an acceptable work

    D. Provide the student with alternative selections that cover the same performance standards that the rest of the class is learning.

    The answer is D. In the case of a student finding a reading offensive, it is the responsibility of the teacher to assign another title. As a general rule, it is always advisable to notify parents if a particularly sensitive piece is to be studied.

91. **Overcrowded classes prevent the individual attention needed to facilitate language development. This drawback can be best overcome by (Skill 7.3, Average Rigor)**

    A. dividing the class into independent study groups.

    B. assigning more study time at home.

    C. using more drill practice in class.

    D. team teaching.

    The answer is A. Dividing a class into small groups fosters peer enthusiasm and evaluation, and sets an atmosphere of warmth and enthusiasm. It is much preferable to divide the class into smaller study groups than to lecture, which will bore students and therefore fail to facilitate curricular goals. Also, it is preferable to do this than to engage the whole class in a general teacher-led discussion because such discussion favors the loquacious and inhibits the shy.

92. **Based on the excerpt below from Kate Chopin's short story "The Story of an Hour," what can students infer about the main character? (Skill 7.3, Rigorous)**

> She did not stop to ask if it were or were not a monstrous joy that held her. A clear and exalted perception enabled her to dismiss the suggestion as trivial. She knew that she would weep again when she saw the kind, tender hands folded in death; the face that had never looked save with love upon her, fixed and gray and dead. But she saw beyond that bitter moment a long procession of years to come that would belong to her absolutely. And she opened and spread her arms out to them in welcome.

   A. She dreaded her life as a widow.

   B. Although she loved her husband, she was glad that he was dead for he had never loved her.

   C. She worried that she was too indifferent to her husband's death.

   D. Although they had both loved each other, she was beginning to appreciate that opportunities had opened because of his death.

The answer is D. Dismissing her feeling of "monstrous joy" as insignificant, the young woman she realizes that she will mourn her husband who had been good to her and had loved her. But that "long procession of years" does not frighten her; instead she recognizes that this new life belongs to her alone and she welcomes it with open arms.

93. **In preparing a speech for a contest, your student has encountered problems with gender specific language. Not wishing to offend either women or men, he seeks your guidance. Which of the following is not an effective strategy? (Skill 8.2, Rigorous)**

    A. Use the generic "he" and explain that people will understand and accept the male pronoun as all-inclusive.

    B. Switch to plural nouns and use "they" as the gender neutral pronoun.

    C. Use passive voice so that the subject is not required.

    D. Use male pronouns for one part of the speech and then use female pronouns for the other part of the speech.

    The answer is B. No longer is the male pronoun considered the universal pronoun. Speakers and writers should choose gender neutral words and avoid nouns and pronouns that inaccurately exclude one gender or another.

94. **Which of the following sentences contains a subject-verb agreement error? (Skill 8.3, Average Rigor)**

    A. Both mother and her two sisters were married in a triple ceremony.

    B. Neither the hen nor the rooster is likely to be served for dinner.

    C. My boss, as well as the company's two personnel directors, have been to Spain.

    D. Amanda and the twins are late again.

    The answer is C. The reason for this is that the true subject of the verb is "My boss," not "two personnel directors."

95. **Writing ideas quickly without interruption of the flow of thoughts or attention to conventions is called (Skill 9.2, Easy)**

    A. brainstorming.

    B. mapping.

    C. listing.

    D. freewriting.

    The answer is D. Freewriting for ten or fifteen minutes allows students to write out their thoughts about a subject. This technique allows the students to develop ideas that they are conscious of, but it also helps them to develop ideas that are lurking in the subconscious. It is important to let the flow of ideas run through the hand. If the students get stuck, they can write the last sentence over again until inspiration returns.

96. **Reading a piece of student writing to assess the overall impression of the product is (Skill 9.2, Easy)**

    A. holistic evaluation.

    B. portfolio assessment.

    C. analytical evaluation.

    D. using a performance system.

    The answer is A. Holistic scoring assesses a piece of writing as a whole. Usually a paper is read quickly through once to get a general impression. The writing is graded according to the impression of the whole work rather than the sum of its parts. Often holistic scoring uses a rubric that establishes the overall criteria for a certain score to evaluate each paper.

97. **Which of the following is the least effective procedure for promoting consciousness of audience? (Skill 9.2, Average Rigor)**

    A. Pairing students during the writing process

    B. Reading all rough drafts before the students write the final copies

    C. Having students compose stories or articles for publication in school literary magazines or newspapers

    D. Writing letters to friends or relatives

    The answer is B. Reading all rough drafts will not encourage the students to take control of their text and might even inhibit their creativity. On the contrary, pairing students will foster their sense of responsibility, and having them compose stories for literary magazines will boost their self esteem as well as their organization skills.

98. **Modeling is a practice that requires students to (Skill 9.2, Average Rigor)**

    A. create a style unique to their own language capabilities.

    B. emulate the writing of professionals.

    C. paraphrase passages from good literature.

    D. peer evaluate the writings of other students.

    The answer is B. Modeling has students analyze the writing of a professional writer and try to reach the same level of syntactical, grammatical and stylistic mastery as the author whom they are studying.

99. **A formative evaluation of student writing (Skill 9.2, Rigorous)**

   A. requires thorough markings of mechanical errors with a pencil or pen.

   B. making comments on the appropriateness of the student's interpretation of the prompt and the degree to which the objective was met.

   C. should require that the student hand in all the materials produced during the process of writing.

   D. several careful readings of the text for content, mechanics, spelling, and usage.

The answer is B. It is important to give students numerous experiences with formative evaluation (evaluation as the student writes the piece). Formative evaluation will assign points to every step of the writing process, even though it is not graded. The criteria for the writing task should be very clear, and the teacher should read each step twice. Responses should be non critical and supportive, and the teacher should involve students in the process of defining criteria, and make it clear that formative and summative evaluations are two distinct processes.

100. **In this paragraph from a student essay, identify the sentence that provides a detail. (Skill 9.3 Rigorous)**

   (1) The poem concerns two different personality types and the human relation between them. (2) Their approach to life is totally different. (3) The neighbor is a very conservative person who follows routines. (4) He follows the traditional wisdom of his father and his father's father. (5) The purpose in fixing the wall and keeping their relationship separate is only because it is all he knows.

   A. Sentence 1

   B. Sentence 3

   C. Sentence 4

   D. Sentence 5

   The answer is C. Sentence 4 provides a detail to sentence 3 by explaining how the neighbor follows routine. Sentence 1 is the thesis sentence, which is the main idea of the paragraph. Sentence 3 provides an example to develop that thesis. Sentence 4 is a reason that explains why.

101. **In general, the most serious drawback of using a computer in writing is that (Skill 9.4, Average Rigor)**

   A. the copy looks so good that students tend to overlook major mistakes.

   B. the spell check and grammar programs discourage students from learning proper spelling and mechanics.

   C. the speed with which corrections can be made detracts from the exploration and contemplation of composing.

   D. the writer loses focus by concentrating on the final product rather than the details.

   The answer is C. Because the process of revising is very quick with the computer, it can discourage contemplation, exploring, and examination, which are very important in the process of writing.

102. Which of the following is most true of expository writing? (Skill 10.1, Easy)

   A. It is mutually exclusive of other forms of discourse.

   B. It can incorporate other forms of discourse in the process of providing supporting details.

   B. It should never employ informal expression.

   D. It should only be scored with a summative evaluation.

The answer is B. Expository writing sets forth an explanation or an argument about any subject.

103. Which of the following is not one of the four forms of discourse? (Skill 10.1, Average Rigor)

   A. Exposition

   B. Description

   C. Rhetoric

   D. Persuasion

The answer is C. Rhetoric is an umbrella term for techniques of expressive and effective speech. Rhetorical figures are ornaments of speech such as anaphora, antithesis, metaphor, etc. The other three choices are specific forms of discourse.

104. **If a student uses slang and expletives, what is the best course of action to take in order to improve the student's formal communication skills? (Skill 10.2, Average Rigor)**

    A. Ask the student to paraphrase their writing, that is, translate it into language appropriate for the school principal to read.

    B. Refuse to read the student's papers until he conforms to a more literate style.

    C. Ask the student to read his work aloud to the class for peer evaluation.

    D. Rewrite the flagrant passages to show the student the right form of expression.

    The answer is A. Asking the student to write for a specific audience will help him become more involved in his writing. If he continues writing to the same audience—the teacher—he will continue seeing writing as just another assignment and he will not apply grammar, vocabulary and syntax the way they should be. By rephrasing his own writing, the student will learn to write for a different public.

105. **Which of the following should not be included in the opening paragraph of an informative essay? (Skill 10.3, Easy)**

    A. Thesis sentence

    B. Details and examples supporting the main idea

    C. Broad general introduction to the topic

    D. A style and tone that grabs the reader's attention

    The answer is B. The introductory paragraph should introduce the topic, capture the reader's interest, state the thesis and prepare the reader for the main points in the essay. Details and examples, however, should be given in the second part of the essay, so as to help develop the thesis presented at the end of the introductory paragraph, following the inverted triangle method consisting of a broad general statement followed by some information, and then the thesis at the end of the paragraph.

106. Explanatory or informative discourse is (Skill 10.3, Average Rigor)

    A.   exposition.

    B.   narration.

    C.   persuasion.

    D.   description.

The answer is A. Exposition sets forth a systematic explanation of any subject. It can also introduce the characters of a literary work, and their situations in the story.

107. Oral debate is most closely associated with which form of discourse? (Skill 10.5, Average Rigor)

    A.   Description

    B.   Exposition

    C.   Narration

    D.   Persuasion

The answer is D. It is extremely important to be convincing while having an oral debate. This is why persuasion is so important, because this is the way that you can influence your audience.

108. **Which of the following is not a fallacy in logic? (Skill 10.5 Rigorous)**

   A. All students in Ms. Suarez's fourth period class are bilingual.
       Beth is in Ms. Suarez's fourth period.
       Beth is bilingual.

   B. All bilingual students are in Ms. Suarez's class.
       Beth is in Ms. Suarez's fourth period.
       Beth is bilingual.

   C. Beth is bilingual.
       Beth is in Ms. Suarez's fourth period.
       All students in Ms. Suarez's fourth period are bilingual.

   D. If Beth is bilingual, then she speaks Spanish.
       Beth speaks French.
       Beth is not bilingual.

The correct answer is A. The second statement, or premise, is tested against the first premise. Both premises are valid and the conclusion is logical. In B, the conclusion is invalid because the first premise does not exclude other students. In C, the conclusion cannot be logically drawn from the preceding premises—you cannot conclude that all students are bilingual based on one example. In D, the conclusion is invalid because the first premise is faulty.

109. Which part of a classical argument is illustrated in this excerpt from the essay "What Should Be Done About Rock Lyrics?" (Skill 10.5, Rigorous)

> But violence against women is greeted by silence. It shouldn't be.
>
> This does not mean censorship, or book (or record) burning. In a society that protects free expression, we understand a lot of stuff will float up out of the sewer. Usually, we recognize the ugly stuff that advocates violence against any group as the garbage it is, and we consider its purveyors as moral lepers. We hold our nose and tolerate it, but we speak out against the values it proffers.
>
> --"What Should Be Done About Rock Lyrics?" Caryl Rivers

A. Narration

B. Confirmation

C. Refutation and concession

D. Summation

The answer is C. The author acknowledges refutes the idea of censorship and concedes that society tolerates offensive lyrics as part of our freedom of speech. Narration provides background material to produce an argument. In confirmation, the author details the argument with claims that support the thesis. In summation, the author concludes the argument by offering the strongest solution.

110. **Identify the type of appeal used by Molly Ivins in this excerpt from her essay "Get a Knife, Get a Dog, But Get Rid of Guns." (Skill 10.5, Rigorous)**

   As a civil libertarian, I, of course, support the Second Amendment. And I believe it means exactly what it says:

   A well regulated militia being necessary to the security of a free state, the right of the people to keep and bear arms shall not be infringed.

   A. Ethos

   B. Pathos

   C. Logos

   D. Mythos

   The answer is A. Ethos is using the credentials of the speaker as a reliable and trustworthy authority. Pathos is an emotional appeal and logos is an emotional appeal. Mythos refers to mythology.

111. **Which sentence below best minimizes the impact of bad news? (Skill 11.3, Rigorous)**

   A. We have denied you permission to attend the event.

   B. Although permission to attend the event cannot be given, you are encouraged to buy the video.

   C. Although you cannot attend the event, we encourage you to buy the video.

   D. Although attending the event is not possible, watching the video is an option.

   The answer is B. Subordinating the bad news and using passive voice minimizes the impact of the bad news. In A, the sentence is active voice and thus too direct. The word "denied" sets a negative tone. In C, the bad news is subordinated but it is still active voice with negative wording. In D, the sentence is too unclear.

112. Which of the following sentences is properly punctuated? (Skill 12.2, Easy)

   A. The more you eat; the more you want.

   B. The authors—John Steinbeck, Ernest Hemingway, and William Faulkner—are staples of modern writing in American literature textbooks.

   C. Handling a wild horse, takes a great deal of skill and patience.

   D. The man, who replaced our teacher, is a comedian.

   The answer is B. Dashes should be used instead of commas when commas are used elsewhere in the sentence for amplification or explanation--here within the dashes.

113. Which of the following sentences contains a capitalization error? (Skill 12.2, Average Rigor)

   A. The commander of the English navy was Admiral Nelson

   B. Napoleon was the president of the French First Republic

   C. Queen Elizabeth II is the Monarch of the British Empire

   D. William the Conqueror led the Normans to victory over the British

   The answer is C. Words that represent titles and offices are not capitalized unless used with a proper name. This is not the case here.

114. **Students have been asked to write a research paper on automobiles and have brainstormed a number of questions they will answer based on their research findings. Which of the following is not an interpretive question to guide research? (Skill 13.1, Rigorous)**

   A. Who were the first ten automotive manufacturers in the United States?

   B. What types of vehicles will be used fifty years from now?

   C. How do automobiles manufactured in the United States compare and contrast with each other?

   D. What do you think is the best solution for the fuel shortage?

   The answer is A. The question asks for objective facts. B is a prediction that asks how something will look or be in the future, based on the way it is now. C asks for similarities and differences, which is a higher-level research activity that requires analysis. D is a judgment question that requires informed opinion.

115. **In preparing a report about William Shakespeare, students are asked to develop a set of interpretive questions to guide their research. Which of the following would not be classified as an interpretive question? (Skill 13.1, Rigorous)**

   A. What would be different today if Shakespeare had not written his plays?

   B. How will the plays of Shakespeare affect future generations?

   C. How does the Shakespeare view nature in *A Midsummer's Night Dream* and *Much Ado About Nothing*?

   D. During the Elizabethan age, what roles did young boys take in dramatizing Shakespeare's plays?

   The answer is D. This question requires research into the historical facts; *Shakespeare in Love* notwithstanding, women did not act In Shakespeare's plays, and their parts were taken by young boys. A and B are hypothetical questions requiring students to provide original thinking and interpretation. C requires comparison and contrast which are interpretive skills.

TEACHER CERTIFICATION STUDY GUIDE

116. **To determine the credibility of information, researchers should do all of the following except (Skill 13.4, Rigorous)**

    A. Establish the authority of the document.

    B. Disregard documents with bias.

    C. Evaluate the currency and reputation of the source.

    D. Use a variety of research sources and methods.

    The answer is B. Keep an open mind. Researchers should examine the assertions, facts and reliability of the information.

117. **Which of the following type of question will not stimulate higher-level critical thinking? (Skill 14.4, Rigorous)**

    A. A hypothetical question

    B. An open-ended question

    C. A close-ended question

    D. A judgment question

    The answer is C. A close-ended question requires a simple answer, like a "yes" or "no." An open-ended question can generate an extended response that would require critical thinking. Both a hypothetical question and a judgment question require deeper thinking skills.

ENGLISH

TEACHER CERTIFICATION STUDY GUIDE

118. **Mr. Ledbetter has instructed his students to prepare a slide presentation that illustrates an event in history. Students are to include pictures, graphics, media clips and links to resources. What competencies will students exhibit at the completion of this project? Skill 15.4, Rigorous)**

    A. Analyze the impact of society on media.

    B. Recognize the media's strategies to inform and persuade.

    C. Demonstrate strategies and creative techniques to prepare presentations using a variety of media.

    D. Identify the aesthetic effects of a media presentation.

    The answer is B. Students will have learned how to use various media to convey a unified message.

119. **For students to prepare for a their roles in a dramatic performance, (Skill 16.3, Average Rigor)**

    A. they should analyze their characters to develop a deeper understanding of the character's attitudes and motivations.

    B. they should attend local plays to study settings and stage design

    C. they should read articles and books on acting methodology

    D. they should practice the way other actors have performed in these roles.

    The answer is A. By examining how their characters feel and think, the students will understand the characters' attitudes and motivation.

ENGLISH

120. **The new teaching intern is developing a unit on creative writing and is trying to encourage her freshman high school students to write poetry. Which of the following would not be an effective technique? (Skill 17.2, Average Rigor)**

   A. In groups, students will draw pictures to illustrate "The Love Song of J. Alfred Prufrock" by T.S. Eliot.

   B. Either individually or in groups, students will compose a song, writing lyrics that try to use poetic devices.

   C. Students will bring to class the lyrics of a popular song and discuss the imagery and figurative language.

   D. Students will read aloud their favorite poems and share their opinions of and responses to the poems.

The answer is A. While drawing is creative, it will not accomplish as much as the other activities to encourage students to write their own poetry. Furthermore, "The Love Song of J. Alfred Prufrock" is not a freshman-level poem. The other activities involve students in music and their own favorites, which will be more appealing.

www.ingramcontent.com/pod-product-compliance
Lightning Source LLC
Chambersburg PA
CBHW080728230426
43665CB00020B/2655